Passeggiata

Passeggiata
Strolling Through Italy

G. G. Husak

2008

Passeggiata

For Al

"Life has taught us
that love does not consist in gazing at each other,
but in looking outward together in the same direction."
Antoine de Saint-Exupery

PROLOGUE

For almost fifteen years, March has signified not only the coming of spring, but my husband Al's and my pilgrimage to Italy. After more than a dozen trips, Italy is no longer foreign to us. We are comfortable there, and its cities, villages and culture seem part of us, even though we know ours is a fringe position and that, as visitors, we have the luxury of a romantic and imaginative perspective. Still, we are pleased that we can stand at a counter in a café in a small town and drink cappuccino with the local folks, pretending that, in our jeans and black jackets, we blend in. We feel as if we belong, at least for the moment.

With each trip we discover more history, more art, more patterns of culture, but there is always more to learn, especially how to live life. We leave our Type-A personalities at home and live in the moment, becoming less aware of watching the clock or being productive or getting things exactly right.

People often ask with wonder and a sense of doubt why we keep going back to Italy, why we don't go to other countries. We tend to shrug off the question, finding it difficult to explain all of the nuances of our Italian trips, and say something vague about the weather being nicer there in March. Recently, when friends once again asked the question, "Why do you keep going back?" Al said simply, "Because we like it." He went on to give his list of things that, he said, "are better in Italy than anywhere else."

It's not that we don't travel elsewhere, but there is something special about returning to a country with so much to see and to learn. Rather than feeling as if we are repeating ourselves and becoming bored, we find that we enjoy the familiarity. Every trip reveals more and suggests other places to visit. Sights we looked at only superficially in the beginning now have deeper meaning because of our increased knowledge. The more we know, the more interesting it becomes.

Visiting Italy is like peeling layers from an old painting or wallpaper which has somehow been covered over. We keep finding new patterns underneath each layer. At the same time the day to day efforts of dealing with cultural differences and logistics, of menus and train schedules, are now easier for us. We can put our energy into finding the Michelangelo sculpture in the out of the way church in Rome or the small mountain town on the Adriatic coast with its stories of medieval miracles.

We have been to popular tourist centers like Rome, Florence, Venice and Naples more than once. It is a wonderful luxury to relax and simply enjoy Rome, for example, by sitting on a stone bench near a fountain and watching children chase pigeons and old people feed them. We don't have to run around frantically like the "real" tourists, seeing all the sights on a tight schedule.

We've visited out of the way places, the smaller hill towns and seacoast villages with fewer tourists, especially in the early years. Wandering small streets and quiet pathways, strolling with a purpose of discovery but without goals, open to what we would see, we've had surprising and lovely experiences in unlikely places. We've learned how to go with the flow in Italian culture, to trust the country and to trust ourselves that we can meet travel challenges along the way.

At some point over these years I realized that this focus on getting to know one country is like becoming intimate with a person. I remember when I was young, looking at older people, parents and other midlife married folks, and thinking how boring it must be to be with the same person day after day for your whole life. For an adolescent it was a disturbing thought. Now at mid-life with the good fortune of an intact marriage and especially during this time of greater togetherness, we can both cherish the familiarities of our relationship and continue to be surprised at how much more there is to know. The more we know about each other, the more surprises and the more depth we find.

In Italy's cities and towns there is a custom of "passeggiata," a kind of walk or stroll, a walk for its own sake, often arm-in-arm with another. Our trips to Italy together have become a kind of passeggiata in which we walk together literally and figuratively learning how to be, not only a couple, but part of the world again.

Our comfort level in this country that reveals itself more and more to us each time we visit is similar to our comfort level as we spend more and more time in this new, intense, and in some ways more intimate phase of married life. As in many phases of marriage, we find it easier to accept the low points, rough paths, rocky roads and steep hills because we know that the high points will be there as well and that eventually the path will level out. Our Italian passeggiata, our strolling through Italy, reflects our passage through life together.

***

The first time we went to Italy together was to visit our oldest daughter, who was spending a semester of her junior year in Florence. 1993 was our empty nest year, the year our younger daughter left for college, and our first year getting used to being just a couple again. We were still accustomed to our parenting role so it was easy to justify planning a trip to Europe to "check on" our oldest. But we were also traveling just as a couple and were testing the waters of our new one-on-one relationship. After twenty-plus years of functioning as Mom and Dad, we felt both excited and anxious about the changes in our lives.

During this first trip, we had our ups and downs and plenty of moments of confusion. But in the process, we discovered Italy and inadvertently discovered a common interest that would enrich the next few years of our relationship. I guess in some ways we also began to rediscover each other. We were just beginning to appreciate this freedom to go and do and to just be who we were, to peel the layers from our parentally defined relationship and see who we were as a couple. On this initial trip, I never knew that we would come back year after year, or that these vacations would enrich this new phase of our married life as much as they have.

CHAPTER ONE

Culture Shock

We left Houston on a sunny spring day in March. Al had been working long hours, which was nothing new, and I was ready for a break from teaching. Although pulled between the excitement of visiting one daughter and the worry of leaving our younger one behind, we were energized by the anticipation of our Italian adventure.

When we arrived in Rome, we plunged headfirst, unprepared, into Italy. There is always an intensity and frenetic energy about Rome that we have come to appreciate, but that first arrival, jet-lagged and with no one to guide us, was overwhelming. Kirsti had given tips on how to get to the train to Rome's Termini Station, but by the time we figured out the signs, worked our way through customs and passport control (always stressful, even now), we had to pass by the line of taxi drivers who spotted us immediately as tired first time tourists and called, "Taxi? Taxi? Roma? Termini?" Trying to look confident, we pulled our bags assertively past the cab drivers hoping to see something, anything, in the way of a sign or arrow that would guide us to the train. We turned left and then right, toward a ramp that went over the busy street outside. A sign that read "trene" looked close enough to train, which kept us moving while dragging our wheel bag and duffle up the ramp to the train tracks and away from the aggressive taxi drivers.

Crotchety, cranky, and still confused, we managed our way to the tabacchi (tobacco) shop near the tracks. Back then it was the only place at the airport station that sold train tickets. At that time in Italy commuters bought bus and train tickets along with candy, cigarettes, magazines and newspapers from local shops. We dragged our luggage into the tiny tabacchi. As in any busy airport newsstand, a line of people wanting to make simple purchases formed behind us. The language, the surroundings and waiting customers intimidated us and we felt pressured to complete our business.

Kirsti had had the foresight to emphasize the name Termini, the main Rome station, several times to us and it was good she did since we later learned there is more than one station in Rome. "Just say, 'Termini,' Mom," she had told me. I cautiously held up two fingers and said "Due tickets, Termini?" The saleswoman answered me in English, "Two for Termini Station?"

We were surprised when the saleswoman spoke English, but quickly discovered that shopkeepers throughout Italy found it more efficient to speak English to the ever increasing number of visitors. Shopkeepers often know basic English words such as numbers and ticket information. Even now in an age where English is more and more the international language, there's no obligation on the part of Italians to learn it, so we try to appreciate that they make an effort to speak our language, rather than take it for granted.

Fortunately we had changed a little money before we left home, but as we pulled out paper bills of 10,000 and 50,000 lire (this was before the Euro), we felt clueless. Foreign exchange can look like play money at first and Italian currency with its big numbers was especially confusing. Kirsti would have been aghast at us flashing through a handful of bills as we tried to figure out which bill would be closest to the cost of a ticket. Unclear about what the price was and how much the currency was worth, I held out some money while other customers waited and Al moved away from me crossly, not comfortable with my lack of control of the situation. Undisturbed, the shopkeeper took several bills and returned several coins along with the receipt and our train tickets in the change dish on the counter.

The saleswoman had told me the price of the tickets in lire, about 20,000, but the number meant nothing to us. When we had time to do the exchange numbers, the cost was about $12.00 so we knew we had been charged correctly. Our first experience with money established some trust since it would have been easy for the busy salesperson to charge us twice as much in our fragmented and confused states of mind.

As we started with our luggage through the turnstile to get on the train, we did not know that we had to stamp our tickets in the time slot in order to make the turnstile let us through. A fellow passenger showed us how to use the machine to stamp our tickets to validate them with the time and date.

Safely in our seats with luggage stowed above us, as the train lurched forward heading toward Rome, we felt a certain satisfaction knowing that we had spent 12 dollars instead of the $60.00 plus tip that a taxi would have cost us. We had made lots of mistakes but had muddled through, and, when the dust settled, we felt a genuine sense of accomplishment to have gotten onto the right train. Our passage was under way and we were launched into our Italian experience together.

We were relieved to finally get on a train and in a compartment of our own. In fact, it almost felt like a let down. The old worn out seats could have been on any bus or train we'd ridden our whole lives and the views from the windows were typical of railroad tracks entering cities in the U.S. Weeds grew along side of vacant lots, as the tracks paralleled highways nearby then moved closer to some buildings, apartment high rises with balconies. Nothing special. So we rested and rode along enjoying the stressless quality of the familiarity of the scene, but waiting and watching for something Italian to show itself.

When we arrived at Termini, it was another story, an abrupt change from our sleepy airport train. Rome's main train station, like the city itself, hums and roars. With more than 15 tracks lined up and trains more or less constantly coming and going, it is similar to an airline hub. All roads led to Rome in the old days and probably still do today. Dazed and overwhelmed again, but with nothing to do but drag our bags off the train, we got our adrenalin moving and went to try to figure out the schedule to Florence which we knew was "Firenze" in Italian. The large yellow boards listed destinations and times, showing several trains to Florence; we chose the first departure available. We found the arrival time and went to call Kirsti so she could meet us at the station when we arrived.

We had managed to get a few coins in our transaction to buy tickets and candy at the airport and thought we had read in a guidebook that a 200-lire coin would operate a phone, just like a dime or quarter used to at home. Al was frustrated. "Look in the book," he said. Struggling to get out the guidebook and leaf through it while holding onto my bags, I found the reference. Al found a coin, but had to pull out his reading glasses to check the number. Another frustration about middle age travel is you can't remember details easily or see without your reading glasses. We found the reddish orange phones with no problems. Then Al said, "There's no place to put the money." The first phone we went to had no coin slot, and we had no phone card, never having used one. In those early years the red public phones were often occupied by callers since not all of the phones worked. Moving to the line with an option to use a coin as well as a card, we waited our turn. But when we stepped up to the front of the line, we couldn't figure out how to work the phone. We would drop in the coin and hear strange noises, but no human voice, not even an Italian operator. Several times we cancelled our call, retrieved our coin, and tried again. Since we were calling Florence, we weren't sure if there was a different process for long distance. Finally, an Italian couple behind us took pity on us. They shrugged off our offer of the coin, inserted their phone card into the card slot, and dialed the number that we gave them, waiting until the connection was made. While hospitality may not have been their motive, they just wanted to use the phone themselves, somehow, with their help, we managed to make a connection with Kirsti.

Once again something as simple as making a phone call became a sign of our incompetence in this culture. "What if we can't get in touch with her?" I thought, even though I knew that eventually we would figure it out. We felt vulnerable. I was paranoid about our luggage since we'd been warned about pickpockets in this train station, and if anyone ever looked like an easy mark fumbling with our lire and looking dazed, it was us.

With Kirsti contacted and our bags still intact, we stepped from the arrival and departure tracks of the station into the terminal itself. It was like a busy Manhattan street at lunch time with continuous throngs of people in constant motion. We broke the crowd like water moving around a large stone and flowing back together. Later we would learn to flow with the moving crowd, but like sightseers in New York, and like the tourists we were, we stood and gawked at the activity around us.

Experiences like these would change forever how we view strangers in our own country. Simple things like buying a newspaper or a coffee were challenges in the busy Roman terminal. I thought, "So this is what it feels like to be in New York or another big American city if you are Japanese or Puerto Rican with little English and trying to order a meal or get directions. People are basically in a hurry. They want you to keep moving or else you are in their way. It makes me glad that more Spanish is spoken now in Houston, to simplify life for those for whom English is hard. A lot of people in Italy have helped us by speaking a little English.

***

Often the trains from Rome to Florence are crowded and require reservations if you don't want to stand in the aisles. But on our first little train ride from Termine to Florence, we took random seats and had a compartment to ourselves. Only later did we discover that we were on a local train, which stopped almost everywhere between Roma and Firenze. What is often a two or two and a half hour ride took us four hours. Although this last leg of our journey was long, it was perfect to calm our culture shock and sedate our jetlagged selves. The train had old seats and open windows. Although it was a slow train, rocking along and making many local stops at small towns, the stucco stations and Italian names along with tile-roofed old villas and distant hill towns overlooking golden-green fields and vineyards made for a soothing and pretty ride.

We sleepily rocked along past the tile roofs and stucco buildings of small towns, stopping at the stations marked Ostiense or Orvieto and others where we would later return. The slow-moving train would roll into a station, stop briefly as an occasional passenger departed or got on, and we would leave. The window was open from the top down, letting in the country air refreshing us after our hours of intercontinental airplane air. We dozed and slept between stops in that pleasantly aware state that jet lag and gentle movement can create. The sliding door of the compartment stayed open and we saw only a few people come and go in the aisle. No conductor came by to check our Eurail pass.

As we pulled into Florence, I recalled my first arrival into Italy years before as a young college graduate, sleepy but in a different way, as having spent a long night on the train. I remembered loving my first impressions, the feeling of the soft air on my skin, the bright light, the subtle mix of odors and sounds, and the feeling of gentle oldness. I thought how I had always loved Italy and thought of it as my favorite country. As the train slowed, we glimpsed neighborhoods on the outskirts of the city, seemingly less dense than the mid-rise apartment buildings that we had passed in Rome. Now Al and I rode gently past stone churches, stucco houses and apartments with laundry hanging out to dry on the small balconies. I remembered thinking that people must do laundry every day. I'll always associate the image of laundry drying on the lines outside apartment windows with Italy.

Sometimes inconveniences become blessings. The long, rocking, inefficient ride on the quiet train had given us the rest and recuperative time that we needed. By the time we arrived at the Santa Maria Novella station in Florence, we were glad to see Kirsti waiting for us.

It's a wonder to fly across an ocean and travel half a continent to a foreign country only to get off a train and see your own grown child in jeans and a sweater, standing as familiar as if she were in your own neighborhood at Christmas. There she stood confidently in Stazione Santa Maria Novella, a station named after a nearby church, typical of how Italy blends the old and new. As we hugged and kissed her, feeling the happiness that parents feel reunited with their children no matter how much they have grown up, she seemed as comfortable in her Italian environment as if she was greeting us on her college campus in New England.

Now that we were in Firenze, Kirsti took over and got us all into a cab. Al and I learned quickly that our English didn't necessarily get much response with taxi drivers, nor did our English pronunciation of Italian. The driver looked confused when I told him the name of our hotel was Villa Carlotta, pronouncing it "carl-ah-ta," until I showed him the name printed on the reservation. With high energy and a grand sweep of his hand to the steering wheel, he repronounced it car-LOW-ta, with exuberance and a big grin. Al smiled for the first time since we arrived and connected with Italian culture in that moment. He can still give a good imitation of our first Italian cabdriver's enthusiasm when he got past our language barrier and understood where we wanted to go.

Later, we followed our daughter through the dark stone streets of Florence, clueless about our mysterious surroundings and seemingly in a no man's land of high walls and wooden doors that all looked the same as we turned corners into other dark alleys where there appeared to be only dead-ends. We suddenly turned into a doorway of a small restaurant adorned with white tablecloths and single roses on each table. The courteous and dignified waiter greeted us, "Buona sera," listened to our daughter, our ambassador, request a table for "tre personas" and then at the table ask for "aqua naturale" and "vino rosso." We heard no English and were impressed that she could get along so well with her basic Italian.

That evening we ate unsalted bread dipped in olive oil and black pepper, learned that if we asked for water they would bring mineral water unless we asked for it, "senza gas." We ate ziti peperoni, a spicy pasta with a red and hot pepper sauce but no meat and thus began to learn the nuances of Italian dishes. Green salads were served after the meal, another custom in Italy, and I discovered that red table wine, usually new wine produced locally, would never give me a headache as at home.

***

At dawn the following day we were back on a train, taking a quick tour because Kirsti had no classes on the weekend. So off to Venice we went, still jetlagged and tired. For Al and me, it was too much too soon, too much experience in too little time. We learned to pace ourselves better in later trips, although I sometimes think that my most vivid memories are created when I'm still in the unreal airy mind-space that jet lag and lack of sleep causes. Maybe the sense of dreamlike reality occurs because our brains would normally be in a sleep state. Instead of our dreams seeming real as they do when we're asleep, our reality seems dreamy during these hours before our circadian rhythms get adjusted to the new time.

Since Kirsti was less experienced about Venetian than Florentine transportation, we didn't know how to buy tickets for the vaporetto, Venice's watery version of a bus-boat. First we weren't sure which boat number to get on, and although a turnstile at the gate required a ticket, we saw no place to buy one. We missed two vaporetti while we figured things out.

Our bad memory of the vaporetto would later be balanced by wonderful memories of boats in the early morning fog, of sitting behind a sea captain and his second in command in Venetian seaman's uniforms and blue seaman's caps as they turned the large-spoked wheel to guide us through the canals. We loved the otherworldly feeling of Venice and we felt like part of an old movie filmed through smoked glass. We would have experiences filmed into memory to be recalled with wonder in later tranquility. The peak experiences and pitfalls of travel tend to arrive back-to-back in this way.

We finally made it to the hotel where we were told our room would be ready in "ten minutes," which in Italy often means "more or less." We settled into overstuffed chairs in the lobby of our lovely and elegant hotel as we gazed out at the Grand Canal and the often photographed dome of Chiesa San Giorgio, the church across the lagoon. When we finally checked in, Al wisely chose a nap, and Kirsti and I walked the quiet back streets and canals of the neighborhoods of Venice, away from the shops and hotels. As we strolled across stone bridges and along footpaths behind Venetian homes, we talked about her plans after graduation, and she shared some of her experiences and concerns about moving on to the next phase of her life. It was a treasured conversation as we walked up and down the small canals lost in the real life of Venice where the best and most characteristic sight was the laundry hung from windows and over the narrow canals. We were in a distant world, so different it seemed a fantasy land, but made real by hanging t-shirts and overalls, sheets and curtains, swinging from upstairs window lines. The laundry formed a good background for talking of the practical realities of going back home.

I often have felt this way in Italy, that we are in a different reality. We observe and become part of ordinary life as people go about their daily tasks of laundering or gardening or vine-tending, but with a sense that we are in another time and dimension because things are so different from what is ordinary to us. In one sense it feels as if we are on a different plane of existence but, in another, life feels more grounded in the real life texture of everyday details.

***

The next morning, we naively accepted a free boat ride offered by our hotel concierge to visit the island of Murano to tour the glass factory. A small craft shuttled us across the lagoon, the blue of the water reflecting sunlight as brightly and with as much shimmer and shine as the elaborate glass collections we would see. It was a sparkling scene. When the boat docked, a warm and gracious Italian helped us from the boat and escorted us into a glass-blowing workshop. This gentleman spoke excellent English and was the most masterful salesman I have ever encountered. He spoke a few words to Kirsti in his Italian and then in English complimented her on her Italian and, after asking where Al and I were from, told us he knew the owner of a well-known restaurant in our home city. Having established a personal rapport with us, he showed us one glassblower at work, explaining the history of Murano glass and the uniqueness of the old methods. We were suitably awed by the skill of the craftsman and the effect of the thin blue flame on the shapes and colors of the glass.

Seeing and admiring the glass working set us up for a required tour of room after room of glass displays, ornate, exquisite, grand, museum pieces, whimsical collector's pieces, and elegant dining crystal with at least some practical use. It was both the friendliest and strongest sales presentation of my life. We had been targeted by the hotel we were staying in as people with some money to spend, and it became more and more evident that we were not getting off this island without a purchase.

We generally do not travel to shop and usually buy little except for small gifts and souvenirs. And we have no interest in glass collecting. Given our normal priorities, we never would have spent time looking at these displays, let alone buy them. But lulled by being in a Venetian setting and hustled by the best salesman, we ordered six etched wine glasses, which cost

$150.00 (our usual wine glasses come from discount stores), and a rose, green flower-patterned and gold-tinted ice bucket for $60.00. Not only had we spent our first morning in Venice, and our first real sightseeing day in Italy, looking at glass displays that none of us were terribly interested in, but we had spent money on glass that we hadn't really wanted.

At the time I resented spending our travel budget for something we didn't want. Al was more forgiving. I think he admired the man's sales technique. (The glass took six months to arrive, I had to call Venice twice to check on the order, and it messed up our credit card bills for that long as we withheld payment until our glass arrived.)

Our purchase seemed an unplanned and extravagant mistake in every way, except that, in spite of it all, we love what we bought. The glasses are a lovely and extravagant piece of our unextravagant Italian vacation. The little glass ice bucket, bought because it was smaller and cheaper than most everything else we were shown, is rarely used for ice but is displayed safely on the top shelf of our bookcase. There is something special about having this little piece of impractical beauty that we never intended to buy. We do use the wine glasses, carefully and only on special occasions, and Kirsti will own them someday as she was our hostess for that trip. Ultimately, Italy didn't let us down.

CHAPTER TWO

On Our Own

Back in Florence after our busy weekend in Venice, Al and I rested and regrouped. We enjoyed the comfort of our hotel and the spring morning pleasantness of drinking our morning coffee as we looked out from our hotel balcony across the Arno River and up to the Piazzale Michelangelo. Taking advantage of our first real leisure time, we planned for a different kind of vacation within this vacation. It was the first day we would spend in Italy on our own.

Kirsti had to go to her Monday classes and besides, at the independent age of twenty-one, she was very ready for a break from entertaining her parents. She had made some suggestions about places we could see on our own for a day. We decided to try to get to the top of the hill where all the pictures of the city and of the Duomo, the cathedral with the red tiled dome that is the focal point of Florence, are taken. From the balcony of our hotel, we could see the Piazzale Michelangelo high on the hill across the Arno River. Al read in a guidebook about a bus across the bridge that went up the hill. "We can have lunch up there," we said to each other, picturing ourselves in a hilltop outdoor cafe looking over the city and the river on this balmy spring day.

We left the comfort of our hotel with a tourist map and started walking in the direction of the bridge. We crossed the bridge on the lookout for a bus stop. But once we were across the bridge, having seen no signs of a bus stop, Al led us, using the map, back from the river toward the hill. When he noticed flights of stairs that seemed to head in the direction of the hilltop, he said, "We can go up this way."

One thing led to another. Al lead the way while I insisted that I was not going to climb those stairs. Even so, we started up. They were broad stairs, obviously used by local people avoiding the busier roads to get from point to point on the hillside. Al, of course, climbed on ahead of me, intrigued by the challenge of seemingly endless stairs, and I quickly discovered, after years of living in a one story house in a city without hills, that my calf and thigh muscles had atrophied. I distracted myself from the pain as much as possible by the pretty views that presented themselves at the landings and tried to act as if I was enjoying the surroundings rather than catching my breath, especially when people much older than I walked easily up past me, often carrying large bags of groceries. Al continued upward and occasionally waited for me, but by the time I caught up, he was ready to go again.

As we climbed and climbed the wide steps with occasional landings, which seemed to go on forever, I periodically tried to look back through the shrubbery and trees. When we finally got to the top, we were rewarded with the view of the city across the Arno. On the opposite side of the hill, we could look down on the wall of the old city winding over the green hills and taking advantage of the natural protection. We got an overview, for the first time, of the pattern of protection that medieval Europe found necessary. Looking away from the city, as the countryside opened out under the sky, we glimpsed the character of the landscape of Tuscany, the area we had heard so much about.

We walked around looking for a hilltop restaurant which, as it turned out, didn't exist. All we saw were snack and souvenir stands and lots of tour buses.

We walked out to the Piazzale Michelangelo, so named because of the sculptured representation of his David. This copy of the David stands in the piazza above the city, a protector and symbol of the Renaissance spirit, challenging the Goliath of medieval power and control. We wandered past an ice cream bar and soft drink carts, avoiding the line up of tour buses stopping to let people look out the windows or wander for a while and take snapshots. We had no camera so looked out at the scene for a while trying to fix the view of the red tile roofs and Brunelleschi's famous cathedral dome in our mind's eye. We enjoyed the deceptive peacefulness of the scene, the relative serenity and breathtaking beauty of the cityscape so different from the intensity of pedestrians and motorbikes in the crowded narrow streets in the city below.

We ended up eating in a small corner restaurant at the bottom of the hill. After all of our hiking and looking, we were long past the standard lunch hour. Still, the owner of the small trattoria greeted us, "Buona sera," since it was now afternoon and seated us at one of the small tables with peach-colored tablecloths and a small vase of flowers as decoration. We were served good pasta with gracious hospitality in a romantic setting. It couldn't have been a nicer lunch, even without the view. We were beginning to learn to take Italy on its own terms.

The next day we went to the Uffizi Gallery. Al insisted that we follow Kirsti's advice and, against my fatigued resistance, got us up early to be among the first standing outside the entrance in the line that developed well before it opened. By then we were relaxed and were getting oriented to our surroundings, so even though we waited for an hour, we enjoyed the morning sights and sounds looking forward to our first taste of the wonders of Italian art. When we joined the orderly flow of people through the galleries, the masterpieces didn't disappoint us.

Later that day, following the advice of a newspaper article that Al had come across in the *New York Times*, we wandered to the other side of the Arno River where we strolled along narrow side streets, passing antique shops and woodworking, weaving and ceramics studios. We walked single file on the narrow sidewalks between the rows of buildings and the streets. Al set the pace in front so neither of us had to hurry or slow down for the other as we wandered through the old neighborhood, enjoying our first venture off the beaten tourist path.

***

Toward the end of the week, with our daughter back in her role as tour guide and taking advantage of Italy's compactness, we set out on another side trip, this time to Verona, a city north and east of Florence. Again we traveled by train, changing once in Bologna on the way. There we got a chance to taste the food and culture of Northern Italy.

I had never visualized ancient Roman buildings anywhere other than in Rome, but in Verona we discovered that Roman ruins are all over the place. We climbed the steps of a Roman amphitheater, the best preserved in Italy with almost all of the circular structure still intact. It was smaller than Rome's Coliseum but felt more substantial. We climbed up one of the aisles to the top to look out over the countryside from the back row and down to the stage toward the front. The Roman arena is still the site of modern productions of plays and operas, with many of the members of the audience sitting on the stone seats that climb to the open air. That morning a school group of Italian teenagers had also climbed to the top row, but across the arena, where they settled down on the ancient stone seats of the theater for a round of singing. The nearest parallel I could think of was a school bus or campfire sing-along at home.

Leaving the amphitheater, we wandered along the pedestrian boulevard past nice shops and the bustle of weekend shoppers. We entered a subtly marked entrance through a short tunnel of brick and stone. Its walls were covered with years of graffiti, colored designs of entwining hearts and lovers' messages. We moved into the courtyard of Juliet's house and balcony. I had read in our guidebook that this compact city was the "fair Verona," the setting for Shakespeare's *Romeo and Juliet*. A main attraction was a brick courtyard and romantic, vine-covered old house with a stone balcony. Without historical basis, tradition and tourism had colluded to refer to it as "Juliet's house." As a tourist destination there was not a lot to see. But the lovely tree-shaded courtyard was a place to capture the imagination. We joined the others who faced the balcony, perched about fourteen feet above the ground, and let ourselves picture Juliet in a flowing gown looking down at Romeo below. And while the realist in us knew that this probably wasn't Juliet's real house, especially since there probably wasn't a real Juliet, we couldn't help but enjoy the experience. When teaching *Romeo and Juliet*, I had never really thought of Shakespeare's Verona, the city of the feuding Montagues and Capulets, as real, but an imaginary place in an imaginary Italy, simply a background for his stage play. Now I realized that Verona was a real city, one of the many Italian city states that had endured struggles between powerful families, and Mantua, the city to which Romeo was banished after killing Tybalt, was also real and only miles down the road. Having taught for decades that the Renaissance, which spread to England, began in Italy, I now had a new understanding of what the connections between cultures meant. What I had read in textbooks and taught about the influence of Italian culture became more meaningful.

***

Tired from juggling going to classes and entertaining her

parents all week, when we went to the hotel, Kirsti went in for a nap and Al and I had an expensive beer at an outdoor café, one of many around Verona's main piazza. We enjoyed just sitting at the small round table, watching waiters move quickly here and there with trays and drinks, beer and coffees, as a large stage and sound system were set up in the square. When we gestured toward the sound stage and asked our waiter, "For what?" he shrugged indifferently.

"Politicos. Talk talk talk," he said, unimpressed.

I finished my drink and walked back to the hotel to visit with Kirsti while Al had another beer on his own and soaked up the atmosphere. Later, from our hotel window, we heard the political rally and even caught a glimpse of the main speaker. He was Senore Berlesconi, not yet, but soon to be, twice elected as Prime Minister. We were present at the beginning of a politically historic era but didn't know it.

The next morning, while Kirsti and I took our time getting dressed and sipping our cappuccinos, Al took a walk on his own, crossed the river, climbed to the ruins of the ancient Roman theater, and listened to a Saturday morning concert in a small church. When Kirsti and I met him after our own walk down the pedestrian-only shopping streets, he was enthusiastic about what a great morning he had had.

*****

Al and I were scheduled to fly out of Rome, and Kirsti told us it would be worth it for us to leave early to spend part of a day there if we could. That would give her time to settle down and get ready for her week. We had done so much, had so much experience and variety in a week. As parents, it was hard to leave but it was time. Al and I had enjoyed being both parents and fellow travelers in this trip. We took the train to Rome, checked our bags at the hotel near the airport and then took the train back to the city. After our earlier confused experience in the Rome station, we were impressed with our ability to manage the Termini trains easily.

On this final afternoon of our trip, we walked around Rome, trying to see the basic sights, confused but stimulated by a city larger than any we had visited. We sampled much of Rome's many treasures. We walked along the Via di Coloseo at the edge of the ancient Roman Forum and looked down into ruins of the ancient city. However, when we arrived at the end of the long boulevard and looked through the gated doors into the Coliseum, we found we had arrived there too late for entrance on a Sunday afternoon. Hiking back past the buildings of the ancient Forum, we looked down wistfully at groups of tourists winding their way through the famous ruins, but discovered that the entrance was a long walk around the site and on the other side of where we were. By the time we would have gotten to the entrance, the Forum, too, would be closed.

We walked past the white-layered wedding cake structure of the Vittorio Emmanuele Monument, which we would come to rely on as a reference point for getting our bearings in that part of the city. Past the palace and on the other side, we walked up Michelangelo's steps to the Piazza del Campidoglio. Beside the stairs, two small wolves in a cage symbolized the story of Romulus and Remus, the mythological founders of Rome.

According to the famous story, the abandoned or orphaned twin babies were nursed by a mother wolf and thus survived to found a civilization somewhere among the seven hills of what would become Rome. The image of the female wolf nursing two little boys is replicated throughout the city, painted or sculpted over doorways, and smaller plastic versions line souvenir carts in Rome. Several years later, we noticed that the caged animals near

Michelangelo's stairs were gone, perhaps in response to animal rights advocacy.

At the top of the broad, gracefully curved stairway, we admired the architecture and design of the small piazza nestled between the buildings that houses the Capitoline museums. As we stood in the Piazza di Campidoglio, Al and I agreed that there was something special and right about the space. There was a sense of grace and balance both looking up at the curved stairway and standing in the piazza. Without being architecturally sophisticated, we got a sense of why the most famous works are significant. Not grandiose or overdone, they communicate a beauty even to us novices. We were struck by the grace and balance and a subtle sense that this was the best way to design this small space.

We wandered randomly into other parts of the city, getting lost again, but not really caring since, on this last afternoon, we had no real plan. We found the famous Trevi Fountain and, along with other Sunday afternoon tourists, followed the old tradition of throwing a coin into the water with the wish to return to Rome someday. We never suspected, as we tossed our coins into the bubbly fountain, that we would come back to Italy and Rome so soon and for so many years. We have maintained this tradition every trip.

We had planned to eat the last of our Italian dinners in Rome, but couldn't find a restaurant that was open. We assumed that because it was Sunday everything was closed but found out later that we were just in the wrong part of town for weekend dining. Instead, we had coffee at a small cafe and then waited for two hours for a bus that never came. We ended up taking an expensive cab ride back to the dining room of our airport hotel, a cab ride that Al enjoyed as much as any sightseeing, sitting on the edge of the seat of the old taxi, grinning and watching every move of the steering wheel and every gesture as the Roman driver dived with others into the circling traffic in what seemed to me a form of "playing chicken." With verbal vehemence and emphatic gestures, he pushed the little Fiat to its limits as we darted past bigger cars and then sped merrily along the highway to the airport. "He knows what he's doing, "Al told me as I clung to my arm rest. "He's a good driver."

It occurred to me that for Al, both the beginning and ending memories of our first trip would always be related to our cabdrivers.

***

In later years we would learn how to get ourselves and our luggage from a hotel in Rome on an early morning bus to the train station where we would take a train to the airport with plenty of time for our two hour check in for an international flight. This time we stayed at the more expensive and less interesting American name brand hotel near the airport to be ready for our early morning departure.

Italy was different in 1993. It felt more like a foreign land than in today's world of the European Union and globalization, especially to us who had not done much international travel. There was more culture shock. When we remember our first trips these many years later, we have a sense of nostalgia for a time with fewer crowds and a greater sense of adventure. And we were more physically sheltered then, more used to our suburban comforts along with the isolation from the general community that came with the hours we spent in our cars. We were less used to leaving our comfort zones in many ways. Yes, Italy has changed, becoming more accessible with phone cards and ATMs, and e-mail. But we have also changed as we learn to leave the confining shell of our lifestyles and habits and ways of seeing the world and become more at ease with differences and unpredictability.

***

After we got back to Houston, we had time to think things over. We realized that we had had a good time in spite of some bad moments and that much of the intensity of the trip was from having so much experience in such a short time. We started to do our homework about Italy.

The first time we went out to dinner with friends and got to talk about our trip, we swung into our narrative, telling them about the slow train to Florence, the vaporetti and glass in Venice, our peek into the closed Coliseum. We described circling the old Jewish neighborhood in Rome trying to find our way to a certain road and getting more and more twisted and tangled in the medieval streets.

An older friend, an experienced traveler herself asked, "Did you have a good time?" But before we could answer, seeming to sense our memories of some trying moments, she laughed and answered her own question, "Sometimes you enjoy your trip more after you get home than you did while you were there." It's true that back home, Al and I have time to sort through the sights and sounds and people and experiences. We can select the highlights and replay them. Certain moments, the best ones, become set in memory.

As Al and I gradually selected the moments to remember, Italy became a bond. Sitting in the comfort and familiarity of our living room, we would recall climbing the stairs to the Piazza Michelangelo or waiting in line at the Uffizi, browsing in the outdoor markets or getting lost in Rome.

We looked through our photographs and shared the highlights with our friends and we started to appreciate our trip more. Not yet realizing that we would be going back so soon and so often, we read more guidebooks, and allowed doors to open up to new intellectual interests; it was the beginning of our mutual hobby. We noticed an article on Venice in the travel section of the Sunday paper, complete with pictures of an old synagogue and the piazza where boys were playing soccer, an article we would have normally skipped over, and read with interest the history of a place we had visited. We followed the Italian election with a sense of connection as we thought of the political rally in Verona. When the narrator of a television show (Rick Steves' PBS spotlight on Florence) stood on the Piazzale Michelangelo looking out over the red tile roofs and the cathedral dome, I would excitedly exclaim, "That's right where we were." As we sat in our family room in the suburbs, we were transported back to Italy.

Our moments to remember, often the less important but somehow more personalized ones, stand out in color and form, the specifics that define the trip as time goes by. Our minds focus on the funny, unusual, or surprising scenes or events that we experienced in the same place at the same time and from the same perspective. We crystallize the specifics of these memories, the gesturing welcome of a waiter, the three kinds of cookies we bought at a bakery, the cat that kept us company in an outdoor restaurant, or even the argument we had on the corner. These memories, selected by an unstated mutual consent, are shared in a kind of private way.

CHAPTER THREE

The Return: Milan

I had to do some selling to get Al to go back the next year. He was used to traveling on business, but for him, travel just for pleasure was an indulgence. I have always loved to travel and don't need a sense of duty to go.

Italy was cheaper in March, I told him, and the weather would be better than most other places we could go. Besides we knew the ropes now. I suggested that we could use frequent flier miles for tickets and always put the miles back into our accounts if we changed our minds. I promised a low-key, nonstressful itinerary, no early morning departures or long train trips, and nice but inexpensive hotels. "I bet it'll be cheaper than taking a vacation here," I said, determined to prove my point.

When, in answer to one of my proposals, Al finally said, "I guess so," I took it to be as close to a "Yes," as I would get and set out to make it happen.

I wanted to avoid our first trip's mistakes of doing too much. With relaxation in mind, I planned a simple itinerary, creating a circular tour with only a few short train trips connecting the dots of our destinations. I used Milan as both an arrival and departure city. I had read that its airport was smaller and simpler, less frenetic than Rome's and that it would be an easier place to transition from home into our Italian vacation.

Milan seems the least glamorous of the big cities in Italy. If Naples is less visited because it is a little more intimidating,

Milan is less highlighted because it seems to offer less for tourists than Rome or Venice or Florence.

But for us, Milan became a favorite stopover. In later trips, if we had started our trip in Rome, we flew home from Milan to take advantage of the airlines' open jaw option to fly into one city and out another. Whether we had spent a couple of days in Milan or just one night on our way to leaving for the airport, we have always enjoyed our time there.

Our first flight into Milan was serenely beautiful as we flew over the snow-capped peaks of the southern Alps and the blue lakes of northern Italy. In the early morning sunlight the sparkling scene of miles of mountain ranges from our airplane window was a perfect awakening experience, more stimulating than our morning coffee. Even though it was only 3:00 a.m. in Houston and we hadn't slept much, we couldn't help but be energized by the sight of the Alps.

When we arrived, in what was, for us, an unusual exit procedure, we carried our luggage down the steps of our 747 jet, walked across the concrete and onto tram buses that took us to the terminal. After our hours crossing the Atlantic, it was refreshing to breathe the cool morning air for a few minutes before going back into the terminal.

At first it seemed that we would have a long wait to get past the windows for passport control. As United States citizens we have to stand in a different line than the European Union passengers, who are able to walk quickly through the entryway with a quick glance at documents by the officials.

When faced with potential delays, Al always wants us to get in two different lines, getting irritated with me when I resist. He wants to be sure that at least one of us doesn't get stuck in the slowest line or the one that comes to a halt while some bureaucratic confusion is resolved. I tend to feel as if it doesn't matter very much whether we have to wait or not. I want to relax right away, letting things like passport lines move us forward at their own pace.

"You get in that line," he said, nodding toward two aisles away.

I thought about readjusting my shoulder bag and pulling my suitcase across the intervening lines of other travelers with their luggage and shook my head. "No." Unfortunately, I also couldn't resist a lecture, "It's not going to make that much difference."

While we were stubbornly and emotionally negotiating the "who was going to stand where and who was in charge of whom" issue, the line moved us along, and, before we had resolved our argument, the passport official behind the glass window waved us through with barely a glance at our documents. Our moods shifted quickly as we moved on to our next challenge of finding transportation into the city.

Unlike Rome, we were not greeted by taxi solicitors. The atmosphere was calm. We pulled our bags and followed the exit signs to the main doors of the terminal. Locating the airport bus that would take us into Milan's main train station was as easy as finding a city airport bus at home. For once, there was nothing confusing about what bus to get on or about the process of buying a ticket. We had planned ahead, knew how we were getting to the hotel and were able to pay the driver using the lire we had brought from home.

On the bus we heard as much English spoken as Italian. I listened to two college girls from Boston plan how many cities they would visit in a couple of days. The newly arrived American girl was amazed that they would be able to take a day trip from Verona to Venice, expressing her disbelief, as her friend tried to explain how close things were and how easy it would be to make the trip by train. I thought nostalgically of our trip with Kirsti the year before.

The bus passed car dealerships and apartment complexes on the highway and then wove into the suburbs and the city itself. Except for the Fiats and Audis and the Italian names of roadside businesses, we could have been on a highway in the U.S. When we got to the train station and walked inside the terminal to get directions to the Metro, we looked around at the station, a beautiful and noteworthy architectural sight with its lofty ceiling and grand sense of space. They say that Mussolini, under whose authority the station was built, made one contribution to Italy and that was to make the trains run on time. The station seemed an appropriate acknowledgment to the importance of train travel in Italy.

For us the station at Milano Centrale provided extra convenience. Not only is it the main stop for the airport bus, but it connects to the underground trains that serve the city. After looking at the posted subway map, Al felt confident that we could take the subway to our hotel. This time, our adventure of getting ourselves to a hotel without a taxi, instead of becoming a disaster of dragging bags and getting lost as sometimes happens, was successful. We descended the stairway to the subway and easily rode the several stops to one near the Duomo or cathedral.

But when we came up the stairs from the underground, we were confused about which direction to walk to our hotel. We knew we were at the right stop but were disoriented with the many possible directions we could take from the Piazza Duomo. Still, we couldn't help but be impressed by the grand piazza crowded with pigeons and people and the cathedral itself with more delicate spires and more detail than any other cathedral we'd seen. The spires that rose against the blue sky reminded me of decoratively dripped cake frosting or the sand castles we used to make at the beach by drizzling wet sand into higher and thinner steeples.

We looked at the map in our guidebook, and, using the front of the Duomo as a reference, Al chose what we hoped were the right bearings. We walked diagonally across the piazza toward the far corner, then across the busy street, down one block and onto the Via Sperinaro. On this narrow street with shops specializing in fruits and vegetables, cheese and dairy, breads, poultry, or meat, we entered another world from the busy piazza, the traffic, the streetcars and buses a few steps behind us.

We passed a tiny pasta shop and found our hotel next to a produce market, a display of fresh arugula and pears and tomatoes standing outside the open door. Only an unobtrusive sign over a closed door showed us the entrance to the small family-owned place. If we hadn't been looking, we would easily have passed it among the other shops.

We opened the door and climbed two flights of stairs, our upward exertion broken with only one tiny landing to reach the reception area. At a reception counter on one wall a couple of people waited to be checked in while others stood at the small coffee and snack bar on the other side of the compact space. We showed our confirmed fax reservation for a room with bath and received our key. Our room was on the fourth floor. The reception area was counted as the first floor and not the second, in spite of all the stairs we had climbed to get there. The entrance on the street level is considered the ground floor, one below first. We climbed several more flights carrying our bags and followed the stairs upward and around in the crooked design of the connected old buildings. Fearing I'd never make it to the top and wondering if Al's knee would give out enroute, I paused to breathe as often as possible. But once we reached our floor, we were pleased to find that we had a pleasant and airy room and even a tiny window with a view. The climb up had been worth it. We caught our breath, dropped our stuff and headed down again, an easier descent without our bags. We relaxed knowing that when we carried our bags down the stairs, we would have gravity on our side.

***

With its own small church, the small street and hotel of the same name has been our anchor of charm and intimacy in Milan. The logistics are perfect, since we can get back on the Metro to sightsee or to get to the airport bus. But the family hospitality and atmosphere of casual camaraderie is what makes this hotel special. Even when we arrived as we did then, tired from our long trip, we relaxed when we reached the small lobby of the Speronari Hotel. Back at the small reception area again, we asked the hotel manager for a map of the city. Overriding our protests, he quickly prepared a fresh cappuccino to welcome us. One year when a friend suggested that a grand hotel on the other side of the piazza was worth its expensive price just for the experience of staying in such historical luxury, we decided to stay with our bargain stop not just to save money but because we liked it better.

We headed back out to the piazza with no real agenda, no expectations, but a guidebook and a sense of curiosity. We walked across the pigeon-covered piazza and watched people buy packets of food to feed the throngs of pigeons. Braver tourists posed for pictures as the pigeons ate from their hands, sat on their arms and flurried around their heads. The pigeons moved across the piazza like waves, often seeming too lazy and well fed to fly except in extreme necessity. They rolled apart as we walked through them and huddled in bunches whenever any type of feeding seemed to be happening. Al would probably have let them eat from his hand, but I preferred to watch from a safe distance. At the end of the piazza farthest away from the church, I photographed the first of the lion statues that I noticed displayed so often in public places as symbols of Italian history.

The Piazza Duomo in Milan is high energy, large and full of people and activity, intensely Italian, yet in a modern way. The more business-like culture of northern Italy prevailed in Milan, feeling more like New York or Chicago than Rome or Florence. Traffic crosses the bottom part of the piazza, but across its broad space a constant flow of people comes and goes. The walkways around the piazza are a way for pedestrians to get places, to do business, to shop, and to meet people, rather than just to stroll quietly.

Al and I surveyed the elegant Duomo rising with its white marble exterior and appearance of dripped icing on its many small spires and sculpted figures. Its spires reached toward and into the heavens. The high steeples reach beyond what the eye can see, if not literally then symbolically. We wandered into the interior of the church, spent a few minutes looking around in the vast darkness, and then followed the small signs to the back entrance from which we would be able to climb to the rooftop. We had read on a sign that we would have the option to take an elevator, but once inside, we learned that the elevator was out of order and didn't go all the way to the narrow top even if it had been in service. Committed to our mission, we began to climb the narrow stone stairs of the interior until we came out on the lower levels of the rooftops. In the open air, we continued to climb across the slanted peaks following designated and marked pathways through the interior of the spires to the highest level possible on foot. It was magical.

Al climbed ahead and, this time, I kept up, thinking with each turn that we were as high as we were going to get, but we continued to find yet another flight of stairs. Being outside on the rooftops was exhilarating, especially on our first day when at moments parts of ourselves were experiencing the occasional rushes of jetlag and adrenaline which intensified our senses.

Looking at the exquisite detail on the spires so far above the ground, I was reminded of a time a geologist friend of Al's told of seeing exquisite and unusual flowers blooming behind rocks in a very out of the way area of the desert and wondering about such beauty being hidden. We chose photography shots from among the white up-shots of these lovely and delicate spires decorated with sculpted depictions of flowers and fruits of the vines.

"I wonder why they decorated way up here where nobody could see it," I asked. Then I answered my own question. "I guess they thought it was for the honor of God above, since the spires reach to the heavens." Even though our modern sense would question the concept of God being physically above the earth and the practicality of creating art that very few could see, Al and I had a special sense about beauty that was not visible to the ordinary perusal of human beings.

We couldn't help but be impressed by a culture which created and appreciated beauty for its own sake and thought that the Divine Creator did too. The walls and facades of the visible parts of the Duomo are lovely as well, and although the details of the roof design were not evident below, there seemed a sense of rightness and perfection in completing the rooftops this way, an effort at transcendence, of rising above the mundane world below, which we would remember when we returned to the ground.

When we reached the highest level, we relaxed in the serene quietness in the pleasant air far above the piazza. Leaning on a balustrade, we realized we were in the company of the statues of saints, which looked out over the busy square below from the white spires of the cathedral. They were surrounded by beauty, white marble, blue sky and birds, and the beauty reflected downward. We stayed for a while, leaning back against one of the slanted roof structures but safely away from any edge, basking in the morning sunlight and the loveliness of it all. When we returned to the busy city, a sense of the beauty and the blessings of the saints above stayed with us.

Across the Piazza Duomo Al and I crossed into the famous Galleria. Here, broad passageways connect multistoried old buildings under the high canopy of glass, the walkways cross under a central dome, under which a circular mosaic of signs of the zodiac decorates the floor. The high arches and canopy of framed glass connect the buildings, creating an indoor/outdoor space, with natural light and the flow of outdoor air.

The famous old Galleria is an integral part of the city's life, rather than separated from it as our indoor malls. Although it is covered, the glass lets in natural light and the broad lanes open into the city as outdoor air flows through. Rather than being surrounded by parking lots, the Galleria is, in fact, a main thoroughfare connecting the Duomo with the Piazza de La Scala, the famous opera house of Milan. Somehow even with the lines of shops and restaurants, the focus of Milan's Galleria seems more on quality of life and community than consumerism. People strolled and looked in shop windows or sat at cafes with coffees and aperitifs and watched others.

Although the space was under cover, natural light and fresh air moved through the wide-open entry passages, making us feel as though we were outside. I watched the comings and goings of men and women as they passed through the Galleria. "It's really different from the malls at home," I said to Al. "Not so much about shopping." He nodded.

Rather than a closed-in food court, cafes lined the pedestrian way, creating another place for strolling and people watching. We chose a small round table at one of the outdoor-style cafes. We quickly discovered that food and drink would cost more here since we had chosen a prime location with full service. But Al said, "It's okay. We're on vacation." We ordered two expensive beers, a bowl of peanuts and two tiny sandwiches.

Having made it across the Atlantic and climbing to the heights of a cathedral roof in less than twenty-four hours, we settled into one of those special moments of shared pleasure. As we drank our beers and nibbled on our expensive snack, we smiled, sharing our feeling of good fortune that we were really in Italy again and had many days ahead of us to look forward to.

By now I was tired, but Al felt energized, so after debating what to do next, Al went to the Castella on his own to see Michelangelo's sculptures, and I went back to the hotel. I walked the short familiar distance to the hotel alone, comfortable that I knew my way in Milan, in a way I would have been afraid to do in Rome at that time, for fear of getting lost. Milan was easier to get around in, even for me.

***

We had hoped on the initial trip to Milan to find an authentic neighborhood away from the busy city center. Al read in a guidebook about an old section of the city called Ticinese, near a canal. We attempted to go there but we decided to travel most of the way via the Metro system to avoid wear and tear on our knees and feet. Once above ground, we again had trouble getting oriented in the small streets and piazzas of the older part of the city. As we walked, we came upon the sculptured arch of an ancient porto and a line of Roman columns in front of the Church of Saint Ambrogia. As I stopped to photograph one of the statues of lions on the steps of the church, Al watched a group of school-age boys playing soccer in the piazza between the line of ancient columns and the church. This was the Italy we had come to see, the ordinariness of everyday life against the backdrop of ancient ruins and medieval churches.

We continued in what we thought was the right direction, turning left instead of right at a crucial corner, but soon realized that we were not nearing the intended canal, so we backtracked.

Al is definitely the leader and the guide for these outings. I could do some things on my own in cities, such as going to museums or churches, but I would never brave the long walks through unfamiliar city landscape on my own. Old neighborhoods are harder to locate than official tourist sights. There are no signs or crowds to lead us. Even when we returned to Milan, we found the area near Ticenese confusing. But we always enjoy both the search for and the discovery of these back streets and real life neighborhoods.

Once headed in the right direction, we soon came to the old canal lined with the shops of the open air market. Booths stretched endlessly along the street as they wound back from the main strip of shops. When we turned into the narrow lanes between the closely packed market stalls, we had the feeling of being in an Arab marketplace. The atmosphere was far more energetic than flea markets we had been to at home. Hucksters stood on their tables or chairs calling out their bargain prices for clothing and musical tapes as we wound our way through the crowded lanes of shoppers. We watched coin and phone card collectors browse intently through displayed merchandise. We passed a "hand is quicker than the eye" street vender who had set up a business on an upside-down box. He would hide a coin under one of three cups and inevitably fool the onlooker about where it was, keeping the customer's coin in the process. The task of following the money looked easy, as it looks easy back home to compete with one of those machines where you grab a toy with tongs in a glass case full of toys, or to hit bottles with a tennis ball at a fair. Feeling confident that I could keep my eye on the coin, since the man's hands were on the table all the time, I wanted to try. But Al shrugged and looked skeptical, "Don't be ridiculous. If they can't do it, you can't." So I kept my coin. The market became a regular stop for us in Milan.

✳✳✳

During our first trip to Milan, the main tourist sight on my list was Leonardo's *Last Supper*. I had made a special trip to see it during my tour through Europe in my twenties and vaguely remembered it being in a room associated with a church, a convent, actually. I had decided to take advantage of a several hour layover while passing through the Milan station. I had taken a taxi on my own, since my travel companion at the time wasn't interested, to run in and see the famous painting. I remembered both the room and the painting being dark, the room poorly lighted and the painting with muted and faded colors. Still, there was a beauty and intimacy about the faces in the painting that surpassed any reproduction. I also remember there was no one else in the room. I was the only visitor.

I had been intrigued, too, by the story that the Milanese had saved the painting on the wall of the convent's confectionary, during the bombings of World War II, by piling sandbags against the wall. While destruction occurred in the city around it, the wall with its painting survived. There was something special and almost mystical about the famous painting with so much history that had withstood the possibility of destruction. In the minds of many, Leonardo's *Last Supper* is as close as they can get to visualizing a real biblical event.

Al wanted to see the famous work, too, so we set out from our hotel one bright morning feeling no need to ask for directions. We had a good map and a guidebook that told us how to get there. We took the Metro, walked farther than we had anticipated along streets with little atmosphere, only apartment buildings and businesses and few helpful signs. Finally, we came around from the front of a church to the piazza that was in front of a smaller building that we thought housed the painting.

We were confused. There were no people around, no sign of tourist activity. The streets were quiet and there was no one to ask. Al insisted that the painting was in the church, but it was closed. Besides, I had read that the fresco wasn't in the church itself, but in the dining room of its convent, which was the traditional location for Last Supper pictures. Finally we saw a sign near the side entrance to what we now know is the convent. It explained that the convent. was "Chiuso restauro" or "Closed for restoration."

Of course, we were disappointed. And we felt stupid. Had we asked at our hotel, we would been told that the painting was under restoration and not viewable. But the long walk through the afternoon and the quest itself had been its own adventure. I was glad to have the memory of Al and me standing on the threshold of the convent alone.

When we did finally visit the painting a couple of years later in its newly restored presentation, the once silent and empty piazza held a long line of tourists while snack vendors and tour guides hustled them for business.

Once inside, Al and I joined a group with an English guide, tagging along at the edges and listening to the commentary. The guide explained that, for devotional reflection during meals, the confectionaries or dining rooms of convents and monasteries were often decorated with a large-sized painting of the Last Supper. Leonardo's idea of using the dining room wall was not new. His famous version was actually painted onto the wall itself, as was common in those days. But Leonardo painted after the plaster was dry instead of following the proven method of applying paint into wet plaster. As a result, the paint of his masterpiece had chipped and faded over time along with the plaster that held it. It seemed amazing that a work of art by an artist who was so famous, had used a technique that was basically a big mistake. We listened for a while to the guide's insights about the composition of the painting, the significance of the arrangement of the main characters around Jesus and the subtleties of Leonardo's use of color, light and shadow. Then Al got tired of what he saw as an art history lecture and we moved to stand in front of the wall sized painting with the other visitors, simply taking in the great work wordlessly and in a more personal way.

And although restoration has improved the painting's colors, and the lighting in the convent dining room is much better now, I enjoyed my shadow of a memory of visiting this room on my own in the quiet and dimness of light and shade so many years ago. I marveled that I had been the only one there.

***

If my first "must see" in Milan was Leonardo's *Last Supper*, Al wanted to see the inside of La Scala, the famous opera house. One fairly cold night we stood outside La Scala. I was dressed in a black skirt and sweater and black flat shoes, and Al had on a dark sports jacket and even wore a tie brought from home, just in case. We had been told that, although performances were always sold out, occasionally standing room was available at the last minute. The night's opera happened to be particularly famous with a famous performer, so by the time we arrived, even standing room was sold out. Later, we learned that standing room at La Scala does not mean that you can see the stage from a standing position in the back, but that you stand shoulder to shoulder in a small room behind the auditorium, able to hear the opera, but not to see it. For a visual person like me that would have been the last thing I would have wanted.

But our attempt at dressing in our travel best wasn't totally wasted. We stood along the walkway outside the front of the theater and watched as the audience of local people arrived, well dressed but not flashy, in wintry fur and leather coats and formal dark suits, their style precise but subdued. As the doors opened and closed, we managed to glance into the old opera house, and could see the red upholstered chairs in the compact theater and the stage lighted up for the performance. Neither the theatergoers nor the formally dressed ushers seemed to mind that we tourists looked inside. It became a quest of Al's, from that evening on, to try to see an opera in Italy.

A couple of years later, we visited the museum associated with the opera house. The museum presents the history of La Scala and Italian composers and operas, and also connects Italian opera to performance art forms such as marionettes and Japanese shadow puppets. The display of large marionettes from Naples, demonstrating as it did an artistic tradition of its own, planted in us the first thought of visiting Naples someday, an example of how travel leads to more travel as each trip suggests other places to visit.

Part of the museum tour was a walk through the balcony of the auditorium of the intimate spaces of the old opera house. For the price of admission to the museum, we could imagine ourselves as part of the audience. We were amazed at how much closer the audience would be traditionally, both to the performers and to each other. While the red upholstered seats look uncomfortably small and stiff for modern tastes, the atmosphere was wonderful. I was reminded of Shakespeare's Globe The-ater, which, as I told my students, was a tightly packed space, in which audience and actors could interact easily. Seeing La Scala made me think that the Italian tradition of cheering "Bravo" for the singers made a lot more sense in the smaller intimacy of the old theater.

Since then, we always check to see what is playing at the opera and I have in mind that someday, even though I don't like opera as Al does, I'll try to get tickets to something ahead of time.

***

The stress-free travel itinerary in this second trip included a one night stopover in Parma, the home of Parmesan cheese, as we discovered when we saw the large cheese wheels and Parma hams hanging in the shop windows. Parma was close to Milan, a short train ride away, but it provided a strong contrast. After we arrived one Sunday morning and checked into our hotel, we joined the pedestrians on their way to church in the town's Cen-tro or center. We were pleasantly surprised at the architectural beauty that was there. We wandered into the mass at the Duomo and then visited the Baptistery, an octagon of marble near the church just off the central piazza of the old town. People were conservatively dressed, in the northern style, wearing wool coats and jackets, the men in suits and ties and women in long wool coats and moderate heels for Sunday. I was in awe of being at a service in the old cathedral where mass had been said for hun-dreds of years.

Back outside, as we walked across the piazza away from the church, Al commented on how many men in dark suits we no-ticed talking into cell phones at a time when they were a luxury item in the U.S. "They get better reception that way," Al said.

"They probably use these instead of regular phones," (a trend which has now become strong at home as well). We strolled with the city folk along the wide streets to the central piazza, found a small round table at a busy café and ordered "birre" and a sandwich. Along with our fellow diners, we were in no hurry to leave as long as the sun was out. Later that evening we went to a restaurant that Al had found in the guidebook, a small, unassuming place with gracious service and excellent food that Al still remembers. Parma had been an unexpected discovery and although we were there only a little more than twenty-four hours, we have good memories.

CHAPTER FOUR

The Italian Riviera

The next day, we continued on to the Cinque Terre or the five lands. When people speak of the Italian Riviera, they picture an Italian version of Cannes, a glamorous area full of sunglassed faces, suntanned skin, movie star looks, elegant yachts floating along the docks, and efficient service in expensive waterside cafes. But unlike Portofino, a fancier Italian resort farther toward the French border, the Cinque Terre is very non resort-like.

In fact, except for the largest of the five towns, Monterosso, and one parking lot above the town of Corniglia, the towns have no roads and no cars. Built on harbors and hillsides that rise almost immediately from the water's edge, the five lands jut out into the sea and are separated from each other by water and mountain. They are connected only by hillside trails, by boat and by short train rides that cut through the intervening mountains. The towns are close together and much of the sightseeing is to view the next town, tucked against the hillside across a tiny harbor, from the perspective of another. Each is recognizably different from the others, distinct as a fishing village at water's edge or cliff side medieval town with high lookouts and old dwellings stacked along the hillside.

The individual villages are defined by their position on the coast, the middle being the highest elevation. The farthest town to the west is Monterosso, where Al and I stayed for two days. Toward the east and the Italian peninsula are Vernazza with its harbor and church, and Corniglia sitting high over hillside vineyards above the sea. There is Manarola with its walkway around the edge of low cliffs, its houses built into the lower foundation of rocky hillside and rows of yellow and pink houses rising sometimes six or seven stories and supporting each other, wall to wall, up the hillsides. Farthest east is Riomaggiore, which like Monterosso, is at sea level, its townscape more gentle than dramatic.

We arrived in Monterosso, the largest of the five towns, on a train from Parma after changing in La Spezia to a local train. Traveling off season, as we were, the weather was pleasantly cool. We seemed to be the only visitors, and our hotel was nearly empty. I reminded myself I had organized our itinerary to be low stress, a wind-down vacation after a busy year, a time when we could actually feel like we were on vacation as well as having the adventure of seeing new parts of the country. For low stress, the Cinque Terre was a good choice.

Kirsti had told us about the Cinque Terre where she had stayed with a friend to walk the trails and goat paths between each of the five villages. Kirsti had also recommended the accommodations, an old villa owned by the hotelier's family for many years before it became a hotel. It was right on a small beach looking out on the deep blue sea. We knew that she had liked it. She even found the name and number of the hotel tucked into the back of her passport. Our host's hospitality was memorable. He took our personal check on a U.S. bank to pay for our room. He gave us some letters to mail for him from the airport, which he said provided quicker service, trusting that we would. And he gave us a lot of personal attention and information not only about the Cinque Terre but about other cities as well.

This hotel manager knew about public relations. He stamped a paper to put in our passports, too, tucking it into a back page so as not to interfere with officialdom. Later when we looked for information to give to other travelers about our tiny hotel in this tiny village, we remembered to look in our passports. When I think how hard it is to dig through our stuff looking for pamphlets and business cards to find one particular address, I realize his cleverness.

One gesture was to send a bottle of wine back to the person in the U.S. who had recommended his hotel. When we visited, he asked how we had heard about his hotel and we told him, "From our daughter."

"What does she look like?" he asked.

We told him, "Blonde, in her twenties." Al added, "She traveled with another tall blonde. From Texas."

"Oh yes, yes. I remember," he told us, although I suspect he says he remembers all of his visitors whether he does or not. "I'll give you a bottle of our good Orvieto wine to take home to her." Later on he did as he said, and, feeling obligated both to him and to her, we carried the heavy bottle all the way back to the U.S. A couple of years later, friends whom we had sent to the hotel brought a bottle of local wine back to us and fixed us dinner to go with it. We sat around the table and talked about the Cinque Terre and about our host. The wine gift may have added extra travel weight but helped us reminisce about our unique experience.

When I had called him early one January morning from my kitchen table in Houston, our host enthusiastically promised us "a beautiful room overlooking the sea." The $100 would include half board of two meals, breakfast and dinner, he said. When I asked for directions from the train station, he told me to walk out of the station, turn right, and walk 100 meters.

At the time I could not picture at all how these directions would work. The hotel owner was only a voice across the ocean, (a leap of faith) from a strange far-away place. Italy was still a relatively unknown adventure. When we arrived at our planned destination, it was always with a sense of breaking through from the darkness of a distant voice into the light of reality, that we put such verbal descriptions, as these directions, into play.

When our train arrived that morning, after passing through several tunnels allowing only occasional glimpses of the bright blue of the Ligurian Sea, we walked out of the one-room station, turned right, walked with our luggage the 100 meters that our host had indicated and arrived at the door of a pink stucco waterfront hotel. Immediately, we felt the unrushed nature of the place; it was almost a letdown from the larger cities and the bustle of travel. As we arrived at the villa on a quiet and small sandy beach, a stone's throw from the water, we couldn't help but relax.

The owner greeted us with gusto, insisting on making us a welcoming cappuccino at his small bar in the tiny lobby before he took us upstairs to our room. Italian hospitality can sometimes make even old Southern style warmth look formal. As we sat and watched milk froth and bubble for our cappuccino, the friendly senore, who spoke excellent English along with his fluency in several other languages, chatted away, welcoming us and explaining the arrangements for breakfast and dinner and talking to us about the area.

When we finished our cappuccino, he took us and our bags up a wide and gracefully curved double staircase to our corner room. In this off season month, we had the best location, with a small balcony that looked out to the sea, as he had promised. The bright room, which without air conditioning might have been uncomfortable in the warmer months depending on the direction of the sea breezes, was for us, at this time of year, just perfect. Our view of the blue sea would have made a good travel poster, but here we were, in reality, at the Riviera of Italy without pretense or hassle.

In the family-sized dining room at one of several small tables, we were served home-cooked meals from the menu of the day by family members recognizable in celebration photographs that were displayed on the walls. A main course was prepared each evening and all guests were served the same menu. As guests, we were treated like family. It was simple and one of our favorite times. We ate some of our best food, and although there were only a few choices, the personal attention in a restaurant was a new experience for us.

The next morning, the hotelier joined us at our breakfast table to help guide us in our sightseeing and future travel plans. He told us what small churches to see in Monterosso and what to look at in the other towns as well as other tourist stops beyond the Cinque Terre. Al took notes on a small piece of paper which he folded and put in his wallet. "Beyond the Cinque Terre," he said, "yes, yes, you should go to Pisa and see the leaning tower, take your picture with all the tourists but that's all there is to that place. It's more significant that you see the cathedral where Galileo did his experiments. The tourists don't always go there." Al and I knew that Galileo had proved that the earth moved around the sun, upsetting the theological idea of the time that said that the earth was the center of the universe. Our host demonstrated, by moving his flattened hand in a gently circular motion, how the great scientist had used a flat circular object hanging from the roof and lightly touching sand, its unmoved base creating a pattern and showing that something outside the structure of the church, namely the earth itself, had moved. Our host criticized the institutional church of the time for its inquisitorial attitude toward Galileo and went on to say ironically, "You know, it was just in the news. The Pope just admitted that Galileo was right."

Leaving the subject of Pisa and Galileo, our host recommended that we stay, not in Pisa, but in Lucca, a town that at that time we had never heard of. "Pisa has a couple of sights," he said, "but Lucca is a better town to stay for a longer time and there are fewer tour buses." Although our itinerary bypassed both Pisa and Lucca that spring, several years later, Al would find the folded paper with the bits of information, and we would follow our host's recommendations and stay in Lucca.

***

In Monterosso, the Cinque Terre seems real and unreal at the same time. The simple life in the villages of the Cinque Terre is real but so different from modern urban life as to seem almost other worldly.

In the historic centro of Monterosso with an occasional small church built of black and white marble squares, narrow shop-lined stone streets, and a more medieval atmosphere to the old buildings, we followed the twists and turns of the streets as they sloped up the hill. We walked with the older folks along the waterfront and past the fishing boats pulled up on the sand in front of the small harbor. The boat area looked like a parking lot and seemed to operate on the honor system. Although we saw no identifying markers, we wondered if the boatmen had their own assigned spaces on the beach. Al looked at the orderly rows. "Everybody seems to have his own spot."

It was in Monterosso that we first ventured into local shopping. Now it seems a simple task, but I felt like I was floundering in unknown territory the first morning when Al sent me into a small grocery to get us ham and cheese, bread and apples and something to drink. By pointing, gesturing and attempting a few Italian words, I managed to get the friendly and patient shopkeeper to understand to slice just enough for two sandwiches. When it came to paying, I trusted in his honesty to take the right amount of money from my hand and to give me the right change. Al and I sat on a park bench under a shade tree and ate our lunch while looking over the quiet sea.

Unlike at home where seacoast property is often a commodity, and to sit near the water's edge requires paying expensive restaurant prices, in the small seacoast towns in Italy that we visited, the coastline is just part of the town. Seaside views in the Cinque Terre are not owned or protected by fences, but, as we would see later in Sicily, are often just background to the town's life. Sometimes city beach fronts, even those that are not dedicated to fishing or trade, are scruffier and less carefully designed than in resort areas of the United States, but community access seemed a better vision of how nature should be shared. Charging money to walk a private beach or to be able to sit and look out at water is like charging for a view of the sky or to breathe air. And while there may well be privately owned waterfront areas that we never saw in Italy, we felt welcome to the small towns' coastlines.

March was allergy season in central Italy. The gentle sea breezes had not blown any of the heavy air away and the beautiful pink and red and white blossoms of fruit trees we had seen were also producing lots of pollen. Al often has hay fever symptoms in season, but even I had them this time, and we weren't alone, having seen in our travels other people who sniffled and carried handkerchiefs.

Five days of blossoms combined with cigarette smoke on our train car had caught up with Al. His sniffles had turned into full blown allergy symptoms, stuffy head, congestion, itchy eyes and a generally draggy feeling. As he lay down to close his watery eyes for a while one afternoon, I set off for the local "farmacia," the pharmacy, looking for an antihistamine or decongestant. I remembered seeing the farmacia sign in the village in Monterosso. I wanted something that would make us feel better but not make us drowsy.

A pharmacy or farmacia in Italy doesn't sell candy bars and beauty products as at home. It is a smaller, more focused medical establishment and pharmacists are knowledgeable about simple ailments and remedies and can prescribe some medicines that would require doctors' approval back home. We had noticed that pharmacists, dressed according to profession in their white coats, seemed to engage personally with each patient, moving freely from behind the low counters into the aisles for consultations. Hesitant as I entered an environment so different from a drugstore at home, but motivated by Al's allergy discomfort, I went to the low counter and through pantomime and a few English words, I tried to explain Al's allergy symptoms. I wanted something that would make both of us feel better but would not make us too sleepy, like so many antihistamines do. The pharmacist spoke only Italian, but in his professional role as health consultant, and with the helpful patience common in small towns, he got out his English dictionary so that we could look together to help understand the details of what I wanted. Finally he chose a standard antihistamine remedy and suggested that we take half of the dosage, which we did. After a long nap, we recovered enough for Al to hike and me to ride between all four villages.

In the Cinque Terre, others were helpful, too. We bought postcards at a small shop and asked where to buy stamps. Stepping into the street, the older woman shopkeeper spoke to us in Italian and with gestures sent us up a hill and under an arch to a tabacchi shop to buy stamps. The man at the tabacchi directed us verbally and with hand motions through the side streets of the village to a bank to change some traveler's checks.

People in the small towns speak less English but are often more friendly. The Cinque Terre gave us confidence that we could make ourselves understood if necessary, that people were kind and helpful, and that small towns would be easier for us even if they weren't set up for tourists and even if we didn't know any Italian.

***

If you are looking for tourist sights or entertainment, don't come to the Cinque Terre. As in many of the best places in Italy the towns themselves are the sights and climbing to the top of each village hill is the ultimate goal. We did very little formal sightseeing, but our awareness of the texture of life in the wonder of its small details enriched us as we strolled through the towns and looked at the water. As has happened with other simple places in Italy, I can still imagine myself walking along a narrow street with a stone wall on one side and blooming gardens on the terraces on the other side or walking along the sea wall in the late afternoon winding along the small empty beach between the wall and sea.

The compactness of road and garden and houses brings us into intimate contact with townspeople. We saw women trimming back grapevines, getting ready for new spring growth, an elderly man tending his tiny backyard garden, his early spring lettuce coming up from the soil. It's rare to see a yard of any size devoted to something as nonproductive as grass. Although we were obviously outsiders, people greeted us, "Buon giorno," "Good morning," as we wandered along the back lanes. Far from feeling like intruders, we felt as if we were a part of local life, at least temporarily.

As we walked, I noticed how close we seemed to the tasks of everyday life. I realized how in the U.S. we live separate from our neighbors, especially in the suburbs with our wooden privacy fences, backyard patios, and gated communities. We in the suburbs all know how hard it is to walk to do an errand, to make a bank deposit or grocery purchase or buy stamps. The distances are too great even if we are willing to make the effort to walk. Even in urban areas, we often live indoors in locked-up apartments or townhomes, often with enclosed garages or condos set back from the street. We seem to have become less pedestrian, especially in newer more sprawling cities, as people use cars not only for commuting but for even the smallest of errands.

I always feel a special kind of loneliness when we come home, not just because Al and I are no longer on vacation together but also because at home it is harder to feel part of a community by simply taking a walk. Al reminds me we probably would get bored spending days and weeks in a small town in Italy, but I maintain my romantic view of village life. People are together in their walks and in their day-to-day living. So much of what we do to fill our need for community requires spending money. We join exercise clubs and organize social events that Italians seem to have built in to their daily lives, enjoying being in the natural outdoors along the way. Part of my vacation goal is to remember these places and ways and to re-experience them in my mind. It's comforting to be reminded that gentle places like this exist in the world.

***

While community connection is built in to the simple daily tasks of life, the more adventuresome activity in the Cinque Terre is to follow the trails that local people have used for years and hike along the hillsides up and over across the vineyards that spread out over the mountainsides between each of the five towns. A modern alternative is to ride the short distance on one of the trains that travel along the coastal route from Genoa to Le Spezia. Twice Al walked the miles over the hillsides while I took the five minute train ride through the dark tunnels to the next sea inlet and waited for him in the next village.

On our first morning in the Cinque Terre, we rode the train to the farthest town from us, a ten minute ride through tunnels and along the sea coast with glimpses again of the blue Ligurian Sea. I had read that the walk from Riomaggiore back to Manarola along the Via dell'Amore or Lover's Way was the easiest hike. A guidebook mentioned a railing along the pathway which was neither too high on the hillside or too close to the sea to be intimidating. As far as I was concerned, the easiest hike still qualified as the adventure of walking between two unconnected villages. Unfortunately for me, when we got to the Via dell'Amore, we found it barricaded with a sign that indicated it was under construction.

Al looked around the barrier and walked a few steps past it. He said, "It's okay. We can probably still do it." I shook my head and headed back down the entry steps. In hindsight, I suspect we could have walked the trail, barricade or not, but at the time did not want to break any official Italian rules, fearing I might have to leap over a hole in the path or rock climb along a cliff when I reached a point of no return along the walkway. I knew enough to know that Al, once committed to the hike, wouldn't turn back easily on my account.

Disappointed in our first effort, we took the train back to explore the town of Vernazza.

***

From the small stazione in Vernazza, we wound down a narrow path-like street that looked as if it had been used at one time for donkeys or goats. Although no cars drove into Vernazza, the small pathway was now paved for pedestrians. At the bottom of the hill the small harbor was framed by a fisherman's church made of gray stone. From inside, worshipers looked from windows at the water that washed against the foundation of the side of the church. The church was a bulkhead against the sea, and looks as if an artist had planned the composition of small rowing-style fishing boats in primary colors, red, blue and yellow, which were pulled up onto the rock and sand of the tiny harbor, complementing the gray of the stone church.

As in Monterosso, the arrangement in rows and an honor system seemed to be the only security for the simple craft. "I wonder how they know where to park," I asked Al. Again the boat owners seemed to have assigned places since things were so orderly.

In Vernazza, we had one of those travel moments frozen in time that all travelers experience, those moments where everything comes together, not because of an important sightseeing experience but just something simple. Al had noticed a small gelato shop opposite the church and bought us each a cone. We climbed onto the large flat rocks at the edge of the blue water. We ate our gelato and looked at the water and felt the sun and looked at the boats and just sat there for awhile. We were not looking at things as much as just being there, part of the scene, and it was fine. The picture was perfect and we were in it. The side of the stone church was behind the boats so if we turned from the sea we saw the town. As we sat in the sun on the warm rock at the edge of the blue water, I was reminded of some Walt Whitman poems in which he became both the participant in a scene and a poetic observer though his notice of sensory detail.

Like Whitman, we were able to observe the scene as we might appear in it, leaning back against the broad rock, eating our gelato and looking at the sea around us. Not only were we taking in the sights and sounds and tastes and smells of the scene around us, but were in it surrounded by images of color and light, sound and taste, and scent and touch, the hard warm rocks beneath us, the balmy sea air on our skin. We were our own picture postcard.

This was one of our first glimpses into the Italian way of living the moments of life to the fullest, of the meaning of the Italian expression, "la dolce far niente," the sweetness of doing nothing. But we had much to learn about this fine art. Coming from busy modern lives, it's hard to let go of purposeful activity for very long. As long as we sat and ate ice cream, we had a purpose. Although we were relaxed in a pleasurable setting, we were doing something. We had a "raison d'etre," a reason to be there. Once our gelato was gone, and we had taken in the sights and atmosphere, Al felt the need to move on.

Al was determined to walk one of the town-to-town trails, in fact the longest one, that afternoon. "We've been here all day and haven't walked a trail yet," he complained. So, while I walked back to the station and waited for the train back to Monterosso and our hotel, he set off for the hour-long narrow hillside trail from Vernazza through the vineyards across the steep hills high above the sea. After arriving at Monterosso, I waited at the other end of the trail and wondered what I would do in this almost all Italian-speaking village if Al didn't show up in a reasonable time. But somehow it didn't worry me too much and soon enough he came striding down off the hill, tired and with sore knees, "from the downhill stress," he complained, but with a sense of accomplishment.

Al was unwavering in his intent to walk between each and every town. I was equally determined not to climb over these hillsides, finding the high paths not good for anyone with fear of heights or vertigo. So for these adventures we parted company and met again. I liked hearing him describe the hillside views and sloping vineyards, but I never regretted not following those narrow paths along the steep hillsides, where the view cascaded down into the sea. There were no windows or railings to separate me visually from the sea, and that would have made me dizzy.

Al liked walking from town to town over the goat paths and across the rows of grapes planted on the hillside. He went across steep, high hillsides, sloped straight down to the water. The only other people he saw on the trail at this time of year, when no tourists were around, were occasional local pedestrians and vine tenders on the hillside. The narrow trails were unmarked except by the feet of the many villagers who used them to traverse the side of the hills high up across working vineyards where vines had been fallow for winter and vine tenders had cut back the vines in readiness for the new season. He was impressed with their ability to work the land on such a steep hill.

While Al walked between the towns, I took the train. I spent time wandering in the towns, looking at the water and the gardens and the people. Although I thought he overdid his hiking, pushing too hard while we were on vacation, our parallel approaches worked fine. I didn't slow him down on the trails. He could go at his own pace. And I had plenty of time to contemplate the views from the harbors without feeling rushed.

The next day Al walked two more trails, between Vernazza and Corniglia, and then, after lunch, on to Manarola, on his way to meeting his goal. Corniglia, the middle town of the five villages, sits high on the hilltop with houses built along the crest in a stepping stone arrangement until it is too steep to build farther down. Al got a headstart on his hike leaving the train at Vernazza, while I took the next train from Vernazza to Corniglia.

CHAPTER FIVE

Discovering the Passeggiata

Although most of Corniglia sits high on a hill, the train stops at the bottom near the water. Al met me at the station, after a hike that he said had been easier than the one the day before. We climbed together up the nearly 400 wide and gracefully turning stairs from the sea level station to the town center. We had read about a small winery even farther above the town, but even Al allowed himself not to go any further. He had taken the train as far as Vernazza and walked across the hillside from Vernazza to Corniglia while I had taken the train the entire way. We stood at the scenic lookout at the top of the stairs taking in the panoramic view of the hills and the colors and shapes of the other towns that jutted into the sea in the distance. We wandered along the crest of the town looking out at the expanse of azure sea, the light shimmering as the sun met the rippling water far below us. From different perspectives of greater height and steeper angles and drop-offs, we looked at the other towns of the Cinque Terre in the distance, looking across Corniglia's small harbor to the town on the next hill that jutted into the sea coast.

Our hotel host had told us he would call ahead to a friend who owned a restaurant in Corniglia with "una bella vista," "a beautiful view." We were the only guests in the small restaurant. Perhaps the place was packed in the summertime, but on this early spring day we had the place to ourselves. We ate at one of the four tables on the tiny veranda at the edge of the hillside down to the sea. We looked out over the hills and rows of vineyards dropping off from beneath us to the sea below. We ate lobster-stuffed ravioli with green salad with a light white Orvieto wine produced from the vineyards before us.

We savored the view of the other towns from our central perch, a rich variety of perspectives of architecture and natural environment all within a small space. Looking down the vine-covered hillside to the sea below, we studied the mechanical pulleys that went up the hillside; these would carefully carry boxes of the harvested grapes a few feet from the ground up the side of the steep hills to the villages and wineries above. We saw a vine tender working along the steep hillside. Al said, "He looks like he'll fall into the water if he stands up or leans back too far." But the worker seemed at ease alone on the hillside above the sea.

We had noticed small vineyards in the miniscule yards of Monterosso and Vernazzo. As in much of Italy, a yard full of grass was unknown. Every foot of space seemed to be cultivated with trees, vines or produce. The seasonal task of spring was to trim back the vines. We noticed the precision that accompanied the simple process and felt the vine tender's closeness to seasonal cycles of natures. Grape growing seems always to require less mechanization and more direct connectedness. My observation was that only a person could decide, piece by piece, what part of the vine to cut and only human hands had a gentle enough touch for harvesting grapes. It seemed to require full attention and a coming into the moment as the vineyards were tended vine by vine.

In Italy wine is produced regionally and although you can order wine that is not grown locally, generally the house wines are local wines. Wine is part of the terrain, geographically and culturally. People don't drink just to drink, there is no legal or illegal drinking age, and people don't tend to get drunk. Wine is the most common drink with meals. We often got a carafe of wine for around three dollars, less than wine by the glass costs at home. Although some Italian wines are produced for export, local wines seem less about commerce and more about supplying the needs of the community. We guessed that people grew the white grapes for themselves as well as to sell larger quantities of the white grapes for Orvieto wine. Being so close to the vineyards, the realities of spring vine tending connected, and we felt less like visitors and more immersed in the process of winemaking that starts with the grapes. We weren't on a tour of a winery being lectured to about vines and grapes and aging processes. The close to the earth aspect of vine tending that we saw on the steep hillsides of the Cinque Terre was somehow more inspiring.

Later when driving through northern California country in Napa and Sonoma, we noticed similar contours of the land with vines curving along them in rows of grapes. After being in Italy, we appreciated the Italian influences of California more and could understand how its climate and terrain drew immigrant Italians to settle there. With more land to work on, the vineyards became production oriented, reflecting American commerce.

As the balmy spring day lingered, we shared the scraps of our lunch with a couple of cats who had kept their distance, hanging around politely until we were finished, and then moved in for any leftovers.

After finishing our memorable outdoor lunch, we drifted down through the town along the local streets, passing a few shops and side-by-side multi-storied houses in colorful stucco that leaned together for support. We saw lines of drying laundry, including a picturesque grouping of 12 small soccer shirts, orange with black numbers, swinging side-by-side in two lines.

Gradually we wound our way down the hillside along the circuitous more picturesque route through the town rather than the direct descent of the 400 stairs. We followed a narrow road along the back of houses and yards and small vineyards along the hillside. As we reached the lower stretches, we saw a couple about our age, also wandering down. At first they seemed to blend in, then Al said, "They must be tourists, too. We haven't seen anybody else just wandering."

Al decided to walk from Corniglia to Manarola, the next town to the east, and the last one of the five for us to visit. As I waited for the train going in that direction, the same couple we had seen on the hillside arrived. We struck up a conversation. I discovered that not only were they from the U.S., but from a city where Al and I had lived for many years. We even knew some of the same people. When I said goodbye as they continued on to Riomaggiore, I couldn't wait to tell Al about the unlikely encounter.

Al and I met the American couple again as we were leaving the Cinque Terre on the train from Le Spezia to Florence. It felt strange but comfortable to connect with familiar lives in this unfamiliar place. "It's amazing," one of them said as the train rolled along, "We're practically the only people on a local train in an out of the way village in Italy in the early spring talking about people we know back home."

But we also talked about Italy. They had returned more often then we had at that time, (although our trip numbers may have surpassed them by now). They had brought their kids once and shared a villa with another family. They had traveled to other countries, but as the husband said, "After all, what can match Italy? Nothing is like it." Those of us who love Italy understand each other's feelings. Like fellow travelers and Italianphiles we met over the years, they validated our own growing feeling for the country and culture.

***

From the train in Manarola, I followed the narrow stone streets, past the layers of buildings built on foundations of other buildings on the hillside, seemingly holding each other upright. Many of the houses looked medieval and their only obvious acknowledgement of modern times was the plethora of television antennas on their roofs. While I figured the houses had been updated with indoor plumbing and electricity, I wondered what they were like inside and thought how fascinating it was to take buildings hundreds of years old and modernize them. Coming down from the station toward the sea, I didn't see Al in the small piazza. Thinking he was still hiking over the hillside, I climbed some stairs to walk out along the catwalk that wrapped around the hill protruding out into the sea, separating the town from the harbor, and providing views of the distant villages to the west. Standing out over the blue sea, this time from a lower perspective, I found my attention focused hypnotically on the sparkling light, on the intense and changing shades of blue of the expanse of rippling water, now the most beautiful part of a quite spectacular view.

The walkway wrapped itself back in a U-shape along the hillside and when I reached the cliff side farthest from the town, I saw Al coming down a slope above me. From this spot, we could look back at the other towns to our west from a different perspective. From the seaward most point of the wrap-around cliff walk, we could look back to see the harbor and rocks, the bright colored fishing boats, and the brightly colored houses on the hillsides of Manarola. On rocks below, we looked down at a lone fisherman. Using a few Italian words and simple gestures, I shared a conversation with an older Italian woman from Milano who had come by herself to visit "la bella mare" as she called the sea. Standing on the catwalk, we shared the beautiful view of the sparkling sea below us and the other towns in the distance to the west. Al moved down to photograph the fisherman, a subject that would have seemed small and insignificant to me but which he felt captured the mood of the afternoon. Thus began a pattern of that subject, fishermen in boats and in mist or alone on rocks or on beaches. Somehow the reflection of light on his subject caught his photographer's eye.

***

Although at the time we had no name for the ritual, it was in the Cinque Terre that we first discovered the local passeggiata, the evening ritual of strolling walks. Inadvertently, we experienced the passeggiata as we strolled with the villagers along the water front before the dinner hour and through the small downtown after dinner. We had simply gone out for a late afternoon walk ourselves and gradually realized that we were a part of a community experience that took place before and sometimes after dinner.

When we walked in the morning or mid-afternoons, we felt we were practically the only people in a quiet and relatively uninhabited town. As we walked along the waterfront near our hotel, we noticed more people than earlier but figured it was late afternoon and people were coming home from work or just enjoying the spring weather.

But by evening we realized that going out for a stroll when everybody else was out was a communal experience. It was quite different from our home experience of walking our dogs or taking exercise walks with our headsets covering our ears.

Life in the small villages has a pattern and there is a ritual to the passeggiata as it occurs in these places. Later, when we mentioned the practice and the timing of the street life to another American traveler, he said, "One thing about Italy, whenever it's time to do something, everybody does it." People shop and eat and then walk at certain times of the day creating a rhythm of life and social activity. The community involvement that, at home, we work hard to establish with our neighbors and in our churches and volunteer activities just happens in the small towns in Italy.

In the early evening, everyone in town seems to be outside, men sitting on benches or standing in small groups, women strolling through the towns, without any real purpose because there is no place to go to in a hurry. They simply enjoy the companionship of bonding with their community, understanding that the most important part of a social experience is not the show or the food or the music, but the people.

The Cinque Terre was the first place where we slowed down, where in spite of Al's hikes across the hillsides from town to town, his goal oriented enjoyment of the conquest of earth, we learned to stroll instead of stride, to stand and look out at water, to sit in the sun and just be for a little while. We learned that we could walk along the same small street, seemingly retracing our steps, but discover new views and experiences, depending on the time of day. Instead of broad strokes and highlights of travel, we had depth and simplicity. For us urban Americans, used to fast paces and goal setting, the rhythms of Italian village life were a contrast.

**

Several years later on a Sunday afternoon in Milan we were witness to a high energy passeggiata, one of the most intense we had experienced. It was early spring and good weather was not guaranteed in northern Italy, as we were reminded when it actually snowed the next day. The sheer numbers of people and the purposeful activity may have been greater because these were the first warm days of spring and the weather was still unpredictable, so a good day was seized as a chance to be outside.

As Al and I randomly explored the variety of avenues from the Piazza Duomo, we accidentally came upon a wide Corso that was full of people, not standing around or sitting in cafes, but in motion, the right and left sides of the crowd moving in opposite directions in the flow but with the same rhythm and sense of purpose. No one was in a hurry, yet people were not ambling either.

Everyone seemed more or less comfortable in the flow and stream of people. Older people walked comfortably along and mothers and fathers pushed toddlers in strollers. Teenage girls walked arm in arm alongside young lovers who did the same. Small groups of young men seemed to move a little faster than the others but without seeming to push ahead. It was not a parade, not a means of exercise, not even a means of seeing and being seen, just a common energy and experience.

Al and I walked with the others, he, for once, settling into the common pace and not needing to move any faster than anyone else. We stopped once for gelato, waiting our turn in line patiently, entertained by the activity all around us. Later, as we continued our walk along the pedestrian corso, Al noticed a coin-operated phone, the only kind we knew how to use, and stopped to check his voice mail back home. I found a wall to lean on, and while I waited, watched the passeggiata pass in both directions, the mostly casual, but stylishly so, mixture of all ages of Italians, many dressed in black leather jackets and fitted black pants and black shoes. I absorbed the intoxicating buzz of people in steady motion and enjoyed the sense of just being.

Milan is a good base for visiting the lake country of Italy, known for its beautiful resorts with views of the snow covered peaks of the Alps even in the summer. Eventually and at the end of our second year, we circled back to Milan, spending the last night in the town of Stresa before flying out of Milan. What in the warmer months would be bustling and busy, the small resort town on Lake Maggiore was in March still very quiet with only a few hotels and restaurants open for the season. Here, we were our own passeggiata, spontaneously strolling random routes around the lake and up the hills behind the harbor. We had the town and the lakeside walkways much to ourselves and although we did the tourist activity of taking a motorboat ride to the islands in the lake, we mostly entertained ourselves by watching the ducks near the shore, walking on the hillside streets with budding spring flowers, and watching a fisherman in the morning haze standing in his rowboat and throwing out his line. And we remember this quiet place more than some of the more famous places we've been.

Twice, when we spent our last evening in Milano, we visited an international exhibit in the museum near the Piazza Duomo and near our hotel. One year we stood in a long line of mostly Milanese in a cold drizzle and finally entered an exhibit of paintings of Impressionist and modern art from Moscow, traveling from behind the walls of the Soviet Union for the first time since the Cold War. As we followed the flow of viewers through the well laid out exhibit of previously not shown Monets and Picassos, the colors and light more than made up for our cold feet and damp jackets. Another year we went to the same museum and saw a special exhibit of art and photography presenting the life and ideals of Mahatma Gandhi told mostly through photographs. After taking in as much as we could of the large-sized photos representing Gandhi's life and contributions to Indian independence, and his death by violence, we stepped out into another damp and cold March evening.

Both of these international exhibits made us think that Europe seemed more in touch with the East in many ways, through geography, history and contemporary life. In both cases we had commented on how Italy seemed connected to Eastern countries and cultures. This was in part because Milan, like London or Paris or New York, was a big international city. But Italy is geographically closer to both Eastern Europe and Asia, and their histories are more connected. This fact gradually took on a deeper meaning and added to our understanding of the larger world in ways we didn't expect. The historical implication of being separated from much of the world by the oceans became more real to us. Leaving our familiar center behind helped us realize that the world looks different when you change the center point.

During one trip, we hit a last day of bad weather in Milan. The cold weather had shortened any local passeggiata and there were few pedestrians around. I was cold even in my layers of clothes and jacket so we gave up walking. We found a local trattoria not too far from the hotel, good enough, although not particular charming and sat in a booth by the window. By the time our food arrived, it had gotten dark outside and as I glanced out at a street light across the way, I was surprised to see snow flurries. "Look, Al, it's snowing," I said. He shook his head, not believing me, and then saw the white flakes blowing in the lights. I went on, "I guess this should make us appreciate how lucky we've been to have good weather in March." We both thought of the sunny skies, blue water and balmy breezes that had been typical. Cold winds and snow flurries wouldn't give us the Italian feeling that we had come to associate with our Italy vacation in early spring. We'd been lucky. We walked back to our hotel along quiet passageways and through the covered Galleria where, now that the weather had shifted, very little was happening. When we crossed the piazza in front of the lighted Duomo, which was empty of both people and pigeons, Al couldn't resist seeing the deserted snow-covered streets as a new adventure. "These would be good pictures," he announced, thinking of the effects of the snow. "I'm cold," I complained, "and we don't have the camera."

Back in our warm and cozy upper-story hotel room, which now felt especially warm and cozy to me, Al found the camera. We had inadvertently bought a roll of black and white film so while I opted to stay in the warmth of the hotel, he went out and about the quiet city for about an hour taking black and white snapshots of the old buildings and streets lighted in the emptiness with snow and damp reflected in the streetlights. I felt like I was living in an old movie as I watched the snow flurries from the little window of our hotel room.

The next morning our plane was delayed in leaving as crews sprayed de-icing materials on its surface. As we watched from the window of our 747 and looked into the wet gray day, one of us said, "So much for sunny Italy." And again, we reminded ourselves not to take our good weather for granted.

CHAPTER SIX

Florence

After our second trip, planning got easier. We had both had a good time and were learning enough about Italy to want to know more. When we got past our initial experiences and impressions, we started to know a place, like a person, in a more complete and deeper way.

Florence was one place we returned to enough to go deeper. After our initial introduction with Kirsti, we went back several times and enjoyed both its familiarity and our continual discoveries. Paradoxically, Florence was both easy and challenging.

Florence was the first city where we had a sense of control. We shared memories of being there with our daughter and celebrated our growing comprehension of the layout of the city. We began to follow a regular route, which we repeated whenever we returned, walking across the city to the river and then across the bridge.

Florence or Firenze is probably the most visited Italian city after Rome. It is smaller and easy to access on foot. It contains layers of history, especially from the early Renaissance. We felt more connected because Kirsti had introduced us to the city from the inside out. Before we saw any of the famous sights, we had plunged into the darkened small streets, and narrow alleys, places that at home we would never go into, following her through the mazes. Since that first time, our trips to Florence have been partly homecomings, as we wander past the apartment where Kirsti stayed, the sights she took us to, the restaurants where we ate, the grocery store where she shopped, taking her own plastic bags because as she said, "They charge you if you don't," and the warehouse-style fruit, vegetable, meat, fish, poultry and cheese market that was our first taste of Italian-style food shopping.

Above Florence, the Piazzale Michelangelo stands immovable as crowds of buses stop to allow tourists to either look out their windows at the view of the city or take a brief walk around to look out over the railings and take photographs. The piazza with its replica of the *David* represents classical dignity combined with the Renaissance spirit and inspiration that was and is Florence. Often tourists passing through are in awe as they photograph the statue of David, thinking it is Michelangelo's original. It is, in fact, only a replica, but stands above the city like a Greek statue of Apollo or Zeus, a young god of the Renaissance, not protective so much as leading in strength, empowering the people, representing the city soul. Every successful wonder-photo or travel poster ever taken of Florence seems to be of the bronze red of the great dome by the architect Brunelleschi and the Duomo itself dominating the cityscape and framed by the same green bushes growing on the edge of the upper hillside. A bit of branch in the foreground to offset and personalize the grandeur of the scene below, the scene is one of the most famous representations of Italy. Later, we would use the same greenery to frame our personal photograph of the rooftops of the city.

Our hikes to the hilltop were worth it, not only because of the view of the city from one side of the piazza, but also to see the ruins of the medieval wall from the other side of the piazza that looked out over the countryside, and the green slopes of the Boboli Gardens of the Pitti Palace that also stands on this side of the Arno River. With Al in the lead, we wandered away from the David replica and the city overlook and discovered vistas and settings richer than what was on the typical tourist agenda. Away from the tourist buses and the souvenir and drink stands, we found our own scenic spot on the other side of the high piazza and looked out for a long time at the quiet greenness of the country and the old stone walls of the medieval city, winding and turning over the rolling hills. Walking further around the curve of the hilltop, we looked up at the decorated facade of a large church that we hadn't known was there, one with even more stairs; one we would come back to climb another time. Still novices as travelers, we learned quickly that the list of tourist highlights wasn't the whole story and that random discoveries enriched our journey.

That first trip Al and I didn't intend to climb; we intended to take a city bus up the hill, but we couldn't find the bus stop. Later we walked up the stairs by choice, climbing the known route to the Piazzale Michelangelo. But that climb and discovery followed by our first lunch together in a small but wonderful little neighborhood restaurant with only two other diners, which we found only after we had hiked back down to the bottom of the hill, set the tone for our later trips.

The dramatic beauty of the cityscape of Florence seen from the piazza above contrasts with its narrow medieval streets that can seem confining, but intriguing, in the dark shadows of the stone buildings. Motorbikes roar through the little streets creating noise and air pollution in what must have once been a quieter, more gentle place. In films such as *A Room with a View* and *Tea with Mussolini*, we get a glimpse of what Florence may have been like for earlier English speaking tourists. These movies show clip-clop of horses pulling wagons and carriages through the stone streets and the sedate movement of pedestrians across the piazza. But today the density of the buildings and streets makes the spacious piazzas in front of the larger churches, which provide spaces for people to stroll and congregate, and the openness of the walkways along the river more appealing. After blocks of walking in close quarters there is always something special about stepping into the openness of the piazzas, the living rooms of the city.

Florence didn't convey to me the balmy warmth that my imagination had associated with the Mediterranean countries, either in its weather, at least in March, or in its culture. People seemed polite but a little more reserved, less demonstrative and more formal than in the warmer Mediterranean South. Like all old medieval cities, much of Florence has small narrow streets, or walkways that pass as streets, where pedestrians, bikers, motorbikes, and Fiats intermingle. That, combined with the high walls of Florence's stone buildings and the exhaust from motorbikes, creates a sense of being closed in at times and gives a strong sense of character to the city and evokes a bit of a fortress atmosphere.

Florence is a walking city. The stone sidewalks are hard, but my feet and legs never feel as tired as when I walk on the concrete back home. My unscientific theory is because the stone is a natural substance.

Most of the city is level, and, most important for us visitors, it is compact. The major sightseeing spots are between the train station and the river and contained in a couple of square miles. We have learned to avoid the busier streets and follow the pedestrian ways that wind between and through the old medieval neighborhoods. While I stall and protest, "This doesn't go anywhere. It's dark that way. I don't see any people," Al heads straight down what seems like a dead end alley only to be proven right by a sharp turn at the end that continues us on our way. The busier streets may feel safer and more direct, but ambling through the back roads deep within the city is not only more interesting but a relief from the gas exhaust from motorbikes that tends to collect in the valleys between the close by, set buildings.

Compared to Rome, where we get lost even on the main streets, Florence is a cinch. If we get off our route, it is easier to find our way by stumbling accidentally back onto a familiar piazza or finding ourselves in front of a recognizable church. We can always head back toward the river to find our bearings.

One time we did get lost and ended up walking along a busy highway in a suburban area. As I maintained a chorus of questions, asking Al "Where are we? How did we get here?" he plodded on looking for a right turn to take us back into the centro, or center of Florence. Although this walk was not picturesque compared to the old city, it reminded us that in real life in Italy, many people do live outside the charm of the city center and commute just as we do at home. Being able to stay in il centro and focus on the historical centers is one of the luxuries of being a visitor.

***

Every time we pull into the Santa Maria Novella Station, we feel comfortable rather than stressed. The station is busy enough to be interesting but is small and feels friendly, especially compared to Rome's Termini. The building reminds me of an old downtown library with its newstands and the interesting mixtures of tourists, students, older people, nuns in traditional habits, travelers and welcomers, coming and going on trips in and out of the city. The station is in town and it's easy enough to stay in a hotel near the station for convenience or for easy side trips. Once we even walked painlessly with our luggage to a hotel a couple blocks away, making an exception to our rule about always taking a taxi from the station.

After we dropped off our bags at our hotel, Al and I head toward the river by way of the compact piazza in front of the Duomo. Coming around a corner, I am always awestruck at seeing this enormous church with its red tile dome and roof and pointed bell tower compactly fitted into the buildings and streets close around it. Part of our enjoyment is our familiarity with the area. One or the other of us says, "Oh, look, there's the Duomo. We're going in the right direction." Approaches to the Duomo from different side streets create different impressions as different angles and facades of the building are framed by other structures. As we walk along the majestic marble side, we look up at the bell tower and always find some new detail to look at, the gargoyles on the sides or the change of colors of the marble in the light.

The Italian word for cathedral, la cattedrale, similar to our English word cathedral, is replaced by the Italian duomo in everyday usage. People seem not to use the formal name of the Cattedrale Santa Maria del Fiore, but simply say they will meet at the Duomo. It's one of many Italian words, originally foreign, which, after our first trip, became simply part of our vocabulary, like pasta or gelato. This wonderful building is one of those sights worth going back to again and again. People who go to the beach or mountains for vacations never say, "Oh, I've seen the waves before," or "I don't want to look at those mountain peaks. I saw them last year." We're the same way about our favorite architecture in Italy. It's like looking at beautiful scenery that you can't get tired of, that always has something new to offer in different light and shadow, perspective and distance.

Many of the old cathedrals have a separate baptistery, a smaller companion building with a center font for baptisms and seats in an intimate arena for family and guests. At the entrance to the octagonal baptistery near the Duomo, we stopped beside other tourists to study the famous doors known as the "Gates of Paradise," with panels sculpted in bronze that depict Old Testament scenes in bas relief and called Ghiberti's panels after its artist. Our first time, Al glanced at the guidebook and told me with authority, "These aren't the real ones." The original panels are safely indoors for protection from the weather and automobile fumes, but we marvel at the excellent replicas. We were new to art history, so we listened as an English speaking tour guide pointed out Bible stories depicted in the small spaces with exquisite detail. We studied the panel of Noah and the Ark, picking out the animal pairs, and we took in the drama of the moment when the angel stopped the hand of Abraham who was about to sacrifice Isaac. The visualization of these artists, their ability to imagine and depict the Bible stories, rivals the imagination and production skills of modern movie directors such as Steven Spielberg and George Lucas. Even though it was a replica, we realized we were looking at one of the great art treasures of Italy.

Inside, Al and I stood looking over the enormous baptismal font. Wondering who had been baptized there, I commented, "I guess it was just for the rich families." This era of Christian art includes a tradition of visually contrasting good and bad, which sometimes seems rather over the top from a modern perspective. We looked up at the ceiling and were amazed by the depiction of a huge monster looking down at us. The monster with its horns and big tongue devouring something rivaled scary monsters in modern movies and could give a child nightmares. This was my first glimpse of the scary side of this era's artistic imagination, "How could they put that in a church?" I asked Al, "I guess it's about good conquering evil, but I'm glad we save our monsters for the movies." Al just shrugged.

Each visit, Al and I continue our regular walk, from the front of the Duomo, where friends meet up with friends and students hang out on the steps, around the side following the marble walls to the back, then enter the stone streets along narrow sidewalks, cutting through the angles and turns of the stone buildings, across vistas and small piazzas often jammed with Fiats and other small cars so close together they have to turn their rear view mirrors in to keep from hitting the next car. I wonder aloud how drivers get in and out of these make-do parking areas as Al comments on the makes and models and design of the local cars, cars that to us would be "foreign." As usual, he notices what's new each year and what's different from other places we've visited.

At another famous church, the Basilica di Santa Croce, we step out from the narrow side street into a larger and more versatile piazza surrounded with small shops of leather and jewelry and souvenirs. It was here that we bought our first Italian street art, two watercolors, which Al later framed and hung; one is of the tower of the Palazzo Vecchio, a Medici palace, from an artist who worked at his easel in the square while we watched. We wandered into the church, less imposing than the Duomo, joining small groups of tourists at the tombs of two of the great figures of the Renaissance, Galileo and Michelangelo. Unless an important sculpture is on a sarcophagus, seeing the tomb of a person is significant mainly to remind us of the reality that these famous people from textbooks had real lives and worked in real places. We feel a sense of pilgrimage, of paying respect to the brilliance of past minds, a need to pause in recognition of their contributions and their place in science and art. Galileo represented a whole new world view as he challenged traditional beliefs by proving that the earth went around the sun, and the great sculptor and painter Michelangelo brought more realistic depictions of the human body into art. Both reflected the major changes of the Renaissance. Seeing the tombs brought us closer to them as real people rather than just textbook names or icons of history.

Once, when we arrived in the Piazza Santa Croce, we came upon a choir of American college students using the church steps as risers and giving a concert of American folk music and spirituals. We felt a sense of national pride that the music-loving Italians in the audience seemed to like the Americans' performance. Another time as we walked across the Piazza Signorini toward the Uffizi Gallery and the river, we came upon a street concert and performance by a group of gypsies. They sang, played fiddles and tambourines, and danced, giving a good show for the public. The only price of admission was when they passed the plate for contributions after they had finished. We would have been happy to buy a tape or CD of their music. They were that good. It was especially nice since we had had an experience years before when a young woman with a baby, whom we were told was a gypsy, attempted to take Al's camera from his belt holder. It was nice to have a positive experience of the sometimes maligned minority population and experience the creativity and beauty of gypsy culture.

After the Duomo, probably the next most central place in Florence is the Piazza Signorini, in front of the Palazzo Vecchio, the old Medici Palace, which now houses a museum. This large piazza was the original site of Michelangelo's *David*. Standing in front of the Palazzo Vecchio, the *David* represented the Renaissance spirit of rising confidence, challenging the arbitrary power of the rulers. Outdoor cafes on the piazza provide a good place to watch pedestrians and a view of the outdoor sculptures of the Uffizi.

Insisting one year that we had to see the original sculpture of the *David*, which today stands indoor in the Gallerie Dell Accademie, I convinced Al that it was worth it to stand in the long line that stretched along the sidewalk. Even though parts of the *David* sculpture were scaffolded at the time we saw it, and even though it was surrounded by lots of people, we agreed that seeing it was worth the wait as it became one of our most dramatic visual and emotional experiences. Once inside, we walked with the others down the hallway that led to the masterpiece, past other great sculptures by Michelangelo, with the respect of entering a religious shrine. We felt the awe of approaching a great work of art that was almost ethereal. We walked around the sculpture, taking in the full experience as completely as possible. The seven foot marble figure of the young David stands looking straight out into space as if staring down his opponent with incredible confidence. Portrayed as idealistically as a Greek god might be, David holds his slingshot over his shoulder, his other hand curled as if with a rock, his eye focused on his target in the distance. This is not a humble shepherd boy but a strong and confident figure taking on arbitrary power wherever it occurs.

The figure dominated the indoor area, but it was easy for us to imagine it standing where Michelangelo intended it to be in the Piazza Signorini in front of the Medici palace where the size and power of the figure could be seen from various vantage points in the piazza and from a distance. In this context, David, the simple boy getting ready to slay the giant with a rock, must have been quite a strong symbol, when placed in the open piazza in front of the palace of the powerful Medici family. We became curious to know more about the politics of the time.

We walked across the side of the Palazzo Vecchio with its squared off tower topped with flags, another often photographed sight symbolizing the history of Florence, thinking that Florence in those days was as much about power as about rebirth. The high stone walls of the city residences still have a fortress feel to them, and architects point out anchors high on the old buildings that supported upper-level crosswalks used by families to get to the homes of friends and allies and to avoid the violence between powerful feuding families who are part of the city's history. I looked up and pointed out to Al where the walkways were built as upper story bridges from one home to another to avoid the fighting in the street.

Past the Piazza Signoria and the Palazzo Vecchio, we often continue past the Uffizi Gallery that houses one of the greatest art collections in the world. In Florence art is integrated into city. We enjoy looking at the famous sculptures displayed in view of the passersby across from the museum entrance. The tumultuous and emotional *Rape of the Sabine Women* with its intensity of emotion and motion; powerful *Hercules* killing the snake that had killed his sons; and victorious *Perseus* standing with his sword in one hand and the head of the Medusa, the snake-haired figure who turned heroes to stone, in the other. These works stand on a raised platform and are protected, but easily seen by the casual passerby.

Walking in Florence is much like an ongoing art walk. The old buildings and historical references are laden with famous art, the way Rome is laden with ancient ruins. It's impossible to visit the city even briefly without feeling the impact of its art history. At first we were casual about being in this intense artistic environment, visiting the most famous sights as tourists, but gradually we developed some understanding about the role that art played in earlier times. It seemed as though art was integrated into medieval and renaissance life, perhaps much as movies and television are in ours today. Art transcends time and provides a kind of immortality in the same way as literature and music and, in modern life, film. In no place was this more dramatized than in Florence.

As we walked past the sculptures, Al said, "Remember, we couldn't see them before. They were covered for repair." They had suffered damage in the bombing of the Uffizi by the frustrated Mafia, who were being seriously prosecuted by the government. I felt a shock to realize we were standing where an internationally reported event had happened. What had seemed a distant drama from our suburban television became real when we saw the intimate and innocuous setting in which the bombing occurred. Seeing the beauty of these sculptures brought home to us the abstract lesson that the great art and architecture of the world should be protected for the benefit of everyone, not just those of its homeland. I understood why the poet John Keats reflected on the universality of art in his "Ode on a Grecian Urn:"

Beauty is truth; truth beauty; That is all ye know on earth and all ye need to know.

***

Our passeggiata continued past the long lines waiting to get into the museum under the shade of the patio along the side. The wide walkway was lined with sidewalk vendors, mostly non-Italians, selling sunglasses and souvenirs displayed on blankets on the ground. At the far end near the Arno River, the pedestrians-only medieval bridge of goldsmiths, the Ponte Vecchio, is another "specialite" of Florence. The shops line both sides of the bridge with small and intimate displays in the windows. Through the open doors, it is easy to see the jewelry cases all the way to the windows at the backs of the shops. Since the tiny shops look out at the river moving underneath the bridge, they have a bright and airy feel. The shops have rooms above with wooden shutters, possibly the homes of shop owners. During World War II, when Hitler ordered the bridges across the river be destroyed to slow down the Allied advance, he saved the Ponte Vecchio because of the goldsmiths. Most of the jewelry in the shops on the Ponte Vecchio is gold, individualized in style rather than mass produced, and exquisite. Earrings, rings, bracelets and necklaces seem to be less showy and more delicate and unique. Al and I do our only gold shopping from the windows. But if I was ever looking for a special occasion gift and had a chance to buy it there, I would. I can't imagine a better selection anywhere.

But it's the atmosphere of being on the bridge that gives the best impression. The very oldness and quaintness of the shops built onto the bridge, the water of the Arno flowing beneath it, and the gold itself always give me a long ago, fairy tale feeling. I am reminded of stories of the princess who spun straw into gold every day. I like to imagine the many goldsmiths working in this small area day after day, in these small elf-like shops. Thoughts of the magic of gold as the purest metal, sought by alchemists and symbolizing love and loyalty, come to mind as well.

At night, shop owners pull down wooden shutters over the windows for protection but there is still a sense of mystery and magic on the Ponte Vecchio, especially seen from down river. One of our favorite photos is of the buildings on the famous old bridge reflected upside down in the river.

We crossed the Ponte Vecchio and the piazza near Kirsti's old apartment. Across the bridge we were on the other side of the Arno and in a neighborhood which Al discovered called Oltrano, translated, (according to Al) "on the other side of the Arno." This is Florence's version of Paris's Left Bank, but more contained and easier to explore. Up the road is the famous Pitti Palace with its art gallery and large terraced Boboli Gardens.

The quiet gardens are a great place to get away from the noise and fumes of the narrow streets of the city. We have walked up and down almost every street in this area, looking for nothing in particular, just glancing into open doors of workshops or looking at small display windows as we pass.

The Oltrano is a working person's area. The small streets hide many workshops of crafts persons, skilled tile makers, marble carvers, woodworkers, leather designers, and paper designers. The small, individually owned workshops, more the size of work stations in people's garages back home, create the beautiful designs seen on buildings and in design centers all over Florence. The quality of work that comes from these rooms, smaller than many bathrooms in the U.S., is exquisite. As Al and I walk single file along the narrow sidewalks, I think about the skills passed down through generations of craftsmen and wonder how much of this talent could be traced to medieval times.

We have, on occasion, strolled there during the lunch hour, only to find closed shops and shuttered windows, although we can hear the clatter of silverware and dishes from upstairs apartments. As in other parts of Italy, the streets in the Oltrano have a decidedly different character when the shops are closed.

Our favorite restaurant in the Oltrano is inexpensive and family run. On a busy lunch hour we will wait in the crowded entry to be seated at the first table with two seats. In the small local restaurant, customers sit at any table with available space and expect that others will join them if there is an extra seat or two. Electricians, workers, carpenters, painters and city maintenance workers mingle with office and shop personnel, leaving no seat unfilled. The lunch hours are not long, but are not rushed either, as people take time to enjoy the full experience of their meal. One time we shared our back corner table with a young laborer, exchanging what pleasant conversation we could, speaking in different languages. Although we understood little of each other's conversation, we enjoyed the easy camaraderie.

It is not unusual for the lunch crowd to have wine or beer with their soup or pasta and main dish. Al and I have speculated what would happen at home if men who planned on climbing on scaffolding in the afternoon openly shared a carafe of wine at lunch. But vino (wine) is an integral part of meals here, and our culture seems to have more obvious problems with alcohol. The only drunk or loud diners we have ever seen in Italy have been Americans or from other English speaking cultures, most often college age young people.

Another of Al's quests was to see the inside of the Santo Spirito Church in the Oltrano. Traditionally, churches, like many businesses, close at noon and open again at 4:00, so the church has yet to be open when we've walked past it. The outside of the church is plain for Italy, more like the stucco facades of the Spanish mission churches we have seen in Texas, New Mexico and California. One cooler day Al and I sat with the locals on the steps and watched the activity in the piazza. On the church steps at the piazza, sitting in the sun on a spring day, we watched kids playing soccer, young lovers, older women with their shopping bags returning home to begin a meal and men leaning on canes, strolling with comrades or chatting with friends standing under a tree. And unlike watching from an outdoor cafe table, the price of admission to the church steps was free.

Churches are an integral part of life, and even those who are not serious Sunday worshippers appreciate having a church as the focal point on a piazza. In fact, it's unusual for a piazza in Italy not to have a church. Many of the old churches were originally large cavernous spaces and many, even today, have no pews, although folding chairs have been added in all churches that hold services. It's hard to imagine how the inside and outsides were used in previous eras, but it occurs to me that sometimes there seemed to be a strong sense of human communality in the outdoors. In Florence the churches are on non-auto accessible piazzas, and sitting on the church steps in the early spring sunshine seems as much of a religious experience as sitting in a darkened church.

Sitting on church steps is standard in Italy for all ages. I try to picture a church anywhere at home with people other than homeless men simply sitting on the front steps. Maybe it's not allowed, maybe there is a concern about muggings or vagrancy, or maybe we're all in our cars and too busy to just sit around anywhere outside, just passing the time, let alone on church steps. But in Italy and in Florence, especially on a sunny day, it's a nice place to be.

Although we are sometimes disappointed because a church is closed and we can't go inside, we sometimes feel released from the need to go sightseeing into the dark interior of a church on a sunny day. In the evenings the churches are open again and in the chilly March air, the candles that light our way into the warm darkness and the quiet are a blessing.

CHAPTER SEVEN

Renaissance

Following our usual pattern, Al will find the smaller, less-touristy sights after I've covered the major ones. Since probably no place has more art than Florence, in later visits, we sought out less famous art stops. One of our favorites is the Medici Chapel. The quiet chapel seems to exist only to house the beauty of the Michelangelo's marble sculptures, the large reclining figures of Night and Dawn.

There is something about the magnificent art that uplifts and transcends in the same manner as looking over the ocean or a hilltop view. Even those of us who do not consider themselves art lovers respond. It was in Florence that we began to appreciate art. We were glad to discover the less famous works of Michelangelo together, to share what we noticed about the sculptures or what we read.

On our later trips we got better about planning our sights and adding to our understanding of art history. The Brancacci Chapel was probably our first venture into a more refined art experience in Florence. Al found the chapel, located on a quiet residential street on the other side of the Arno, listed in a guidebook on a list of lesser known sights.

Masaccio, the painter of the Brancacci Chapel, was a little known forerunner of the Renaissance painters to come. His biblical enactments in large frescoes (paint that is put into the stucco while it is still wet) include realistic scenes of merchants or shopkeepers, women, children and dogs. The pictures are easy to identify as major biblical moments, such as the nativity, the flight into Egypt, the offering or blessing of the young baby in the temple. But the background scene of town life and human activity represents the artist's own times and provides a tangible sense of his reality. The paintings show a shift from the emphasis on the heavenly world of haloed figures so typical of the Middle Ages to images of ordinary life. The early Renaissance began a shift from ethereal depictions in which subjects of art seem suspended in time, to the concreteness of daily life. We had never heard of Masaccio, but we both enjoyed our discovery of his work.

Back home months later, we caught an episode of Sister Wendy's PBS art series that featured the Brancacci Chapel. Her comments focused on the painting we had seen of Adam and Eve leaving the garden, she considered it a momentous painting. The sadness in this painting, she said, was not so much about guilt for eating from the Tree of Knowledge or the trauma in the loss of paradise, which was emphasized in the earlier fall of man and woman paintings, but rather in Masaccio's version, they leave the garden to take up responsibility for their lives. The painting recognizes that human life includes suffering. It suggests a new understanding of human beings, at least in Western culture, that they too would take more responsibility for their lives through education and greater freedom. Who would have thought one painting could say so much?

An art docent friend once told me, "In Italy, people live with their art, even in the small towns and villages." The Brancacci Chapel is typical of how you find art in Italy and in Florence, not on canvasses that can be put into museums, but on church walls and ceilings for inspiration of the worshippers and celebrant. In Florence, the dark stones of the old palazzos and

smaller museums house sculpture and paintings in small unobtrusive streets and entryways. Works that would be showcased
prominently in American museums are often just footnotes to
art in Florence. You get used to seeing really wonderful art everywhere, in an almost casual way.

In a later visit we sought out another art sight, this one in an
outdoor niche of an old guildsman's hall. Following a guidebook
map, Al led us on a cool breezy afternoon along a busy sidewalk to
find the black marble sculpture of Saint Thomas by Verrocchio.
In the midst of city life, a traditional religious subject was used to
make a public statement in much the same way as Michelangelo's
David. The apostle known as Doubting Thomas, because he said
he would only believe in Jesus's Resurrection if he could touch his
wound, looks for proof from Jesus Himself. Stepping forward
with confidence, Thomas seems to ask Jesus, "Are you real?" as he
reaches his hand to touch the wounds.

As we came along the busy sidewalk, Al and I overheard a
guide explaining to a small tour group, "His foot is partially out
of the enclosure of the niche. He seems to be stepping out of his
enclave on the side of the building into the crowded streets." As
we stood in the late afternoon cold looking up at the sculpture
from the sidewalk, we felt a full dimensional connection with
the scene and the strength of the Renaissance artist's need for a
direct experience of reality.

Florence seems the most likely place to suffer from a phe-
nomenon known as the Stendhal Syndrome, a state of feeling
overwhelmed by the sensations of seeing too much wonderful
art from too many artists and historical periods in too short a
time. The intensity creates overload; the names, dates, figures,
colors and design can seem too much to process.

At some point for us, as much as we want to see more, we
just can't take it all in. For art lovers Florence is like being a kid

in a candy store with unlimited supplies of money. But we can all eat too much candy. I've learned to notice when I've reached my saturation point. When we feel overloaded, I have to hope that these sights and experiences are filed away in my mind and that I will be able to rewind and play back at least some of it when we get home.

***

On our most recent trip to Florence, we went to the Museo di San Marco, originally a Dominican monastery. For the monks who lived there, the lay people who visited in the past, and even us modern tourists, it was and still is a quiet retreat within the city. In the courtyard we joined a tour group with an English speaking guide, speaking in front of a wall-sized painting of the Crucifixion, the figure of Jesus on the cross surrounded by saints. According to the guide, since this was a Dominican monastery, and since there was a rivalry at the time between the Dominicans and the Franciscans, St. Dominic was placed closer to Jesus on the cross than St. Francis. By this time we had seen other depictions of the famous saints of Umbria and Tuscany. The sensibilities of the times when it came to religious art were different from ours. We were intrigued by the politics and symbols of the times. Paintings of St. Dominic showed the dark colored robes of his order and vividly portrayed the gash made in his head when he was martyred. The visual depiction of his violent end was a way to honor him and identify with the suffering of Jesus.

We followed the tour group upstairs where we were greeted, above the arched entrance to the monks' dormitory, by Fra Angelico's *Annunciation*, the moment when the young Mary learns that she will bear a child. The guide pointed out the signs of the early Renaissance painting as the angel greets Mary with this unexpected news. Placed in a contemporary setting, Mary is portrayed, not as a medieval Madonna, looking outward under a golden halo from a heavenly throne to symbolize her holiness, but realistically as a young woman, who faces the angel. Mary here seems very human, not like a holy figure but like a real person, surprised and wondering what's happening. An angel could arrive anywhere and interrupt one's life with a message: changing everything forever. "We usually think of bad things as upending our lives," I thought, "but a wonderful thing can do the same." The realism was somehow more moving than earlier Madonnas.

Al and I stood on the landing and looked at the fresco that we had never even heard of before. We shared the same reaction. "There's something special about it, don't you think?" and "It's really nice." I thought again that great art draws us in to its transcendence in spite of our lack of background, knowledge, or even interest. All we have to do is really look.

Down the hallways of the monastery were the monks' cells, simple austere spaces of four walls, rooms to sleep and pray and meditate. As we walked along the hallways and glanced into the small rooms, we noticed simple but colorful paintings. The guide said that each monk could choose the biblical theme for the fresco on the wall of his room. Fra Angelico, the early Renaissance painter whose small detailed works and use of vivid colors most enlightens this museum, used a kinder gentler treatment of the old subjects. These biblical figures seem more human and less other-worldly.

My favorites were the gentler renditions of Jesus walking on water while calming the frightened apostles in the stormy seas, and Jesus praying in the Garden of Gethsemane with the sleeping apostles in the background. The natural details of the garden and the tired disciples sleeping on the ground seemed realistic and empathetically human. The rose and red color pigments brightened the religious themes. Even depictions of the suffering of Jesus seemed less violent, more gentle and serene than many larger crucifixion scenes we had seen. The brush strokes and color of Fra Angelica's paintings gave them a magical beauty.

At the end of each hallway we walked into two personalized cells. One was a double-sized cell, the equivalent of a suite, but still very small, the size of a walk-in closet by today's standards. It belonged to Cosimo Medici and provided him with a private place for prayer and retreat. The guide stressed that in those years, even the rich and powerful withdrew into the monastic world from time to time. The only other personalized cell in the monastery was that of Savonarola, the Dominican monk who took on the Medici in the 1500s and rallied many converts to an early style of fundamentalism, creating an intense religious revival in Tuscany.

In the story of Savonarola, we glimpsed again some of the darker side of Italian history. This fiery preacher was eventually burned at the stake in the Piazza Signorini in front of the Medici Palace, the same place where Michelangelo would eventually put the statue of David to challenge the power of the Medici. The story was that Savonarola's enemies put his bones into the river to prevent them from becoming holy relics, which might have inspired a new wave of religious fervor. Stories such as his create an eerie feeling since today we walk across the same piazzas where he preached and was later executed. "It's eerie that he got burned at the stake near all those cafes," I said.

The odd practice of preserving body parts of saints seems strange to us, but was common practice in earlier times. In fact, to have the heart or head of a holy figure encased or entombed in your church was seen as a way to bring grace from the saint to the community on earth. We echo this practice in modern life when we pay millions of dollars for clothing or personal belongings of famous or important people, a practice that might easily seem strange to future generations.

Ultimately, as sometimes happens with journeys into the past, our tour of the monastery was inspiring and yet disturbing, too, pulling us into the intensity of another time and place. I was glad to get back outside into the sunlight of modern Florence, sit down in an outdoor cafe and let my emotions settle back to normal.

With the energy of modern Florence around us, we could reflect on the lives and issues of the past as not so different from today. The sun came up every morning then as well as now. While Galileo was in a quarrel with the church over whether the earth or the sun was the center of things, maybe most people didn't worry about political or religious confrontations, or whether they were going around the sun or the sun was going around them. They were just getting on with their lives.

***

Florence has my kind of shopping: outdoor markets where I can browse and where, when I buy, I can convince myself that I'm getting a bargain. Shopping in the outdoor markets in Florence is less serious than in the more expensive shops even if the quality is less. I walk along the stalls of leather goods making comparisons and getting the feel of things. Al has learned to find his own spot, a stone to sit on or a wall to lean against as I wander. Before the arrival of the Euro, when the exchange rate was to our advantage, we could buy a leather jacket in Florence in the market for $100. Leather items such as purses, briefcases, shoes, boots, wallets and belts are great purchases as well as silk ties and silk or wool scarves. Leather gloves are easy to carry gifts for our daughters in New England. I love the Florentine floral designs of stationary and cards, journals and picture frames and buy several each time for gifts since they also are easy to pack and carry.

Al and I also enjoy wandering through the warehouse-style market with meat and fish and cheese stalls on the first floor and upstairs, fruits and vegetables, small fresh picked strawberries, new lettuce and arugula, garlic and eggplants and mushroom stalls that specialize in every kind of mushroom. Late one afternoon a woman insisted that she peel a blood orange for us to taste. "Very sweet," she kept telling us. Al accepted the section of orange that she offered, nodded in agreement with her, "Si, very sweet," and bought a sack full. This was our first experience of buying our traveling snacks at the local markets. They were indeed very sweet, once we got past the unusual name and the red color of the fruit. I would look for blood oranges at home and eventually found some to try, but they were never as good.

On a morning in Florence one year, just before we were to leave for the train station, we headed out for a last stroll. We walked out of the door of our pensione on the Arno and walked along the river, down one side, across the Ponte Trinite and back up the other side, crossing back over the Ponte Vecchio and home again. The afternoon before, it had been cold and windy, so much so that we had finally given up and come back to our tiny room to try to get warm in the poorly heated space. It had been colder than we had expected during the last few days of our vacation that year. Feeling discouraged about the uncomfortable weather, I was having the unusual feeling of being ready to get back home to physical comfort and warmth.

But on that Sunday morning the gusty northern wind stopped, the sun came out in full, the air cleared and even though it was still brisk, the day was beautiful. Church bells rang often and randomly from different churches, out of rhythm with one another but creating a joyful Sunday morning celebration of sound. Men in suits, women in dresses and heels, and children in their best clothes, walked to church, enjoying the spring sunshine, adding to the sense of Sunday bustle and celebration. As Al and I in our travel-sturdy blue jeans strolled down one side of the river and back up the other, we saw the city and its surroundings in sparkling sunlight against blue sky. The hilltop statue of the David looking out from the Piazza Michelangelo; the shuttered windows of the elfish shops on the Ponte Vecchio seen from the perspective of the bridge down the river; our hotel from the opposite side of the river, the large wooden doors and heavy handles defining it in the road; the gray stones of the buildings of the city from the other side; the closed-up shops on the gold bridge and the young people in black, staring self-consciously from the bridge into the river in meditative silence. No longer ready to leave, we felt the pull of a day full of life and promise.

Moments like these are what we remember, especially after we've have a day of fatigue or frustration or in this case just bad weather. They are moments, not of being tourists but of being fully tuned into life. Unplanned, an experience, often full of color and sound and people, comes fully together, when, simultaneously, we become both observers of the life of a place and participants in it, if only for a little while. It feels wonderful. Like a performer who knows when to play his best music, Florence, in this short time, left us with a sense that, although we were leaving her, we wanted more and would be back.

CHAPTER EIGHT

Traveling Light

Traveling light is essential to our travel pattern. We only take what we can carry onto a plane and up or down several flights of stairs, if necessary. Traveling with carry-on luggage reduces us to minimalist living. What a relief to have only necessities and less "stuff" to carry around.

Traveling light for me means carrying four or fewer mixable outfits with minimal extras. Our clothes have to be comfortable but look reasonably nice as we attempt to blend with local attire. We need options for the changeable weather of early spring. A sweatshirt and exercise pants double as sleepwear in a cold hotel room or cover-up for going down the hall to a bath or early morning coffee. I can't take my new blue sweater set just because I like it. Rather I bring a black turtle neck with a heavy black cardigan. Dressed in black, both men and women can look passably good in a city, except for special events or expensive restaurants, which we don't attend anyway. We plan on one pair of walking shoes and an all purpose sweater or jacket, and wash clothes as we go, as needed. We carry the smallest travel-size shampoo and toothpaste; I take minimal make-up. I even empty my wallet, leaving behind unnecessary credit, museum, and identification cards. Every ounce less of weight helps when I have to carry it all. We devote any extra space to camera, film, guidebooks, and magazines. I carry a small notebook to use as a mini journal and a tiny address book along with several paperbacks to read, dreading getting overseas and not liking my next book well enough to get into it. Other than that luxury and Al's stash of magazines, we stay pretty trimmed down.

We divide responsibilities. I get the plane tickets, copies of itineraries with hotel addresses, guidebooks and money, but Al wears the money belt and carries both passports. We start out in a state of mutual dependency. But I carry a copy of our passports, "just in case," I say, and we divide the money between us in case some gets lost or taken.

There is something liberating about having everything you plan to use for 10 or 12 days in one flight size bag and a shoulder purse or satchel and leaving everything else behind. Once we are packed and on our way, carrying only what we need, nothing non-essential, we feel free.

Once I'm on the plane, I can relax. My stress is in getting ready to leave home, focusing on details like addresses, vitamins, itineraries, making sure that people can find us and packing just the right things. I've become less compulsive about the details of our leave-taking and less anxious about the separation, especially from our girls now that they are older and independent. In one part of my mind, I used to feel slightly guilty, a mother leaving her kids behind even though they were grown. Gradually, I came to realize they handled their lives just as well when we are in Italy as when we are on their side of the Atlantic.

The transition into vacation mode is always harder for Al. He works more intensely right up to our leaving. He goes from full speed to sudden stop, but he can't unwind immediately. Sometimes he stops at the office the day we leave or is on the phone at the airport arranging for co-workers to problem solve while he is gone. It will take a couple of days before he settles in. But in spite of checking his work-related voice mail, and now emails, and an occasional phone call, he can separate himself from work by crossing an ocean and enjoys his breaks.

We've gotten better handling the transition as we leave our normal lives behind.

We've gotten better, too, at handling the differences in our readiness to relax. As we settle on the plane, Al studying his *New York Times* crossword puzzle and I leafing through travel articles in the airline magazines, we start our vacation. I try to keep my chatter to a minimum since he is still on full speed ahead and needs to decompress.

Even if we are traveling on an American carrier across the Atlantic, once on the international flight segment, we start to hear bilingual announcements as well as conversations in Italian and other foreign languages as we join the world of the international traveler. Given my choice, I would rather take European airlines; they feel that much closer to the mood of our destination. On an Alatalia flight, the food is Italian. We drink some wine, eat dinner and try to sleep a little rather than watch a movie. While we still feel awake and ready to enjoy the evening, it is already becoming one and three and four o'clock in the morning as we cross the Atlantic. Trying to sleep, I occasionally open an eye to glance at the televised map showing our position. As we leave Newfoundland and Iceland behind, I picture us crossing the open ocean as little as possible as we reach for the coast of Ireland, then England, France and the Alps into Italy. As experienced trans-oceanic travelers, we now have a better sense of what to expect and how to pace ourselves. But we still have some uncomfortable moments on the long trip, moments when we wonder why we are willing to put ourselves voluntarily in such small uncomfortable coach seats and call it a vacation.

***

Arrival still feels abrupt as we, our bodies still operating on circadian rhythms of home, land on a continent with different time zones. As soon as we get off the plane, we are pulled hours forward into fully functioning and alert society, while everyone we know at home is still asleep. Once, when we raced to make a connection to Venice after going through customs in Rome, we made it onto an Alatalia flight just before the doors closed. It was a Friday morning and travelers were almost all business types, men in suits and ties. Seemingly, the concept of casual Friday had not taken hold in Italy. We breathlessly dragged our stuff down the aisle looking bedraggled and confused as we claimed our seats near the back of the plane. Bumping and twisting our carry-ons past the well-dressed men with briefcases placed carefully under their seats, we found the overheads full of their carry-on bags. Somehow we managed to jam our carry-ons under the seats in front of us, but not without an awkward struggle. We felt like the American tourists of the Chevy Chase movie, *European Vacation*, klutzes bumbling down the narrow aisle as the morning passengers watched quietly and the crew held up the departure while we got settled. Most likely, we felt our awkwardness more than our fellow passengers. Al, who is often one of the suited early morning business travelers, felt the contrast more than I did, but managed to settle in, and while I chatted with one of the few women on the plane, he was sound asleep.

My seatmate, a grandmother visiting family near Venice, was kindly and we discussed the beauty of Venice "bella...bella Venezia," and our home of the United States, "America" she called it, like many Europeans skipping over the distinction between nation and continent. In spite of our language differences, she made me feel welcome. Once again I wished to be better at languages and resolved to at least try to take an Italian class.

With Al's nap and my friendly seatmate, our temporary loss of dignity and coolness had faded once the plane landed.

Arriving in a new Italian city used to stress us out, but no more. We expect a few moments of confusion when in our fatigued state, we arrive in a strange environment. But we realize that although things may seem overwhelming at first, that nothing really bad is going to happen, and we will be able to figure out what to do next even if we don't speak Italian. A particularly sheltered high school student once told me about her family's arrival in Rome, where she said, "...you can't find anyone who can talk." On the contrary, we have found plenty of people who can talk to us and many who can speak English. We know that we will find a way to get to our hotel one way or another.

Some of our more difficult experiences have been trying to take a crowded bus or walk to our hotel dragging our luggage. Once we argued our way across the bouncy cobblestones of Florence from the station to the hotel near the river, Al insisting on loading his duffle bag on top of my new wheeler, loosening the wheels enough to require a replacement when we got home. I had thought the hotel hadn't looked far on the map and proceeded to misdirect us through the confusing streets. Another time in Rome we got on a familiar but crowded bus to our hotel only to get off when we realized how impossible it was to hold on to our luggage amidst the throngs of bodies on board. Now we almost always take a cab to the hotel from the station when we first arrive. Dragging luggage on a bus or subway when you are in new territory makes for more frustration than we want. Once our luggage is safely stored and we have gotten our bearings and a good map, we are free to use public transportation and our feet.

Even in a cab we learned the hard way. One year, before the adoption of the Euro made money easier to manage, we paid the equivalent of $25 in lire for a very short ride. After that, we learned to ask the driver, "How much? Quando?" before we left the airport, sealing the deal first. Even if the driver has a meter, he can usually estimate the price for us and will honor it. Although many taxi drivers speak and understand some English, Al's and my pronunciation of hotel names is often way off, so it helps to have hotel names in writing to show the driver.

***

Friends often want to know, "How do you get around in Italy?" Without giving us a chance to answer, they will ask, almost automatically, "Do you rent a car?"

As Americans we tend to assume that cars are the best transportation. Cars do provide a flexibility that is hard to have any other way. Having your own car means that you can manage your own luggage, go to out of the way places, follow your own time schedule, change your itinerary on a whim and explore back roads and byways on your own. Movies and travelogues visualize for us the romance of traveling independently around Italy, cruising into small villages with one's bags in the back of a car or van.

But even though we are used to being a two-car couple back home and appreciate the advantages of car travel, we always answer "No," to the rental car question. People ask, "Well, how do you get around without a car?" and we answer in unison, "We take the train."

We sometimes imagine how many more small villages we might see if we had a car and we haven't ruled out a driving trip someday. But cars are also an encumbrance that we do not have to deal with. We don't have to read road maps, get directions or find parking. Once you drive to a city you'll be walking and leaving the driving to the locals anyway.

Cars may work better on major roads and freeways or as a way to get to out of the way villages, but the thought of pulling into an Italian city with a car boggles my mind. I know many people figure out how to get to their hotels or at least to a parking lot. But it can be hard to follow even the best maps into the center of town. In the hill towns, visitor parking is at the bottom of the hill, close to the train stops, and a driver has to figure out how to take a bus or tram to the town on the top.

The other reason Al and I don't rent a car is that it would change the dynamics of our vacation. At home Al, who likes to be in control and drives with intensity and focus, almost always drives when we're together. If I drive, Al, not easily adaptable to giving up control of the wheel, can't help but participate, telling me when to go, which lane to take, which way to turn. Then we have the radio issue. As far as Al is concerned, whoever is driving controls the radio, and if I complain that the music is too loud or not what I like, he feels I am interfering with his space.

When we drive in unfamiliar places, my job is to navigate. Navigation is not as easy as it sounds. When he asks me, "Why didn't you tell me that was the left turn street?" as we sail past it, I try to tell him that it's hard to see the signs when he's still going sixty.

On trains, once we're underway, we sit as equals side by side or facing one another. We are both passengers and can leave the driving to others. We both get to relax, gaze out the windows at the passing scenes, read or doze. I wonder how many who enjoy car trips in Europe do it because they are used to having a car in the U.S. and how many would give it up if they tried the trains. I think part of the reason Al relaxes is because he doesn't have to drive. And even though he says he doesn't mind driving at home, for him it's still related to routines of work, transportation to meetings and the airport. Not driving puts us in a different place attitude-wise as well as physically.

***

For us, as many travelers in Europe, discovering train travel is one of the pleasures of the journey. In spite of what people used to say about the laid-back Italian ways of life, the trains usually do run on time. True, there are vagaries, for example, the not unusual one day strikes or slowdowns in which rail workers protest wage or work issues. Our travels in Italy have taught us to accept the unusual, the surprising. With the right attitude this disruption can add to the adventure.

Once on one of our lowest budget trips, we planned to take a very inexpensive, local train from Stresa on Lake Maggiore to the town where we would transfer to our airport bus to Malpensa Airport outside of Milan. We had decided that a last night in Stresa rather than in a less pleasant hotel closer to the airport would make it more enjoyable. Our flight out wasn't until ten and the 7:00 a. m. train only took an hour along what we had been told was a pretty route. The plan seemed flawless.

On the morning of our departure, our hotelier, without apologies, told us over our farewell cappuccino that there was a train strike that day and that all trains were cancelled, and that he had already called us a taxi to take us to the airport an hour and a half away. As Americans it's hard to imagine an event like a train strike without news coverage and traveler uproars, but in Italy a day strike or slow down is just part of life. Our friendly driver, after tisk-tisking about the train strike, happily gave us a narrated tour of the lakeside as we passed by. Everything about our plan worked except the means of travel and the lire spent. We enjoyed our lovely ride through the hills and past the Alpine lake and got to the airport on time. Although we went many lire over our budget, we had door-to-door service and contributed to the local economy. We got our money's worth.

A second strike experience just missed us in Naples. We had gone to the station one mid-morning to check our schedule and buy our tickets for the next day's departure. The station seemed very quiet at what should have been a busy time of day. "I wonder why it's so empty. I wonder what's going on?" Al asked.

"I know. It's usually so hectic. Maybe it's a slow time," I responded.

But Al knew better. "I'll bet it's another strike."

In spite of the deserted platforms, the information office was open and full of concerned travelers, so we waited in line with the others, mostly young tourists who were trying to find out what was going on. One young man heard Al and me talking, walked over to us and asked cautiously, "Do you speak English?" and then anxiously, "Do you know what's happening? Can you explain to me what's going on?" Americans have a hard time understanding that when there is a full strike, Italians don't expect a customer service desk to work out alternatives. Strikes are a part of life. That's just the way it is.

We were flattered, maybe because of our lack of luggage or the beard Al was growing that trip, to blend in well enough for an American to think we were Italian. The good news was that although we couldn't speak Italian and couldn't get the details, we did know what was going on, having been there before. We understood enough to know that transportation workers had called a day strike and it would last "uno giorno" until "domani," tomorrow, and there would be nothing to do about it. This strike included buses as well as trains. The bottom line was that there was no way that day to leave Naples on public transportation for any destination.

We stood in line with the backpack-laden students as they agonized over how they would get back to Rome. One young couple planned to meet a friend coming from California who was already on the trans-Atlantic plane, expecting to be met at the Fumicino airport that night. Al suggested they call his home in the states, explain what had happened, and hope that he would think to call home and get the message. We were glad that we were not planning to leave that day and not dealing with being stuck with our luggage and no plan. Since we were only looking for time of departures and connections for the next day, we got what we came for in the information office. Looking at travelers with the largest suitcases who were now stranded, Al said, "That's another reason to travel light. You never know when your plans will change."

I answered, "I bet we wouldn't be so cool and calm if today was our day to travel."

As Americans, we appreciate that what just happens to be our native tongue is, through no virtue of ours, fast becoming the language of the world. It seems that almost everywhere we go, people speak some English. But the other side of this easy access to communication is that we Americans often feel surprised when employees in official capacities speak no English and feel no need to apologize. We are spoiled. In Italy, with a few simple words, even mispronounced, some hand gestures, and occasionally resorting to writing the names of destinations, dates, times and prices, we can always find a way to communicate with a patient station agent about the essentials.

In another of the typical divisions of labor that occur in a marriage, reading the bright yellow and black train schedules posted both inside stations and outside near the tracks is Al's job. Major stops are written in larger letters with the intervening stops in smaller print. Posted golden schedules identify a train as an express or an intercity or a locale which determines departure times, how many stops and how long the trip will take. The fine print at the bottom that I tended to ignore sometimes makes exceptions for holidays or weekends.

The all important track number is printed in black on the yellow schedule and in the larger stations also appears on a flashing board for last minute confirmation. The track numbers can change at the last minute, leaving us standing at the wrong place at the right time, having to run to the correct track. When we are confused or in any doubt, I ask a fellow passenger to confirm that we are on the right train. Mentioning our destination, "Firenze?" to a fellow passenger to see if he or she responds, "Si Si Firenze," for example. People on trains are helpful. When there are several stops in a city or if we're at all in doubt about the right station, I ask again. Asking to confirm that we have reached our destination always makes me feel better, and Al, who like most men, hates to ask for directions back home, seems not to mind any more that I double check in Italy.

Compartments on trains seat six with windows that open, sliding glass doors that open to the hallway and a luggage rack overhead. Surprisingly, large bags do fit in the racks, although periodically Al had to convince me, as I protested, that, "No, they won't fall on you." Sometimes we have a whole compartment to ourselves and other times are glad we have reserved a seat when every seat is taken during the entire trip. When smoking on trains was allowed, we were careful to choose non-smoking cars. Now the painted no smoking symbols are obsolete since smoking is not allowed in any indoor area in Italy.

Once we're comfortably in our assigned seats, we can relax and let the forward motion of the train carry us on our journey. Train travel gives us down time. While we're on the train, we don't have to make any decisions, consult roadmaps or read street signs. We write postcards, read travel books and the Italian edition of the *International Herald Tribune*, which we can often pick up at a station news stand. We look at travel maps only to follow our route out of curiosity about towns along the way and to see where we get off.

Train travel feels less claustrophobic, less confining somehow than air travel, even though occasionally a crowded train might involve standing in the aisle or sitting on your suitcase. We've learned to avoid that by avoiding busy travel times and purchasing a reserved seat if we have our doubts. On one trip from Florence to Bologna, standing in a crowded and smoky aisle for three hours was enough to make us wary. But even that experience had a fun side as we watched people cheerfully climb over each other and each other's suitcases to get on or off, and hold on to each other laughing as the train went down hills, through tunnels or around curves.

In many aspects of comfort, train travel is easier than both driving and flying. Unlike driving, once are on the right train, we simply can't get lost. On the tracks, we always know where we are. Like the local people, we bring snacks or sandwiches and something to drink so as not to depend exclusively on the snack carts going through the aisles. Although we can't spontaneously stop in a town for lunch or make a detour to see a sight, we can move around more. Without annoying others, we can stroll down the car and stand in the aisles and look out open windows breathing the fresh air of the passing countryside. There is rarely a wait for the restrooms at the end of cars. When we arrive, trains go right into the center of cities, unlike airports, which are at a distance. And instead of waiting for airline ground crews to bring up a walkway and for closely packed passengers to deplane, we open the doors at the ends of each car and get off easily.

In the relaxed setting of train compartments, we hear more Italian, talk to more people and have had some of our most enjoyable interactions. Lots of Italians either speak good English or want to practice their English. On a train from Rome to Assisi, a Roman business traveler in government tourism who spoke excellent English and had a friend in Houston, shared his opinions on the history of the Papacy and current events relating to the Clinton presidential scandals. After we exchanged phone numbers, he put his large portfolios in the trunk of his cab and treated us to a free ride up to the hilltop city of Assisi.

Once on a train to Lecce, much less of a tourist area, four giggling schoolgirls, on their way home from their college classes to a neighboring town, practiced their "pretty good" and "a little" English with many apologies for not understanding us "Americanos."

From our companions, we get tips for sights to see or to avoid, suggestions for local restaurants, neighborhoods and churches to visit. We share candy when fellow passengers offer it to us, following the local rules of hospitality and enjoying the opportunity to break our childhood rule about taking candy from strangers. Sometimes we just read quietly, nap, or watch and listen to Italian conversations, ones that we don't understand and would probably not be terribly interested in if we heard them in English at home. The background patter of commonplace conversation in Italian might be mundane in content but its rhythm helps us feel immersed in a different culture.

We see the countryside and small towns from the train, effortlessly expanding our tour. We have gone through long dark tunnels and across high bridges to get across the mountain range and have been so close to seacoasts that we could see fish pulled from the water. On our trip south along the Adriatic Sea, Al slept deeply in the quiet, empty compartment leaving me alone with views of seaside fishing structures and then, as we moved inland, groves of olive trees so old that they seemed mystical. Another time while leaving a hill country town, the train stopped for about an hour. We finally saw the problem: a herd of sheep on the tracks.

We were surprised the first time we rode a train without a conductor even checking our tickets, only to learn that this happens relatively often in Italy, especially on short trips. It's not exactly an honor system, although it sometimes feels that way when you get off a train having had no one look at your ticket and thinking that you could have ridden for free. On one of our early trips we bought our tickets and got on the train only to get into a big debate with the conductor about the validity of our ticket. We had bought the passes in the U.S. and thought he didn't understand us, foolishly assuming that the official didn't know the details of his job. The conversation was complicated by the fact that he spoke Italian and we struggled in English to explain our side. With gestures and the help of a fellow passenger, he finally managed to explain to us that we were supposed to get the ticket stamped with the time and date before we got on the train. Convinced that we had made an honest mistake, the conductor moved on. From this experience, we learned that all tickets have to be validated with a date and time punch right before they are used. We learned the habit of putting our tickets, like a time card, into the yellow machines near the tracks to show that the ticket was being used that day.

Another lesson we learned by experience was about smoking versus non-smoking cars. Lots of people in Europe still smoked when we first went to Italy, and if we didn't choose a non smoking car, we could end up in a six passenger compartment with four serious smokers who also liked the windows and door closed to avoid any draft. During one particularly heavy pollen season, on a very crowded train to Florence, we breathed enough secondary smoke that both of us suffered from itchy eyes and scratchy throats by the time we got off the train. At the time we felt the contrast to the non-smoking environment we were used to at home and became wary of getting on any train car that was not marked plainly on the outside with a no smoking symbol. In recent years, the pendulum went the opposite way and the Italians banned all indoor smoking, creating a more inclusive non-smoking environment than in the U.S.

Once we understood the trains, they formed the basis of our vacation. We like going to the station, feeling the anticipation of a new leg of our journey. We like the feeling of mastery as we confidently punch our tickets with the date and time to validate them and then walk down the length of the track toward the second class cars. Even if the train is not there yet, Al has gotten good at anticipating where the train's second class cars will stop, usually a little farther out from the terminal, and we wait there if the train hasn't arrived.

The stations themselves are fun. In the larger cities the bustle and hum of energy as the international and domestic travelers stride purposely to and from the tracks is particularly intense in the morning and evening as commuters travel from town to city and home again. In the larger stations, if the train has a long layover or is at its originating station, you can get on ahead of time, find your seat, and relax, read or nap, unlike in airports where we stand at the gate waiting for a flight to be called. In the smaller stations, when the train comes, we get on and it leaves. Unlike boarding a jetliner, we don't sit and wait as people store their luggage or for standbys to be called. Smaller stations have one or two outside benches. A few people wait, enjoying the fresh air and singing birds outside or a quick cappuccino and pastry in the cafe inside. In Italy people don't stay on the phone until the train is called as we do back in the States while waiting for planes in airports. They don't try to stay productive, reading the paper or working on laptops until the last minute. They don't mind standing outside beside the track just waiting, without entertainment, TV monitors or armchair video games. Especially in the small stations, waiting in the fresh air for a train is time to be appreciated, time to just be.

Al gradually mastered the public pay phones, getting a connection to his voice mail more often than not. Sometimes he uses the down time of train waiting to check messages, if the phone buttons cooperate. One of my favorite images is of Al standing by an orange phone beside the outdoor train platform of a small station checking his voice messages. With his index finger he carefully and slowly punched one number of his access code at a time hoping to convince the temperamental phone to cooperate. Somehow standing at a pay phone outside a small station in Italy didn't seem much like labor. "Not a bad way to work," I thought, as I looked at green country hillsides across the tracks and heard morning birdsongs.

When trains don't go where we want to go, we take the bus. Bus tickets or "biglietti" also have to be validated but often the machines are on the bus. Usually no one asks to see our tickets, although occasionally an inspector will board, walk through and check for validations. You can have a whole pocket full of unused tickets, but if a ticket was not time-punched and validated when you got on, you can be fined. On the plus side, a validated ticket is good for 90 minutes, making transfers within a city easier to manage.

Finding the right bus stop can be harder than with the trains and Al is in charge of figuring out the schedules and routes, using guide book information and watching for posted signs. Mostly I just follow along.

As in other aspects of our travels in Italy, once we got some experience, bus travel became relatively convenient. Using the local orange buses within cities, we can get nearer to a sight than walking the whole way across town, an approach that has had more appeal as our knees have aged. We can take side trips from a city on the intercity blue buses, which gives us more range even without a car. With a little patience and willingness to ask questions and take chances we have learned to get around easily and cheaply.

In Rome and even more so in Milan, the Metros have been helpful, but we know to hang on to wallets and purses especially in Rome and especially if the subways are crowded. The vaporetti in Venice, where public boats move up and down the canals, use the same tickets as the buses elsewhere. Plenty of tourists, like us, opt to save money and be part of the culture by using public transportation.

Rather than an essential luxury, cars feel isolating after traveling by public transportation. On public buses and boats, we see the ordinary life of citizens used to using public transportation, going about their normal lives. We see the variety of life stages from the elderly, the families, young people in groups, business people and shoppers. In the U. S. we trade independence and a certain type of control and convenience for positive participation in the common life. While convenience has its advantages at home when we need flexibility to meet demanding schedules, on vacation we are glad for the chance to mingle.

Our first bus trip was the local bus from Orvieto to Civita. We had checked with the travel information bureau in Orvieto, got a bus schedule to go and return and had a picturesque ride on a half empty bus winding through the countryside and stopping at crossroads to let people on or off. We enjoyed the adventure and the ease of getting off the beaten path. Our only mistake was assuming that the bus would be leaving from the same spot where it dropped us off. We were dropped off in a small piazza and assumed that we would be picked up there or at the bus stop sign across the street. But unlike trains that stay on the tracks, buses have their own routes. It wasn't until later that we figured out that the bus stopped on a different corner when returning through town. Waiting beside the wrong sign, we missed our return bus and had to wait two hours for the next. Finally, we found two teenage girls who said they spoke no English but who were able to answer our question of "Orvieto? Autobus? Dove? Where?"

It got cold that afternoon and I remember how slowly the time passed and the relief I felt when we got on the bus. Once we were on the return, it was fun again as in the late afternoon lots of teenagers were boarding with their backpacks and being dropped off at their various stops as they sang and chattered standing in the aisles even though there were plenty of seats; girls chatted together in seats, boys stood in the aisles holding a pole or chair back as they balanced in the aisles around the bends in the road until they coolly departed at their stops with a wave and "Ciao" to their friends.

We got better at using the buses, although we still some-times missed a stop, or had to run to catch a departing bus or wait a long time because we had misread the symbols on a sched-ule. We learned that some buses and trains only go on holidays while others are commuters and don't operate on weekends. But every one of our mistakes opened the door to another adventure, for example, the girls in Orvieto. And we both remember the small middle-aged man who assured us over and over in Italian that "Si, si, bus, Foggia," indicating that we were at the right stop to get back to our Foggia base. His example showed us what little patience we have as he remained calm and relaxed, nonplussed even though the bus was more than thirty minutes late. As in train stations, Italians don't seem so impatient about this kind of waiting, but seem to include this time as just part of life, part of the flow of time and the interweave of existence. The bus is late. It just is. But it will come by and by. And it always makes me realize how much stress we bring on ourselves at home by assuming that such things are problems. I find myself thinking that maybe the problem is not so much that our plane is late or that we are stuck in traffic, but our attitude about it.

Not that Italians don't get excited about things. They do, for example, when a taxi driver competes for your lane of traffic. Maybe it's public transportation in general that requires patience no matter where we live. And for people who have to ride public transportation in cities at home, late buses are more than an inconvenience. Maybe it's the simplicity of the life that the small towns represent that enables the easier attitude. But in Italy over the years, I find myself stepping back from my impatience and so does Al. We try to carry this change of attitude into our lives at home reminding ourselves that time is just time after all. And in many circumstances being a few minutes late is simply not very important.

Occasionally we have become complacent, thinking we understand the system especially in the small towns, only to be surprised. On the way back from a nearby town to the small city of Foggia on the Adriatic Sea, we stopped in the late afternoon at a bus stop along a two lane country road across from a little church. We had read a brief paragraph about its history and black Madonna painting and hopped off the bus thinking, logically, that we could get the next bus that came along the road to continue our return trip. The caretaker showed us around the church, explained the significance of the black Madonna painting, then directed us to the old cemetery where we wandered in the quiet until the caretaker locked the church door and motioned for us that it was time to leave the grounds. As he climbed on his bicycle to go home, we gestured to our watches and asked "Bus? Foggia?" only to be dismayed when he told us, "No bus. No bus. Finished." Having relayed that information, he rode off down the two lane road. In the fading afternoon light, we realized we were stuck.

We had no car, there was no bus, and we were a very long way from town. We had seen no houses nearby, but Al had noticed a small rail station a short distance back, away from the road, so with no other option, we headed back. Just as we neared the platform of the single track, we heard a train, a three car local, but it seemed to be headed in the direction of Foggia. There were no other passengers, but luckily the train stopped. Not knowing where we would end up for sure, we got on an empty car, figuring we had nothing to loose. A few minutes later we were in the Foggia train station a few blocks from our hotel. Grateful to have found a solution so quickly and easily, we speculated on what we would have done if we and the little train hadn't connected. It wasn't a long ride back to town, but too long to walk. Our only solution would have been to hitchhike on a road that had very little traffic. But thinking of the people we had met and the general feel of the small towns we were caught between, we would probably have been fine. Still, the experience cautioned us against taking too much for granted when it came to transportation. Now, in similar circumstances, we ask the driver before we get off if the bus will return and where it will stop.

***

Between train trips and bus rides, we walk, sometimes on the small streets, behind or beyond the famous sights, taking in local architecture that is less well-known but often as interesting. Without a car to park or worry about, we have more freedom. It's often easier to walk to a sight than to take the bus or the metro. We see the inner streets taking alleyways and walkways where cars wouldn't go. Like the locals, we sometimes stop for a quick coffee as we pass a cafe, opting to sit on the church steps in a piazza and watch boys play soccer, following our whims rather than a schedule. Being on foot allows a different kind of freedom from traveling in cars. Unlike at home where walking is a form of exercise undertaken in sneakers and shorts or sweats, we have gotten used to the idea of walking as a means of transportation. We walk in Italy to get from one place to another and the whole idea of planned exercise time recedes since we get tons of exercise this way without trying. We never put on weight on these trips even though we eat well. We just keep burning it off.

We appreciate the transportation value of good shoes and good legs to get us around. We realize that as we get older, pounding the hard stones of old cities may take its toll on our knees. So we pace ourselves a little more now, taking a bus or subway to cover the long distances from one part of a city to another and saving our energy for the block to block explorations of a neighborhood or historical area. Traveling light applies to the day to day, too. We carry only a cloth bag with guidebooks, camera, water and an occasional snack, sharing our resources, merging our efforts rather than holding on to independence. This bonds us a little more on these trips than we do at home. Walking together we carry things mutually, not carrying two if one will do. We become more interdependent in getting around and now realize it's a very nice way to travel.

CHAPTER NINE

Hill Towns

Al and I had heard about hill towns in Italy, but we weren't quite sure what they were. Visiting small towns again was an appealing prospect, so the year after our trip to the sea coast towns of the Cinque Terre, I decided it was time to include a hill town experience in our itinerary. Partly I wanted to justify another trip to Italy. I told Al, "We have to go back. We can't say we've seen Italy until we've been to the hill towns."

We had seen from our train windows through the countryside of Umbria and Tuscany, the towns rising up from the tops of hills like castles in the distance. According to our guidebooks, their origins could be traced to the ancient Etruscans who took advantage of natural vantage points, which allowed for a view of the countryside from all sides and prevented easy attack or invasion. They were primarily defensive in purpose. As we rode through open country, it wasn't hard to imagine that in older, more threatening times, living on the tops of the hill would have been better than in the vulnerability of the plains below.

I imagined an original hillside encampment used by early tribes as protection against invaders, a place to see who might be coming at them from the land around. On the top of the sheer rock, a town would grow up, complete with a wall and even towers that provided further protection during the chaotic years of feuding city states. Now the same old structures provide the backdrop for modern life.

In most hill towns, the train station is far below the "centro," the historical town center. Usually, a bus or cab will take you up the cliff-like hills on roads that wind and twist to navigate the steep hillside. Out of town drivers are encouraged or required to leave their cars in parking lots at the bottom of the hill to avoid the narrow alleyways in the old towns above. Modern businesses, gas stations, small supermarkets and hardware supply stores are on the lower slopes of the hills in the "new town" or "lower town," while the main piazza, cathedral, other old churches, art and tourist sights are up high. Al and I explored both, observing the contrast between old and new, and how the processes of everyday life went on in both.

Above, the historic centers of the old town rise even higher, places of retreat, often small villas or religious sanctuaries. Since Al always wants to go to the top, we've done a lot of hiking in the hill towns.

***

Our first stay was in Orvieto, a city about an hour north of Rome. The plan was to use Orvieto, on the main rail line, as a stopping off place to reach our real destination, Civita, a truly tiny hilltop town, maybe about a mile square. The trip to Civita would require a local bus trip out through the countryside, since no train line went there. In fact, the bus would only take us to the lower town, Bagnoregio. The only way for us to get to Civita itself was to walk.

Looking back to that visit, I realize we were still novices in our Italian travels, following our guidebook's instructions to the letter. We were used to trains that stopped in the middle of a city. Here, to get to the town above the station, we would need to find other transportation, a bus, or in Orvieto, a hillside tram to carry us up. We knew by then that finding public transportation was not always as easy as it seemed. Anxious about how we would get to the top, I thought, "I hope we don't have to walk up;" the prospect of having to climb up to the hill town would be daunting, even to Al.

It was a nice morning and as we ended the short train ride from Rome, we followed our guidebook's instructions: Get off the train, buy a bus ticket at the ticket window in the station, walk out the door, turn left and cross the parking lot, look for the tram, get on the tram. Fortunately, since we were dragging and carrying our luggage, we easily found the incline, climbed on and let it haul us up the side of the steep hill to the town far above.

From the tram at the top of the hill we stepped out onto a relatively quiet square. The surroundings seemed ordinary, except for the old buildings and enormous cathedral that dominated the piazza. There was a feeling of anti-climax after all the bustle of travel. We had a sense of being out of sync, since on that midmorning March day in Orvieto, it was business as usual. People were at work, in their shops or offices or homes, and here we stood with our bags in the empty square, feeling out of place. We looked around, trying to figure out where to find the tourist office to get a map or to guess which small street off of the piazza would lead us to our hotel.

Noticing a souvenir shop with an open door, I asked directions to the hotel where I had made reservations. With only two turns down the small streets, we easily found the address. But before we could congratulate ourselves, we tried the door, then the doorbell, only to find that the door was locked and there was no response. Confused and disoriented, I went into the grocery stop across the street and asked for help from the middle-aged man in a full white apron behind the deli counter. I gestured questioningly towards the hotel only to be told as he shook his head, "No," by the pleasant storekeeper that it was still "chiuso," or closed for the season. "So much for planning ahead," I thought, as I went back outside to tell Al. Later, I realized I must have mistakenly asked on the phone for a reservation in "maggio," the Italian word for May instead of "marzo," which was March. I had not confirmed by fax, since there was no fax number listed. Al asked the obvious question, "Well, what should we do now?"

Even though my best laid plan had gone wrong, Al and I avoided any confrontation. Fortunately, we were past our jet-lagged, winding down period, having been in Italy for several days before we arrived in Orvieto. And we needed to work together to find a solution since we now had no place to stay.

After a few minutes of feeling disappointed and disoriented, we pulled out our guidebook, picked out another hotel name, and headed to the address on the piazza at the side of Orvieto's cathedral. This hotel was open and they had several rooms. The price was a little higher than my budgeted choice, but not much since it was still the off season. We congratulated ourselves. Not only did we have a place to stay, but our room looked directly out onto the cathedral on the piazza. We had what in the tourist season might easily be one of the most sought after rooms in town. "Yea," said Al, thinking of the empty shops and cafes and quiet piazza, "but it would be a lot noisier, too. It's probably better now."

Later, remembering the friendly little grocery on the side street across from our original hotel, we went back and bought cheese and bread and lunched on that for the rest of the week trusting that the cheese would stay cool enough in the daytime to re-chill on the window sill at night. We felt at home.

***

Hill towns come in various sizes. Orvieto is not a tiny medieval village, but a vibrant and prosperous looking town. For the first time we experienced the less tourist influenced, more workaday aspect of Italian life. To us present-day city dwellers, seeing modern activity go on in seemingly medieval surroundings was surreal. As in much of Italy, the town's anchor in old, ancient, roots creates not only a unique backdrop, but a sense of integration between the modern and the old. This is quite a contrast to the U.S. where newness seems to consistently override the old.

Away from the cathedral, men in business suits, women in skirts and heels, and mothers with baby strollers walked purposely through the streets. I watched women purchase bread, produce and meat for the evening meal, which seemed easier than driving to the grocery store weekly and piling grocery bags in the back seat, often full of things that I don't really need or at least don't need that day. Walking means that errands have to be done more often, and carrying purchases limits what can be bought, but I found it was more pleasant to walk to the bank or post office than to be cooped up in a car.

Walking up hills or stairways creates its own cardio workout, and muscle building comes from carrying groceries rather than lifting weights. Exercise through living seems much more natural, more interesting and somehow less difficult. No wonder Al and I lose weight rather than gain it when we are in Italy.

Still, there were cars in Orvieto and we learned quickly not to assume that a small road under an archway or from behind a church was just a quiet alley. As we crossed a quiet piazza, suddenly several cars would speed toward us, seemingly from nowhere.

Cars and pedestrians seemed to coexist in piazzas and alleyways such as this, and we often walked in areas that required us to be wary of engine noises coming from unseen spaces, especially after dark.

Cars were parked in unlikely places, including garages under old buildings that looked as if they had been carved out of the rock of the hillside. Some may have been Etruscan caves. These garages, carved from the rock of the hillside under medieval buildings, defined the hill town as something new built both on and into the old.

***

The smallest hill town we visited was one recommended by Rick Steves in his Travels in Europe series on public television. Rick, as his fans refer to him, is good at finding out of the way places that are easy enough to get to often without a car. In the beginning we followed Rick's instructions as closely as possible, but as with all guidebooks, we still had to fill in a few blanks. We knew there was a bus from the piazza in the old town from Orvieto to Bagnoregio which was the base town to get to Civita. But to find out when and where it left, we went to the local tourist office. Although it was the off season and we were the only visitors to the tourist office, we were still encouraged by the large posters of the tiny hilltop town that decorated the wall. Obviously we weren't the only ones who wanted to go there. Gesturing toward the posters, we said, "Bella, beautiful." The agent answered, "Si, Si, multa bella."

We inquired about the bus schedule and Al wrote down the times both going and returning. We strolled around the streets of Orvieto until it was time for the bus, then went to the bus stop on the piazza.

When we asked if this was the bus to Bagnoregio, the bus driver told us, "Si, Si," so we climbed on and took a seat toward the back. We studied the view from our window as we wound down the hill, past the train station and out into the countryside, looking at small vineyards, old stone farm houses, fruit orchards and gardens. We rolled through the countryside making turns onto unnamed roads and occasionally stopping for a woman carrying a shopping bag or a man saying goodbye to a friend. At one stop on a country road, a group of teenagers filled the small bus with their energy, their backpacks and the overlapping rhythm of their Italian conversations. Even though there were plenty of seats, several of them stood, gathering in the aisle around those who were seated to form a tight group of talking and laughing boys and girls cheerful and upbeat, heading home from school for their midday lunch break, we guessed. I pointed out to Al, "They're just like teenagers at home. The most important part of their day is socializing."

While I was watching the teenagers, Al was watching the roadside for signs and finally saw one indicating our near arrival in Bagnoregio. When the bus stopped on a small piazza, we got off. Al carefully noted where we had been dropped off so that we would know where we would be picked up for the return. Calculating the return schedule, Al said, "We've got about two hours." Feeling confident in our planning, we started on our short hike to Civita.

***

We walked through the town along a promenade under a canopy of shade trees to the upper end of the town and saw the ramp-like bridge to Civita, which stood ahead and high above us on the top of a sheer-sided hill. We paused to focus on the architectural charm of the small tower and compact grouping of buildings standing against the backdrop of the blue sky with a few white clouds. We recognized the perspective of the town from the photographs on the travel posters in Orvieto. The hill looks like the steep side of a very high castle and the tiny town is built on top of that. We noted the approach from the lower town up the ramp, the sense of its height far above us, the realization that without a ramp it would be almost impossible to get there. Al studied the modern ramp, narrow enough that only the smallest vehicle could pass, and said, "We sure couldn't drive up here." As we began our walk up the gradual slope of the ramp, we looked alternately up at the sheer walls of the hill and out at the valley around us. At one point, a bicycler passed us, pedaling up the ramp, but no vehicle larger than a golf cart could have passed.

As we climbed, I wondered out loud, "How did people get up here a long time ago, when there wasn't a ramp?" Al didn't have a ready answer. We saw no alternative road or route to the top.

As we entered the town, we sensed the quiet. Italy may seem overcrowded to visitors to Rome or Florence, but the smaller towns in those years seemed almost uninhabited, especially in the midday hours in March. In the crisp air of early spring Civita was breathtakingly quiet. There were subtle signs of modern life, of construction and reconstruction within the small town and even a building marked with the name of an American university. The town was inhabited, but gently so. Occasionally we saw an elderly man walking through the narrow streets or a woman sweeping a walkway, but mostly we were alone.

In some ways, it felt almost too quiet and I was disappointed that the few tourist highlights and amenities we had read about in our guidebook were still closed for the winter. After our long trip to get here, our experience was different from what I had anticipated.

But Al was unphased. We had set out to see this hill town and we would see it. As we started to walk, we quickly realized that there was something special about having the little town almost to ourselves. For us, this wasn't just a tourist sight, but instead, gave us the feeling of a real medieval town. We could see why early dwellers felt relatively safe at the top of these hills.

Hill towns tend to be light and airy places, open as they are to the sky. The narrow walkways between the houses and buildings were typical of other medieval towns but instead of the paths being dark, the height of the town kept them bright. Thinking of architectural designs of houses at home where living and kitchen areas are on the top floor to take advantage of the light, I told Al, "They're like beach houses."

"Or high rises," he said, and I thought of the views from upper floors of apartment buildings that command the highest rent. Even office buildings reserve upper floors for their executives because of the brighter light and better views.

I was left with questions as well as impressions. I asked Al, "Why would people build a town way up here?"

"They never knew who was coming at them," he answered. His questions were more practical. He wondered about logistics. "I wonder how they brought their food up here and where they stored it? Also, where's their water supply?"

The views of the valley from lookout spots were wonderful. We walked from parapet to parapet as in a medieval castle, the base of which was made by nature. We walked around the edges of the town, defined by a waist-high wall and steep sides that dropped off into the broad green valleys far below, which lead to hills in the distance and lovely countryside around and below and beyond. There was no such thing as sprawl or outlying suburbs. There was simply no place to go other than straight down.

Castles and mansions were often built on hills, for the views, the fresh air, the separation from whatever annoyances or threats were below and perhaps the sense of superiority. Hill towns gave us the airy feeling of being on top of the mountain looking down but without a castle's sense of confinement. We walked the medieval streets of stone past the old stone buildings in this tiny town with no cars and few people.

Although some of the hill towns we visited had a fortress feeling, this one seemed too gentle and too small. It reminded me of being on the rooftop of the cathedral in Milan. Maybe Civita was not about having a defensive position. Maybe its residents just wanted to be closer to heaven, their hilltop position similar to the spires of cathedrals, rising above the earth, and enjoying a sense of transcendence.

It seemed unreal to us, two middle-aged Americans in blue jeans and black jackets, walking the quiet pavement up one street and down the other. It felt other worldly as the structures were so old and the walkways so empty, as if visiting Sleeping Beauty's castle when time had stopped. Although someone occasionally walked past us, we could have been in a timeless world. We knew that no one at home would be able to picture us here or understand our description of it later, but we knew that we would share this memory in its simplicity.

The quietness tended to quiet us as well, internally and externally. I chattered less, had fewer opinions to offer, and Al slowed down his pace. We seemed to be just walking to walk, not to get anywhere special since we were already there. Our goal was simply to continue moving, up and down the quiet walkways between the old stucco buildings, hearing our own footsteps and feeling our own presence. It felt a little like being out in the snow when no one else has come to upset the serenity.

There is one moment in Rick Steves's Travel in Italy program when he looks over the valley and a rooster crows in the background. On the sunny day that we were there, we heard what sounded like the same rooster (possibly a relative). In the quiet of a small town high above the quiet countryside, with no cars and very few people, a rooster crowing is quite dramatic as its volume fills the silence and echoes through the valley below. The rooster's crow is unmistakable, a siren breaking into the serenity with its announcements. Its call had a sense of robustness and made me appreciate the many references to the cock's crowing in literature. I thought of Chanticleer, the rooster in Chaucer's *Canterbury Tales,* who almost got eaten by a fox because he was so proud of his crowing. Hearing it for myself, I understood the ego of a small creature impressed that he could make such large and dramatic sounds in a quiet landscape.

I also thought about the Keats poem, "To a Nightingale." He says that the same nightingale sings now that sang hundreds of years before, using the song of the bird as a symbol of the transcendence of time and a connection with the past. Hearing the melodic "cockadoddle dooooo" echo through the valley below us, I thought of the rooster in the same way.

Both Orvieto and Civita gave us experiences of different kinds of hill towns in a low key off season way that might have been disappointing to some sightseers. But we enjoyed both places. Civita was another adventure where we tried going off the regular tourist track. Although it takes time and effort just getting to an out of the way place, and although the sights at the end of the journey may not be as defined as seeing a church or museum, the destination itself is often special. For example, the opportunity to be high above the surrounding countryside and wander this medieval town, distant from and yet attached to the earth, was a special experience. The present day location provided a trip to the past. At the same time we had ventured above the earth while still being attached to it. We were both glad we had made the trip.

Leaving the other worldliness of Civita, we retraced our steps back down the ramp to the more real life atmosphere of Bagnoregio and finished our tour of the town well before the scheduled time. We stood waiting for our bus, assuming that like a train it would pick us up where it dropped us off. Across the piazza on the main road, we saw a blue intercity bus come down the hill and drive on by without turning into the parking area where it had dropped us off. It didn't dawn on either of us until later that we had just missed our return bus. We learned another lesson in getting around Italy, that buses aren't like trains, that the stop where you get off a bus is not where you get on or even across the street. Eventually we found out where to stand for the next bus, but our well planned return trip ended up being two hours later than we had expected.

In Orvieto we wandered in the ancient but contemporary setting, walking around the historical city center. We stopped at the small Etruscan museum where we were welcomed enthusiastically by the Italian speaking guide who gave us a lesson in ancient history. I learned the Etruscans had lived in these caves and used the hills for protection. They also developed a distinct art form in pottery and sculpture. He pointed to the Roman numeral century markers under the displays and said the simple words, "Greco," "Etrusca," "Romano," and explained how the differences in color and design patterns of the rustic orange and black figures painted on water jars and vases were influenced by the Greeks but were uniquely Etruscan. We got a mini-lecture in art history without speaking any of the same language.

We had walked around the outside of the cathedral earlier, but after our museum tour we took the time to notice the elaborate mosaics on the front facing into the piazza. The facade rose up from the compact square to such a height that the only full view was from down one of the small streets that faced it. A couple of years later when there was a major earthquake in central Italy, we read that the mosaics of Orvieto's cathedral had been damaged. We guessed that its height may have made it more vulnerable to the stress of even a distant tremor, since the city itself is built on top of the hill and the cathedral rises high above it.

When visiting a large old cathedral, we had learned to focus on the art that our guidebooks highlighted as special, since not every statue or fresco is significant. Following our guidebook, we found the small Chapel of the Holy Eucharist, along the side aisle of the large cathedral. Several paintings depicted the story of a bishop said to have witnessed a faith-enhancing miracle. It was said that, during a time when he experienced doubt about Christ's presence in the Eucharist, he saw the blood of Christ on his altar cloth during a mass. To honor the miracle, the pope at that time instructed the bishop to build a cathedral. Although the subject matter seemed more inspirational to the worldview of the Middle Ages than to us moderns, the paintings sequentially told the story of the religious event visually, making it clear to understand.

In Orvieto we were just beginning to apply some simple concepts to our understanding of art. We had a better understanding of the stories of miracles, politics of the time and place and attitudes of the church reflected in the art. This was more fascinating to me than the details of style and technique that Al noticed.

"We should appreciate what they believed in the context of their time," I said to Al. "They were trying to teach people who couldn't read. The miracle stories are nice." The paintings seemed to express an authentic faith rather than an attempt to control people. Besides, who were we to judge the beliefs of the past if they were sincere? As I struggled with these philosophical thoughts, trying to establish how I really felt about these "inspirational" messages of miracles, Al just raised his eyebrows, shrugged, and wondered, "Why do they put these big pictures back in this corner where you can't see them very well?"

CHAPTER TEN

Siena, Lucca and Umbria

We had been told that Siena, as a medieval city, makes an ideal contrast to Florence's Renaissance history and art. In the historical competition between the two cities, Florence had ultimately won in terms of power and commerce, but Siena maintained a certain charm that made many people like it better. From Orvieto we took the train north and after a quick transfer in Florence, arrived in Siena.

We arrived at the station in Siena with a hotel reservation, a guidebook map and bravado. We were sure that this time we could easily walk from the station to the hotel, which appeared to be only a couple of blocks away. We had used the morning for travel, and, at the halfway point of our vacation, wanted to get to the hotel, drop our stuff and get back to sightseeing. So we set out, Al in the lead. As we headed in the direction of what we thought was a direct line from the station to our hotel, we came up against an old wall, which as it turned out, stands between the station and the rest of the city. Naively, we followed the wall, thinking we would go through the first opening and circle back. After walking quite a bit farther along the outer wall than we had planned, we entered what we thought was an entrance into the city center and attempted to double back toward our hotel. Instead we ended up in the middle of a large Saturday morning market where throngs of people meandered past clothing stalls and food stands. We stood in their midst and argued, our rage rising as we thrashed around in the confusion of streets and alleys like two-year-olds having a tantrum, all energy and motion, but not really accomplishing anything or getting anywhere. "Let's go this way."…"No, go that way."…"You should know which way to go."…"No, you should know. You have the map."

Al stubbornly stalked off down an alleyway, based on our map, which was clearly marked "not to scale," he seemed to be heading in the right direction. Trying to placate him, but giving up, I broke what were the unspoken rules of the quest and asked for directions. I approached a woman selling fruit and coffee and pointed to the street name of our hotel on my itinerary. Al had continued down what turned out to be a blind but busy alley, dragging his bag determinedly through throngs of Saturday bargain shoppers, themselves moving slowly if at all, unconcerned about getting anywhere in a hurry. Finally, I managed to catch up with him and point to the return direction. He barely heard my explanation through his frustration and annoyance. We backtracked out of the Saturday market, walked two more blocks to make the parallel turn we had looked for, and found our hotel, barely a stone's throw from the train station, if you had been able to climb over the protective wall.

Fortunately, the hotel was one of our nicer choices, tucked onto a quiet street on the fringes of the old city. Greeted with hospitality by the desk staff, we calmed down and rallied quickly from our traumatic entrance to the city. We took our bags to our room, washed up and set out to explore Siena.

Siena is famous for the Palio, the dramatic horse races that take place every summer as they have for hundreds of years. Each "contrada" or neighborhood is represented by colorful banners that proclaim their identity. These art posters displayed throughout the city compete for the honor of their group. Like Mardi Gras traditions which are evident in New Orleans throughout the year, or Kentucky Derby mementos that are visible in Louisville, the Palio is reflected throughout the city, regardless of the season.

Looking out over Il Campo, the space used for the races, Al and I tried to imagine the density of horses and riders in what seemed to be a small area for a racing event. Reaching for reference points, we compared the space to a thoroughbred race track, which is not only bigger but more open. Although horses on a track may bunch up against each other, there is still room to maneuver. "It looks too small for horses," I said to Al.

Looking at the surrounding buildings, I added, "It must really be crowded, too." I tried to comprehend the speed and energy of a horse race so close to the packed and enthusiastic audience. "Who," I wondered, "would be part of such an event?" Although probably not as intense as the running of the bulls at Pamplona, I decided that I didn't need to be at a Palio, that imagining the event in the Campo would be enough.

Unusual for Italy, the Campo is anchored by a government building instead of a cathedral, but is also defined by cafes, restaurants and people quietly enjoying life. Al and I wandered across the broad piazza sloping toward the large civic building past students and tourists, mostly young, sitting and lounging on the stones in the warmth of the sunny areas. We found the city tower and hiked to the top of its winding stairways. At each level of our turn up the stairs of the tower were lookout windows, allowing us broader and grander views. We enjoyed seeing a wider vista at each level, the same red tiled roofs from different perspectives framed out of the smaller and smaller windows as the stairs become narrower. At the top the cityscape, the valley fell out below us, expanding in the distance.

I would have stopped climbing as the space of the tower closed in more tightly, happy to see the wonderful cityscape views from closer to the ground, but Al, who wasn't about to stop as long as there was another flight of stairs to climb, kept going. The views from the top, looking over the red roofs of the old city, were probably our most beautiful memory of Siena.

By the year of our visit to Siena, Al and I had begun to focus on learning as a primary part of travel, so we made a point of visiting the art museum. Art, like architecture in Siena was recognizably medieval even to us novices. It provided clear and dramatic contrast to the Renaissance art of nearby Florence. In Siena, we stepped back an era. Paintings tended to be more simple and stylized with less realism. Nativity scenes showed Mary seated in the center holding the baby Jesus in front of her on her lap. Typically, both figures faced directly outward and both wore golden haloes.

We've all learned in high school that Renaissance means rebirth and that the era had something to do with a rediscovery of classical learning, but the radical new focus during the Renaissance period on what it meant to be a human being living in this world received less emphasis. However, the change in art is dramatic and for the modern generation of visual learners, seeing is understanding. Having by now seen plenty of Renaissance art, we could step back and see how primitive the style of art had been before, but with a beauty of its own in its simplicity.

After seeing the Sienese paintings, it was easy to have my high school students compare the pictures of a medieval saint in our literature book to a reproduction of Michelangelo's paintings in the Sistine Chapel. The muscles and sinews and body structure is so much more real than the ethereal medieval Madonnas, I wondered why I never really noticed it before. The earlier art in its primitive bright colors and stylized nature is almost like a fairy tale or a cartoon version of human beings and human life. Things are representative and golden. It's interesting too how the Madonna was so central to the earlier art. Some might see a suggestion of the divine as maternal as well as paternal even in those patriarchal times.

After our sightseeing and art visit, we ate dinner in Siena in a nice restaurant where we were the only diners. Colorfully designed coats of arms representing the Sienese neighborhoods and dramatic photos of the annual race covered the walls. Here, we ate our first homemade pasta "faggiatelle," a hearty, egg-based pasta, which we ordered when the waiter insisted that it was a special. It was a simple meal, but memorable, maybe because of all of the stair-climbing that we had done before.

For many people, Siena is a favorite city. As for us, we enjoyed Siena, saw a lot, learned a lot, but somehow didn't connect with it as others have. Even for Italy lovers such as us, not everything clicks to the same extent. We have friends who, like us, love Italy and go back often, but haven't yet really enjoyed Venice, one of our favorites. Maybe it was the time of year, still a little cool for sitting out on the large people-friendly Campo. Or maybe we were just at a low point in our trip or tired or got lost too often. Some days are like that, even on the best of trips. And although we may be less enthusiastic than others about Siena, we wouldn't have missed going there.

***

If Siena was just okay, Lucca surpassed our expectations. Our hotel host in Monterrosso the year before had told us to visit Lucca. He said, "Everybody goes to Pisa to see the Leaning Tower and take a picture. And yes, you see the Duomo where Galileo did experiments to show that the earth moved around the sun and got church officials upset in the process. But then what do you do?" he shrugged. "Lucca is better," he told us. "You should spend time in Lucca."

We followed his advice. Al had saved the slip of paper where he had written what our host had told us to see in Lucca, so based on nothing but his recommendation, we went.

Lucca, a well-preserved walled city, lies on the plains behind an old fortress. The flat top of the wide walls is now used for a walking, jogging and biking paths. For us, it was the perfect blend of history and everyday life, not inundated with tourists, at least that March. Built on a more level area and protected by a wall, Lucca seemed easier to navigate than the hill towns, although the remains of old defenses was evident from the jogging path along the top of the old walls of the fortress. From the wide tree-lined boulevard used by hikers and bikers, we could see far and wide. In the late afternoon we walked the wall circle with the town's after work crowd, feeling the coolness of the early spring. Middle-aged women with headsets on, men in jogging clothes, young bikers and skaters exercised after work just as in any urban park in the U.S.

Unlike in the hill towns, the train station was on the same level as the town, so we walked through a tunnel under the old wall to get into the town. Managing our bags with relative ease, we crossed several piazzas and filed down narrow lanes, arriving safely at the Hotel Puccini in about twenty minutes.

After our welcome at the Hotel Puccini, which was located on a quiet residential street, we were directed to our first sightseeing stop in Lucca, the home of Puccini. It was just across the street from the hotel. Later, as we walked through the two-story town house, we peaked into small period-furnished rooms where he wrote his operas. We looked at displays of musical instruments and sheet music while a recording of an aria played in the background. We received a quick education on Puccini's life and most famous creations. Being the only visitors that morning in the small, but tasteful, town home where a great composer had worked, gave us reason to be interested in learning more about him and his music. Several years later when Al talked me into joining some friends in getting season tickets to the opera back home, we saw *La Traviata*, *La Boheme*, and *Tosca*, and could picture the rooms where Puccini lived and composed.

Lucca's Duomo houses a simple but wonderfully carved crucifix of wood, one of the most moving art works we had seen, a medium appropriate for a carpenter's son. It is enclosed in a dim area of the nave and hard to see in the minimal light, that filters through the windows into the church. Yet somehow, the relative darkness and the enclosure that allows you to get very close creates a sense of quiet and intimacy that is compelling. Unlike the more dramatic crucifixes we had seen in Florence, Lucca's did not portray agony and suffering, but rather a calm humanity and depth of character, especially conveyed in the gentle face. This depiction of Jesus seemed down to earth and deep at the same time. It always amazes me that after all of the sights and all of the art that we have seen, certain ones are remembered in such a special way, even after we're back home. Al and I both liked it and would like to see it again.

We read that the wood of the sculpture was not a local variety but came from the East. Who the artist was and how it came to Lucca remain mysteries. According to tradition, the crucifix was brought from the Holy Land by Joseph of Arimathea, the biblical figure who provided for the burial of Jesus. We wondered how anyone could prove that. But proof of course isn't the point. All religions have stories of miracles that provide a sense of a spiritual dimension to life and inspire many. As modern thinkers, we are skeptics and believers at the same time. If we don't believe in the literalism of the stories, as people might have in the past, still we appreciate the inspiration behind the stories, and enjoy the sense of mystery and transcendence they convey.

In Italy we learned stories were best accepted for what they were and left in the realm of mystery.

During a celebrated religious festival in Lucca, the life-size wooden figure of Jesus is dressed in an array of costumes and carried through the streets, the focus of an annual pageant. This spectacle is a local way of honoring this special work of art along with the spiritual traditions that it represents. In the small museum adjacent to the cathedral, we studied the costumes and gold jewelry displayed under glass and then looked at photographs of people lining the streets, watching the dressed-up figure on the cross pass by in Lucca's colorful annual pageant. To a modern viewer, the pageantry suggests a blending of pre-Christian festivals and present day celebration. Although Al and I agreed it would be fun to be part of the festival sometime, I was glad we had seen the lovely carved figure in the quiet and personal space of the church, in its moving simplicity without the adornments displayed in the festival photographs.

Lucca lacked the intensity of a city like Rome or Florence but made up for it with its relaxed feeling. We strolled along the streets of Lucca crossing the small piazzas, enjoying blending into the everyday life. We agreed that Lucca would be a good town to settle into for a while and feel at home, a good base for an extended stay in Italy.

We ate pizza one night in a noisy and popular neighborhood place, ordering from the counter and drinking beer at a small booth, a good spot to watch the Friday night gathering of the mostly young people who filled the busy but friendly place. Another night we ate at a small and mostly empty restaurant. From our table, among the seven or so in the space, we watched the chef, Francesco, who was also the owner, through an open space, a window into the kitchen at the back. He stirred sauces in large pans and lifted pasta with a slotted spoon from a steaming pot. His wife brought the dishes to us as soon as he put food on our plates. We felt like we were part of the family.

As we ate, a man dining alone at a table near us struck up a conversation even though he spoke no English and we knew no Italian to speak of. He insisted that we share some of his wine. Walking over to the shelves of wine bottles in a corner of the little restaurant, he pointed at labels of wine bottles and with gestures and simple phrases explained that Chianti from Tuscany got all the attention but that Montepulciano had excellent red wine, too. He insisted enthusiastically, "Buono vino rosso," and poured us more from his bottle in spite of our protests and our own glasses of house wine. He insisted that we drink some with him since, after all, he gestured, he had a whole bottle open on his table and was not going to drink it all himself, then he laughed.

Francesco's placemats featured a drawing, red lines on antiqued looking rust colored paper, which was a pretty good likeness of himself. At home Al found a frame for the extra and clean copy that he asked for and it hangs in our bedroom. The drawing reminds us of the simple meal, the good food, the friendly atmosphere.

The most popular outdoor area in the city was the old Roman circus, defined by the old buildings, which housed shops and cafes, around the open oval space that had been the circus arena. As I browsed in a souvenir shop on a quiet morning, the saleswoman told us that on weekends and in the summer, the shops are busy and outdoor cafes are popular with local people as jugglers and mimes and musicians provide entertainment.

Like so many places in Italy, a simple open space, a square or a circle in front of a church or on an ancient site, provides a focal point for social life. Tourists can enjoy these places, but essentially they belong to the Italians. These public spaces become living rooms for the whole community. Combining people, shops, entertainers, sunshine and fresh air in a space defined by facades of old buildings that hold it all together, life just happens. In the U.S. we often try to duplicate these people places, creating our own piazzas and squares modeled after those in older societies such as Italy, but our public spaces often seem to be more about shopping than just gathering places. And yet community spaces add so much to life in any city, the chance to be out and about where others are doing the same. At its heart it's about community more than consumerism, a concept we need more of in the U.S.

***

There were other sights to see in Lucca. In an excavation in progress of an old Roman bath under street level, we saw how new structures had been built on top of old ruins and understood how ancient structures could just disappear under the layers of time. But the most Luccan sight was the tower.

As in Florence, during violent periods, families lived in towers and visited allied families by walking high bridges from tower to tower rather than risk going into the streets. One of the many towers in Lucca had survived intact. Families kept animals and stored grain on the lower floors and cooked and had living quarters in the higher levels. Again we climbed, this time through the series of square rooms stacked one on top of another. I told Al, "They must have been claustrophobic." Then on the very top we came out onto an open sun deck area, a place to get fresh air and to take in the sky and surrounding vistas of nature. The view of the red roofs of Lucca contrasted to the golden walled stucco of the buildings, less dramatic and more subtly lovely than the reddish clay coloring of the other Tuscan towns, and gave Lucca a softer glow. The use of clay rather than stone may be why Lucca seemed gentler and more benevolent than some Tuscan towns.

A young Chinese man asked us to take his picture with his traveling companion in front of the cityscape and Al enthusiastically set up the shot in front of the single rooftop tree that grew out of a large pot. Then Al, who doesn't like to pose for photographs, had to go along when the young man insisted on reciprocating and taking a photo of us in the same spot. As a result we have a souvenir photograph of us together overlooking the rooftops of Lucca.

***

Hill towns in Umbria seem somehow less imposing. The Umbrian countryside is more gently rolling than Tuscany and hills rise up more gradually, less like sheer-sided rock fortresses and more like a large mound of earth. Hills provided Umbrian towns with the same lofty base, and as in Tuscany, threats of violence in past times warranted these defensive positions. Maybe it's the religious tone, the focus on saints such as St. Francis of Assisi, or just some feeling in the land and in the air that make Umbria seem a kinder, gentler place.

Our stops in Umbria were several years into our Italian odysseys. Al and I were more comfortable about venturing to smaller towns on our own and figuring out what to do when we got there. I had researched and pondered and finally picked Spoleto as a base, partly for location, partly for its reputation as "pretty," and finally because I was actually able to find a hotel that seemed close to the town center as well as accessible by bus to the train station below. We used Spoleto as a base for two days, went one day to Assisi and one day to Cortona.

In Spoleto, our hotel window opened over the red tile rooftops and views of valleys in the distance with plenty of sky to fill the room with light. After dropping our bags at the hotel, we set out to explore. First we climbed from the hillside hotel up to the old town and then higher still. Once again we were looking for a place outside to eat lunch. After exploring the town for a while we realized that al fresco dining was not in evidence at this time of year so, when we heard the sound of silverware and saw a small trattoria sign pointing to the second story of an old building, we opted for a good Italian lunch indoors. After lunch, the town seemed quiet, so without any destination, we wandered farther up the hill, looking down at the cathedral, which was closed for repairs. We climbed past a five-star hotel, then higher still, moving along a broad walkway where benches looked out over the beautiful view of the valley. By now, we were out of the town itself, but continued to walk along the path of the ridge until we saw an old Roman aqueduct crossing to the other side of the valley.

In spite of my hesitation for following an unmarked path, we walked across the aqueduct, which formed a bridge over the valley below and then followed a two kilometer walk along the opposite side of the hill. I generally resist the path to the unknown while Al forges ahead, reluctant to miss anything. More used to what to expect in Italy by now, we were more adventuresome in walking beyond the known routes. I was learning what Al already knew, that you could put trust into luck and good sense to find your way even if there were no trail markings. I can't say that I was becoming a risk taker, but at least a little less cautious and willing to try the unknown.

We gradually drifted down to an old church with an interesting, primitive-looking sculpture on the facade. A closer look revealed child-like figures, representing the most visual of the Bible stories. We stood for awhile studying the facade of the seemingly deserted church, picking out the stories we recognized, Noah's Ark and Jonah being swallowed by his big fish among them. It seemed that early artists knew which stories were easiest to illustrate. Just like art in a children's Bible school class, visualizing makes the stories concrete in a way that creates interesting art but may have contributed to their being interpreted too literally. I wondered if the ability to visualize a story makes it stand out as more important and if the artists' choices have influenced which stories have been selected over time to hand down to us. Seeing these early depictions made me both reconsider their meanings and appreciate the early artists who made them.

Later, Al read a reference in a guidebook to this small, seemingly unremarkable medieval church of San Paola. The reference was to the primitive art on the facade. Al and I felt like insiders for having discovered it ourselves and art aficionados for having instinctively appreciated something unique about the sculptures.

In our unplanned wanderings we enjoyed our discoveries even more because we hadn't read about them in any guidebook or heard about them from someone else. Even though we don't always know what we are looking at when we find an ancient ruin or old church off the path, we feel as if we are having a unique experience as we try to piece together its meaning for ourselves.

Across from the small church where we studied the facades was some farm land and a cow that grazed several feet away. For some reason I can still picture the stance of the lone cow in the grassy space, almost as well as the church. We walked along the plot of pasture back to the road, crossed a busy road to get back to our side of the valley, and climbed back up the hillside stairs, then hiked all the way back to our hotel. Steepness is one of the protective aspects of the hill towns. It is never easy to get to the top in these towns and that, of course, is the whole idea. Even the local people usually find another way to get from the lower town to the upper. Although the walk was possible, it was not easy. We had started by climbing and ended by climbing.

Spoleto was a little too quiet in the preseason, but it gave us another chance to experience real Italian small town life. Setting out later from our hotel, to eat dinner in a quiet place on the old square, we walked along a dark alleyway threaded between stone walls and buildings about six feet across. The first time we saw headlights and heard the roar of an engine coming from the dark passageway, we were startled. But as in other old towns, we learned to pay attention. Therefore, when we heard the sound of a car, we knew to stand against a building or walk single file until it passed. Completing our transit along the narrow passage shared with the occasional moving car, we turned a sharp corner that led up a series of hillside stairs and into the open area of the piazza. From the side of the piazza, we looked down into an excavation of a small Roman theater still used for music performances in summer. We read in our guidebook that the teatro had long ago been the site of a gruesome execution of a large group of dissidents during an early struggle for power, reminding us again of the violence of the past. The next morning, as we waited at the bus stop beside the theater in the pleasant spring air, I said to Al, "It's so weird to be standing here where people were killed."

Resisting my tendency to do too much analyzing out loud, I thought, "How sad that the executions were related to religious loyalties as well as power politics." Here in the peaceful atmosphere of a quiet hill town was evidence of the violence that had prevailed in both Church and State, violence that would stand as a contrast to the peaceful teachings of Saint Francis of Assisi.

CHAPTER ELEVEN

Assisi

Assisi was our first daytrip from Spoleto. Riding on the train in seats facing each other, I looked ahead while Al looked back as we rode through the Umbrian countryside. Other hill towns, seen from the level of the tracks, appeared first as natural formations rising from the flatlands and plains on sloping hills that gradually became steeper until sheer-sided rock carried our gaze up to the silhouette of medieval towers and churches against the sky. It was easy to picture earlier humans seeking the hilltops as protection from enemies coming across the plains. From their superior position on the top of their hill, town dwellers could look out on the surroundings and be able to see who was coming at them. Instead of building castles with walls and moats, they built their towns high enough to create a defensive advantage. And when they weren't being threatened by aggressors, they could enjoy the light, airy and beautiful views from the lookout points and defining edges of their town.

Since there was no direct train from Spoleto to Assisi, we made a connection in Foligno, a larger town that was a small hub for Umbrian train routes. Making the connection required planning ahead. Following the schedule from the book Al had requested at the Spoleto station, we got off one train and almost immediately onto the another. The change took almost no time. Our plan had worked easily and we were on the train to Assisi.

Assisi was only a couple of stops so we didn't bother to sit down on the second train, but stood in an open area behind the seats at the back of the car, rocking gently in the moving corridor near the doors, and chatted with a well-dressed Roman gentleman, a tourist director on his way to Assisi on business. He was multi-lingual and spoke English fluently. He was interested in talking with us about Italy, our travels and our perspectives on the United States.

We talked about how much we had enjoyed his city and our interest in visiting Saint Peter's Square and seeing the Pope. In turn, he told us about his memories of Rome in the old days when the papacy was treated with more of the trappings of a monarchy. He had seen a previous Pope carried in on a raised chair by his uniformed Swiss Guard rather than riding in a motored vehicle. Al mentioned the cleaning and restorations underway on the facades of the old buildings that we had seen in Rome. Our companion said, "Yes, it's nice to clean the buildings," although he had reservations about some of these preparations for the Jubilee, the Vatican's year 2000 celebrations, which would encourage pilgrims from around the world to come to Rome during the millennium year. Considering the less inspirational but more practical side, he was concerned that the regular tourists might stay away during the religious celebration, wary of crowds of pilgrims and that it could be bad for Italy's tourist industry.

Some Italians we had met seemed to have a different relationship with the Vatican than the rest of Christendom and the world, interpreting its actions and effects on their own country. They also seemed a little more realistic about church politics, seeing the institution through human eyes rather than the expectations of American idealism. The Pope's apology for any negligence on the part of the Church to do more to help the Jews during the World War II and the Shoah or Holocaust had recently been in the news. Our companion hadn't thought much of the Pope's apology, believing that the old Pope knew what was going on but had remained silent in a self-protective kind of way. He thought the Pope's statement of apology was too late.

From the politics of the Vatican the senore moved the conversation to the U.S. Also in the news that spring were revelations of the more embarrassing details of the Clinton "sex scandal." He questioned us about why the sordid details of President Clinton's personal life were being published in the newspapers. He compared the scandalous reaction in the United States to the public acceptance of the French president's mistress, symbolized by her presence at his funeral, another story in the paper recently. Like many Europeans, he was not so much shocked by the improper activity in a leader as about the detailed reporting of it in the American press. "Why are these journalists doing this?" was his indignant question in reference to a front page story in Al's *International Herald Tribune*. "He is an important man." There was no sense of being embarrassed by sexual misbehavior, but just amazement that these details would be in the newspapers for people to read about. He went on to criticize the lack of priorities in undermining the image of the president who had more important responsibilities. Al and I had nothing to say that could him help him understand the politics and journalism of the U.S. at that time.

The train began to slow down as the town of Assisi came into view, its large basilica standing out on the edge of the town, a little lower and separate from the other tightly connected buildings whose outline formed a silhouette against the sky. This church, too, was covered with scaffolding, not because of the preparation for the Jubilee, but because of the 1997 earthquake that had done such damage in this part of Italy. As we got off the train and began to look for transportation from the ground level station up to Assisi, our new acquaintance offered to share his taxi up the hill. "I'm going anyway," he said gesturing for us to climb into the back of the mini cab as he got in the front with his portfolios and briefcase. The mini cab wound quickly up the switchbacks of the hillside, across the crest and into the town. Knowing exactly where to take tourists, the taxi driver dropped us off at the entrance to the Basilica of Saint Francis. When Al pulled out money to pay for our share of the cab ride, the senore hospitably shrugged him away. "My treat," he said. We exchanged addresses and extended an invitation to visit us if he was ever in the U.S. Later Al and I agreed that this gentleman in the tourist business had made a positive and permanent impression on us tourists simply by being friendly.

Our visit to Assisi was one of our most memorable, a peak experience in more ways than one. We were not pilgrims by intention, but we were moved nevertheless by being in the setting of the stories of St. Francis. Maybe it's better to be inadvertent pilgrims, without expectations, able to experience the surprise of wonder. As in other aspects of life, sometimes when we go purposely to look for the sacred, we are disappointed, but sometimes we find it in unexpected ways and places.

A spiritual atmosphere drifts through Assisi, in spite of the commercialism that comes with tourism. Without attempting to analyze what elements of the story of St. Francis are historical and what is inspirational legend, we found ourselves inspired by it. The values and ideals that the saint has come to represent, simplicity, mysticism and a desire for some personal experience of God, seemed to transfer well to modern times. His felt like a message we all needed to hear.

We wandered into the sunlit courtyard and joined a group of middle-aged Americans listening to a presentation by Father George, an American monk, dressed in the robes of the Franciscan order. He stood in front of the scaffolded entrance to a damaged part of the cathedral. He gave an introduction to the life of St. Francis, and told of the much later building of the basilica, famous in art history for the frescoes of the late medieval painter Giotto. The monk shared the drama of his experience during the recent earthquake, how the tremor had felt, how it was a matter of luck and grace that a large number of people had not been inside the church during an aftershock.

The earthquake of the previous fall had done enormous damage to the structure and especially to the frescoes, the painted plaster having fallen, along with the ceiling of the upper church. Everyone had been lucky that the second shock of the earthquake hadn't brought the whole upper church down. I remembered seeing on television how workers were salvaging bits and pieces of the frescoes by Giotto. In Italy, the heritage of the past is important enough to save regardless of cost and difficulty. Protecting against loss of life was the first priority, but avoiding loss of art was next.

According to Father George, the earthquake had devastated central Italy and, now, months later, many people had not been able to return to their homes. He asked for a donation to help those in the smaller, less accessible areas where help was slower to come.

According to our presenter, Francis, as Father George called him, was depicted in a life size painting over a door in the church as a little guy with big ears. At a time when Europeans, including church figures, were into power and money and fighting each other, Francis embraced the simple life. He left his well-to-do home, walked away from his businessman father and comfortable family lifestyle and took up a humble existence. It's believed that Francis witnessed human suffering during his experience in the Crusades, but ended up being associated with peace both within and outside his community. And although some of his spiritual experiences, such as hearing the voice of Jesus asking him to build a church when he was young, and, toward the end of his life, the manifestation of the stigmata, or wounds of Jesus on his own body, may seem strange to us in modern times, the message that comes through to visitors to Assisi is inspirational, positive and healing.

At home many of us are familiar with the garden sculptures of St. Francis, often without knowing the story of the figure he represents. Still, the variations of the figure standing calmly in a simple robe, wearing sandals, and recognizable by the birds he holds and who perch on his shoulders, touch us in some special way. More familiar to many than the standing or seated Buddhas of Asian heritage, St. Francis sculptures convey the same sense of peace and harmony. Although it is not clear that Francis wrote it, the often recited and sung "Prayer of St. Francis," which begins, "Lord, make me an instrument of thy peace," conveys his sense of compassion for all things. And the song/poem, "Canticle of Creation," in which Francis refers to his "Brother Sun and Sister Moon" as sharing the creation, also touches us in the modern world, as we learn to see ourselves as residents of a single planet and part of the universe beyond. In his emphasis on the connection of all things in nature, St. Francis reminded me of American naturalist and philosopher Henry David Thoreau, often cited as an early environmentalist, who wrote about transcendental ideals and the unity and sense of divinity in nature.

Al and I connected with the idea of St. Francis in another way. Ecumenical groups today use Assisi as a meeting place which symbolizes their mission. Francis was known for his overtures to Muslim leaders at a time when fear of and confrontation with Islam, (the attitude of the Crusades), was the sign of the times. While still believing that his faith was the only true one, he reached beyond its boundaries, visiting and conversing respectfully with Muslim leaders in Egypt.

As many married couples who grew up in different traditions, (Al with his Protestant roots and I with my Catholic ones), we experienced in our relationship a similar desire and ability to transcend, at times, the specifics and limitations of religion. Having grown up in a time and place where even Christian denominations had more conflict and less equanimity, we had a special appreciation for this kind of message.

A friend who had visited Assisi heard a lecture comparing Francis to the Buddha. Stories tell of the Buddha having been sheltered from the world by his wealthy father before he saw suffering and left the comforts of home to find a way to overcome it. His emphasis on simplicity, the spiritual life over the materialism, (what Buddhists might refer to as detachment), and his insistence on unconditional love and peace even toward the natural world echo as well. The impact on his society was also powerful.

Back home that year, Al and I rented movie director Franco Zeffirelli's *Brother Sun and Sister Moon*, which shows in an artistic but believable way what young Francis' journey might have been like in his time. The film depicts visually the contrast between the comfortable lives and religious experience of the well-to-do with that of the poor. The poor seemed to be left out of the picture. In one poignant scene the peasants stand in the back of the church silent and in awe of the ritual at the front of the church.

In his life of simplicity and poverty, Francis appealed to the common folk. He related to nature, talked to birds, tamed a wolf. He walked barefoot through the mountains in winter to bring his message to another village. He owned nothing and lived from the food given to him along the way. St. Francis is credited with creating the Christmas manger scene to illustrate the New Testament story of the Nativity for uneducated people. He wanted to tell the story of God's love for the poorest people who he felt had not been included in the community and hadn't been told the "Good News" in a way they could understand.

When the brown-robed Franciscan had finished, we entered the ground floor of the church that was hardly damaged by the earthquake. The Basilica of St. Francis has three levels. Because of the earthquake damage, we couldn't go into the upper chapel to see the majority of the famous Giotto paintings but were able to see the ground level. I told Al, "In some ways it's easier not to have so much to look at." We were able to focus more on what was there. We studied the paintings by the medieval artist Giotto, whose work was known to us only from books. We had read that his angels, painted with human and earthly faces who looked out at us from their winged flight, signified a shift from the Medieval focus of literalism in regard to the spiritual world to a greater focus on what it meant to be human, the beginning of a new way of looking at the world that would come to flower during the Renaissance. We walked around the altar, studying the four frescoes depicting the life of St. Francis. One showed his marriage to the blonde, draped in white, female figure of Lady Poverty. It represented, we read, not so much a rejection of human marriage as a separation from the materialism, greed and power of the time. According to the story, Francis had stripped off his nice clothes in the town piazza, to publicly let his father know that he was serious about shedding his old life of material comfort.

To the side of the main altar, Al pointed to the life-size skeletal figure of death beside the door leading outside. We stopped to look at the figure of Francis, the bones without skin and muscle, standing side by side with a figure of Death, whom he referred to as "Sister." I recalled the famous prayer of St. Francis which begins, "Lord, make me an instrument of thy peace," and remembered that its last line was, "It is in dying that we are restored to eternal life."

Francis's body was kept hidden for generations. His followers were fearful that it would be stolen, since during that time the bodies and even body parts of holy people were thought to have a special value both for miraculous protection and for their ability to draw pilgrims to a place. Still intact under the main church was the underground crypt, the holy place where the tomb of St. Francis is kept.

We went down the stairs to the lower level and sat quietly in the small chapel, taking in the reverent atmosphere. A tour guide speaking in German brought her group of sightseers past the signs which stated clearly "silencio" or silence, since this is a holy place of prayer. However in full voice, she began detailing facts to her people about the chapel and its history. Quickly another Franciscan monk clothed in a brown robe with rope belt, sandaled and toch-headed, came forward with indignation from the chapel. He waved his hands vehemently, telling her to be quiet, that this was a holy place. Although he spoke in Italian, there was no doubt about what he was saying to her. Glancing around the crypt at those kneeling in silence, we, too, were reminded that many people make serious pilgrimages to these places and that the concentration of those kneeling in devotion in the small chapel should be respected.

As tourists, we walk a fine line in such holy places. I found myself thinking of an article I had read about how Native Americans thought of certain mountains as holy and how they feel it to be disrespectful when adventurers rock climb on them. I think of pictures I've seen of Hindus bathing in the River Ganges or observing other devotions at holy places. Or the holy relics of Islam that we later saw in Istanbul, their meaning maybe unfamiliar to us, but they are still worthy of respect. Often, holy places and objects of other cultures seem less so to us. Our American brand of Christianity and even Catholicism tends to be more practical, with less emphasis on holy relics and religious pilgrimages. But as travelers we can respect holy places no matter whose they are and whether or not they seem holy to us.

In Assisi, the followers of St. Francis were called the "Jugglers of God." I thought that juggling suggested happiness and perhaps a freedom from excessive concerns with the problems of day to day life. Successful juggling requires a Zen-like focus on the present. As an activity, it seems unproductive but joyful. They say that Saint Francis would not be happy with the elaborate church built in his name. His message was simplicity. He was so wary of becoming part of the establishment that he didn't even want his followers to be formed into a religious order. He seemed to understand that formalizing his ideals would lead to less freedom and spontaneity of spirit, and more towards trappings of institutionalization.

Many years after Francis' death, Chaucer in *The Canterbury Tales* described the life of an English friar of the Franciscan order. Chaucer's Friar is more of a traveling salesman, using his "license to beg," to gather money from "even the poorest widow." The ironic description of the begging friar in England several hundred years later was Chaucer's way of showing how crooked some friars had become and how the original ideals of the founder had been corrupted. Chaucer's Friar lives quite differently from the simple life of the original followers of St. Francis.

As we went outside to explore the town, we noticed again how much of the basilica was covered with scaffolding, the dome and sides covered with support structures. Many of the smaller buildings we passed as we walked up and down the narrow streets were supported by metal braces notched together. The earthquake had had a major impact on the town. The technology of modern times was supporting and saving the structures of the past until reconstruction could occur.

I asked Al, "How did they get all this sophisticated equipment into this small town?"

Al moved his hand in a broad gesture, "They come from all over the place," referring to seismic specialists who rush from all over the world to respond to a major earthquake, ready to assess damage and salvage as much as possible. Seeing both the earthquake damage and the response to it in Assisi made me more aware of similar events in other places. Here again Italy was, for us, a window to the greater world.

Our nicest time in Assisi was our walk up the hill. Having seen the main sights, we now walked just to enjoy the spring air, the light, the songs of birds, to just be, in motion but not to get somewhere. Even Al was focused more on the pleasure and sense of the moment than the need to get to the top or to see something specific. There was no exact destination above Assisi. We just followed the walkways strolling along a path heading gradually higher above the town, feeling the sun and fresh air, hearing the spring songs of birds, who were no doubt descendants of the ones Saint Francis and his followers heard on these same hillsides.

It may have been the stories that we had heard, but we felt the spirituality of the hills. Again I thought of English poet John Keats' "Ode to a Nightingale," describing the song of a nightingale as symbolic of the unity of life transcending time and generations.

We heard the distant sounds of the town below and the gentle quietness somehow around us. Occasionally, a helicopter circled the area of construction around the cathedral. Stopping along the path and looking down at the basilica being repaired, we could see that the grand structure was a bit much for a nonmaterialistic figure like Francis. We were glad we had hiked up to see it from a higher perspective.

Most profound emotions or insights cannot be described in words, and it may be that the places we like the best are the hardest to write about, the most intangible. The feeling of standing quietly in the spring air taking in the experience was simplicity itself. Even the distant helicopter and scaffolded basilica were part of the quiet beauty of the scene. The moments passed, and though we are often restless, we stood in the stillness for a long time.

Finally when enough time had passed, the ordinariness of life reasserted itself. The helicopter seemed to become noisier. I thought again of a poem, this time "Stopping by Woods on a Snowy Evening" by Robert Frost when the harness bells of his horse pulls him away from the experience of a scene of beauty. Besides, we were hungry. We left our scenic spot, wound our way down the hill, drifting through the sloping alley ways past shops and small dwellings into the center of town. In early March we saw no tourists but passed men and women in Franciscan robes, who, rather than standing out as different as in a city back home, were an integral part of their town.

We found a café with a couple of outdoor tables on a narrow piazza near the town center. We ordered beer and panini and when we finished, we moved to sit on the wall near a fountain in the sun. I could have stayed, settling in again to the experience of the moment, but Al was restless and ready to move on. Down from the hilltop and back to the level of the town, he wanted to continue sightseeing.

After our walk above the city and our lunch break, we came back to the realities of earth. We walked to the other end of the town from the basilica to the church honoring St. Clare, who started an order for women to follow the way of simplicity of St. Francis. This church was also supported by metal, covered with scaffolding and closed temporarily because of structural damage from the earthquake. For a while, we leaned against the wall at the edge of the hill looking out over the green hills and tree covered areas of Umbria in the distance. We listened as a large group of teenagers entertained themselves by boisterously singing their school songs in the piazza in front of the church. When the teenagers moved on, I sat on a bench while Al found one of the red phones and checked his messages via voice mail, mastering their bulky punchable numbers and halting technology.

Coming back from Assisi, our serenity was jolted when we missed our train connection in Foligno and got stuck for a couple of hours in a non touristy town. We knew the connection would be brief, no more than ten minutes, but we didn't expect that when we arrived the train would have come and gone. We waited for a while beside the track. When the train seemed unreasonably late, Al studied the posted yellow schedule only to find that it differed from our train booklet schedule by an essential few minutes. Seeing a uniformed agent in the quiet station, Al pointed to the destination we were looking for and asked, "Quando?" when? The agent shrugged, saying in Italian, "It's gone." Al showed the official the schedule in our booklet and showed the connection we were trying to make, but the agent just lifted his hands outward with a gesture that said there was nothing to be done.

Sitting in the open on the Umbrian plains rather than on a hill, Foligno serves as a railway hub for the region. With four unplanned hours until the next train to Spoleto, we experienced life in a town that was not a tourist center. Our romantic view of hill towns was replaced by a confrontation with real life. We followed the standard Centro signs to the central piazza, which, fortunately for us, was an easy walk.

Without the aura of a tourist town like Assisi or the views of Spoleto, Foligno felt a little more worn, a little less other-worldly than the hill towns we had visited. Its cathedral, piazza and buildings were old but with less charm and mystery. The difference between looking at antique furniture and furniture that is just old comes to mind.

Looking at the cathedral on the piazza, we saw obvious damage from the earthquake. Although repairs had been started, there seemed no urgency about the restoration. Pieces of their cathedral had fallen down into the piazza. We had no time to explore beyond the piazza.

Spending a few hours in a town with more suggestion of struggle and damage from the earthquake, less tourist attraction and more of the crunch of real life around us, became one of our memorable experiences, a reference point for our hill country tour. We were reminded that we often see the best and prettiest of the places we visit and that the ordinary life of working people is not always beautiful and romantic and that life can be difficult in Italy as well as joyous.

Still and all, Italy being Italy, even in a real life-town, we easily found a cafe across the piazza that faced the church and had gelato and cappuccino as we watched the late afternoon pedestrians and occasional lone dog cross the piazza. It was quiet because of the hour and the afternoon chill, but the pace began to pick up around 4:00 when the stores reopened. Weekends are probably a little more laid back, and passeggiata time probably brings out people here as elsewhere. By then our time here had passed and we set off back to the station to catch the later train back to Spoleto.

***

I read once that a vacation is over when it's over and that when you unpack, you must abruptly return to ordinary life. But I think differently. When we got back home, I found myself drifting back to the hill town settings, walking on medieval streets or sitting in outdoor cafes, having flashes of memory that defined our vacation. Easily in the random replays of my imagination, I could be there again. It seemed to me that certain places and moments became part of a file, an investment in memory that may serve us well someday, when we need to be able to use those memories. Relaxation techniques sometimes ask people to put themselves in a beautiful or peaceful or relaxing place, to take a mental vacation of sorts. Our hill town experiences, with tangible sensations, became part of this file to be drawn from again and again.

I remember a woman telling me years ago that travel money was always well spent. You always had it. At the time I didn't understand what she meant and didn't believe it. It seemed like a vacation was one of life's fleeting pleasures, an escape from everyday life, more luxurious or frivolous. Over the years I've come to understand what this friend meant by seeing travel as something that, "You will always have." We still have these trips to be pulled out and recalled at will, able to relive them more vividly than a skiing or beach vacation. Travel opens doors and windows to all kinds of impressions, renews our knowledge of our history and art, and gives us new perspectives. We are reminded of places and people and events all the time in things we read or see on television. Although our travel isn't over yet, and I want to go again, I like being able to return to Italy in memory. It helps my restlessness at having to wait a whole year before I can return.

CHAPTER TWELVE

Simplicity

When I first talked Al into returning to Italy, my rationale was direct. Let's see how cheaply we can go and still have a good time. I thought, "If I can prove to him that Italy is not a luxury vacation but is, in fact, less expensive than some of the places we visit in the U.S., we'll be able to go back more often. And we'll get much more travel experience for our money." I had figured out after our first trip that the only two ways we could save significant lire and still have a good time was by planning ahead for budget hotels and avoiding unnecessary cab rides. I really don't like to stay in depressing, gloomy places, but I figured that if I looked at the guidebooks carefully I'd be able to find the non-travel agent hotels, the family-owned ones that would also be close to the centers where we wanted to be. Those would save us cab fare, too. We learned early that a long walk or cab ride back to an out of the way hotel, even if it is in a pretty setting or a nicer building, is a hardship.

My usual approach is to get names and numbers from guidebooks, some bought and some looked at in the bookstores. I have been known to sit on the floor between shelves leafing through books copying down names, fax numbers and later e-mail addresses. Sometimes hotels are better and sometimes worse than the descriptions, but we have never had a really bad experience. Travel guides are pretty reliable if you read comments carefully so I check to see what hotel names turn up in more than one book. Then I start calling before work in the mornings.

Now that I'm used to booking ahead, I have to remind myself how hard it seemed at the beginning. Figuring out the towns we wanted to visit from sketchy descriptions in guide-books and finding names of budget hotels that were in the right parts of town was like reaching far off into the unknown. I was intimidated by the transatlantic phone numbers, the inter-national code, country code and city codes. I was tongue-tied about speaking in English to an Italian hotel owner, hoping he or she would understand me. I had to force myself past my tele-phone resistance. I made the calls at 6:00 in the morning when it was still dark outside because in Italy that was 1:00 in the afternoon. I would call and get strange beeps, operator mes-sages in Italian, wrong numbers, no answer, or what sounded like somebody's home and would feel like I was leaping into the dark across the ocean. Gradually, I was able to piece together our itinerary with a map on the table in front of me, changing our destinations depending on who did or did not answer the phone and where I could book a reservation.

As soon as someone answers, "Prego," I ask, "Do you speak English, por favore?" Often the speaker hesitantly responds "a little" or speaks in Italian to someone else who comes to the phone. As best we can, we discuss the dates and rates and of-ten arrange to fax confirmations. Since in smaller hotels and pensiones, reservations are often written by hand in a book in pencil, I picture the pause on the phone not as an agent wearing earphones but a hotelier leafing through his big book, checking which rooms are occupied for which dates.

My early morning calls across the Atlantic are, as much as anything, a test. It soothes me to know that if I call a certain number, someone will answer the telephone.

I worry sometimes about being contacted away from home. Although I feel more comfortable if I speak in English with someone at the hotel, I know not to expect message lights on the phones or voice mail to the rooms. I give the numbers to my daughters and other family members, knowing, in a real pinch, someone will be able to find us.

Unlike young backpackers who jump on trains and decide on the spur of the moment where to go, Al and I do better with a plan. For them it's an adventure to be spontaneous. For us, it would be one more issue to deal with when what we are trying to do is get away from decisions and just be. Occasionally our plans make it hard to be spontaneous and follow a whim, and sometimes we've wished we didn't have to spend another night in Ravenna or that we could stay an extra day in Florence instead of heading for Milan. But following whims can be just as time consuming as following a schedule. I'm always glad that I have made the reservations ahead. Following our itinerary is like following a treasure map. We know our goals and put our energy into reaching our destinations and finding our towns and hotels.

Whenever we think we have gotten good at hotel logistics, we'll get a reminder to tread cautiously, such as getting lost or finding that the walk to a hotel is straight up hill. We try to remember next time to ask directions, to avoid overconfidence in finding our way around old cities. We have also learned to distrust the scale on maps. When we arrive we try to expect the unexpected and go with the flow instead of getting so frustrated until we get settled.

Places to stay are important in some ways but not in others. We aren't the type of people who sit around and enjoy the ambiance of our hotel room. Rather, Italy is for us the type of place to put our suitcases, sleep comfortably, look out a window if possible. Our best hotels are cheerful with minimalist furnishings, tile floors, a comfortable bed, a table, sometimes a dresser or bureau with rods for hanging clothes, a sink and a bathroom or shower.

Actually the bathroom is a luxury. In Europe, the tradition in many hotels is to have the bathroom down the hall. On a few occasions we have used the bathroom down the hall, saving many lire in the process. But there is something about midlife, maybe it's a need for more space or privacy, or maybe it's having to get up in the middle of the night, but the adventure of padding across the hall at two in the morning in uncombed disarray isn't what I want. So I feel guilty and extravagant and uncomfortably American, because it is the Americans after all who introduced this strange idea of the private bath to European hotels.

Even with private baths, our accommodations are lessons in simplicity and minimalism. Showers sometimes have no curtain and no frame, just a shower on the wall in the tiled floor of the bathroom. It's usually better to leave towels outside and an advantage to be first in the shower since the second will have wetter surroundings. But a shower head, intact tile and a good drain are surprisingly functional. At home we complicate our lives more than we realize surrounded as we are with messages of seeking higher material standards in our homes. I guess selling shower doors, curtains and curtain rods has kept our economy booming along.

Europeans are way ahead of us in conservation of energy use. In the minimalist rooms, lighting may be less bright than at home and the temperature may not be as warm or cool as we are used to. We always realize how much more we use than we need to be comfortable and resolve to use less electricity when we get home. Much is what we get used to. If a room feels dark when we go into it, we know to open the heavy wooden shutters and let in plenty of light, often looking out over a garden or rooftops rather than focusing on the lack of finery in the room.

Al sometimes misses English language television, but we can usually figure out any important news stories in Italian, although we don't always get the details. Part of our vacation is to break out of our ten o'clock news routine, and early morning newspaper fixes, and just be on another country's time. It's part of our magic of being there. We may not really be away from the world, but if we don't know every detail of the news, it feels like it. Occasionally we do get a station catering to English speakers or stay in a hotel with CNN. And we have watched reruns of Lassie without missing any of the plot since the action is all visual. But mostly we read and sleep and are ready to go early in the morning, with no late show distractions to keep us up at night.

The stairs are a challenge since we sometimes have to climb one or two flights of stairs just to get into a pensione. We have learned to remember that the first floor is one above ground level in Italy. Elevators barely hold two people, one with luggage, and they move slowly and sometimes jerkily upward. But the small hotels where we have stayed all felt quiet, safe and welcoming. There seems a closer more familial feel to these family run lodgings, which are clean and convenient and friendly.

Budget travelers tend to bond in their economy, knowing they are lucky to be traveling at all and take pride in their attempts to travel European-style and not insist on American standards of sterility and comfort. We have sat in dining rooms looking over rivers and into gardens eating croissants and drinking cafe au lait and cappuccino. We have exchanged tour tips with fellow travelers in these small rooms. Somehow in a large hotel chain coffee shop or dining room it would seem less easy to strike up a conversation with strangers. We know (or think we know) that we're having a better time than the people on tour buses with all their logistics and luggage taken care of for them. We like the fact that we are a little more immersed in the culture.

In Foggia, at a large hotel comfortably designed more for business travelers than tourists, we learned from an English speaking agent that a double means twin beds and for a double bed we need a "matrimoniale," a bed for married couples. It's a musical word and I liked hearing this expression at this stage of our journey. It reinforced the idea of marriage as sharing a way of living. And it also explained why whenever I asked for a double room we always got twin beds.

Al and I do get along pretty well together in our closet-sized rooms. After our initial adjustment, we can almost enjoy the physical closeness of spending all our hours together in a small space within several feet of each other. Of course not having pressures of work and real life helps to keep our positive side up, while life at home will always be more complex.

CHAPTER THIRTEEN

Magic and Mystery

"Venice is like Disneyland for adults," a friend once told us. Entering Venice, we enter a world of magic and wonder, but Venice is real. It is a place of silence and mysterious beauty, of old palaces and grand canals. A world with no cars.

Looking at a map of Venice shows its uniqueness. The city stands on a series of closely knit islands. Only a long causeway connects it to the solidity of the mainland. At its end, all roads stop and cars can go no further. From there, the Grand Canal turns broadly through the city where it opens into the wider Canale de San Marcos and the lagoon.

By the time Al and I returned to Venice, after our two day culture shock trip the first year with Kirsti, we were fairly used to traveling in Italy. We had continued our trans-Atlantic journey from Rome to Venice for an additional cost of only $3.00 per ticket. The extension saved us money and travel time as we continued to the farthest city first. But adding an extra flight to our journey had made for a long trip.

As Al gestured toward the airport bus that would take us to the city, I moved toward the cab stand, reminding him that we still had a long way to go and that we were more tired than we felt. We had learned the hard way not to overextend ourselves when we were jetlagged. Al followed me to the waiting taxi, and our driver raced us across the causeway, his Fiat flying past the cheaper but slower bus.

The taxi ride was worth it since we would need our energy on the other side of the causeway. In Venice we couldn't take our taxi to our hotel. At the edge of this city of canals, all cars either retrace their paths back to the mainland or are parked in a large city lot. The rest of the journey is by water or on foot. Although it might sound inconvenient at first, one of the wonders of Venice is that there are no cars.

Having splurged with our taxi from the airport, we decided not to take a private water taxi to our hotel, but to attempt to master the vaporetti, taking advantage of our earlier experiences in Venice with Kirsti. Our hotel was a short walk from the Rialto Bridge on the Grand Canal. At the ticket window for the vaporetti, Al felt like a regular as he bought our tickets to the Rialto stop. Paying with lire bills of high numbers, the only ones we had, he kept track during the slow count of his change. Obviously newly arrived tourists, encumbered with our luggage and looking tired, we seemed like an easy mark for a 30,000 lire ($20 dollar) short change from the agent. But Al stood his ground and pointedly kept his hand out until he got his money.

It takes a while to get oriented in Venice. The Grand Canal loops around the city and, until you get used to a few landmarks, it's easy to head off in the wrong direction since, unlike street buses, the stop is on the same side of the canal regardless of which direction you are going. Depending on which of two lines you stand in, you will get a boat going in one or the other directions along the canal.

We walked down to the sheltered waiting area at the water's edge and Al studied the posted map of the Grand Canal. While I was convinced we should be on the right side of the divided area, he promptly backtracked, and got in the line on the other side. This time I followed him with only a minor protest, having learned by then to accept that he would be right more often than I about directions. Still, as the small ferry boat slid sideways up to the small dock, I surreptitiously asked another passenger, "Rialto?" I wanted to be sure we were getting on the right boat. I was relieved when she nodded, "Si, Si. Rialto."

The uniformed ferryman unhooked the chain and after others had exited, we walked on. Although there were empty seats in the closed cabin, we pulled our luggage onto the open deck of the ferry and stood with the local commuters feeling both the sea air and the magic of Venice come upon us.

The workaday reality of a Venetian morning presented itself with a sense of magic and other-worldliness. We heard the rush of water as the vaporetto moved past the old buildings and into the bustle of boats moving through the broad canal. Breeze on our faces, light sparkled on the water and we felt a surge of energy. The sights and sounds pulled us fully into the moment as the majesty of the old city enveloped us. I said to Al, "This wouldn't be a bad way to go to work."

Every vaporetto ride feels like an adventure. We pay for the transportation but also for the fun of watching old Venetian palazzos, ripples of water moving gently against their facades, as we pass by, feeling the breeze and hearing the water moving beneath us as the low throttled motors create a softened wake. The vaporetto is part of the whole magic and uniqueness of Venice.

Historically the city developed where it did as protection from conflicts and invasions. Having water around provided a deterrent to whoever might have intended harm. Similar to the more fortress-like hill towns, the sea provided an obstacle for invaders as well as a defensive advantage. The sea still provides protection, but now from much of the turmoil of modern life.

Living as they have on these islands for hundreds of years, Venetians are used to conducting business on water. Even emergency responses are provided by boats, (police boats, ambulance boats and fire boats with sirens). There are gondolas used mostly for tourists, but most common along the canals and in the lagoon are commercial boats, which, like small delivery trucks, ferry sea-food, fresh produce, canned and boxed groceries, hardware and lumber to destinations within the city. Its beauty remains, but, with the exception of the food from the sea waters, most day-to-day necessities are imported from the mainland by boat.

As we traversed the city canals, we saw these small crafts with a crew of one or two cruising past our vaporetto on their way to deliver large bottles of wine or water, wrapped in netting for easier handling. Sometimes they carried cases of soft drinks or beer or stacked boxes of household items such as laundry soap, reflecting the details of commerce and everyday life in this city built on water.

From the perspective of an American urban dweller the silence and atmosphere of a city built entirely on canals and with no cars is amazing. Everything that modern city dwellers do in cars, Venetians do in boats or on foot. No cars means less air pollution, a quieter atmosphere. However, the constant wake of the many boats causes concern about settlement and foundation problems and wear and tear on the old buildings. Al had read about attempts to try new kinds of engines with less turbulence and less exhaust to solve the ongoing problem, and speeds are limited in the canal. Al pointed to the foundations of the old building as we passed. "They're sinking. The water line is higher than it used to be." The city itself is Venice's best investment, since its oldness and charm make tourism a major industry, so attention is paid to protect it.

Al and I got off the vaporetto at the Rialto Bridge, a major landmark with its high arch and broad views of the canal in both directions. The Rialto bustles with energy, boats coming and going under the bridge, tourists taking pictures, local people returning during the early morning hours from the open air seafood and produce market on the other side. It is a genuine old neighborhood filled with local people, but its charm is overlaid with tourist attractions.

As much as we enjoyed riding the vaporetto, they often stopped on the wrong side of the canal from our destination. Our hotel was on the other side of the bridge so we needed to cross over. The center of the bridge has wide steps that follow its arch, lined with shops, mostly for the tourist market. On the outside of the buildings, other stairs avoid the shoppers' fray and stay open to the view of the busy canal.

We now had to decide whether to walk with our luggage on the outer or inner stairs to get to the other side of the Rialto Bridge. Enthralled with the beauty and drama of it all, the morning sunlight glimmering brightly on the moving water as boats of all kinds moved up and down the canal, I wanted to take in the view as we walked. I wanted to start vacationing now; Al wanted to find the hotel first.

"You'll get lost," he said. "You don't know where you're going."

"The stairs go to the same place," I answered. "I want to look at the view."

We ended up taking parallel routes, Al on the inner steps and I on the outside ones, and I paused from time to time to try to enjoy the drama of the canal activity.

Once we were on the other side of the canal, we gathered our remaining mental energy to find the hotel. Luckily, the walk to our pensione from the bridge was only two short blocks. We watched carefully for the street sign to the small walkway to the right, as indicated on our map. Down the alleyway we found the address of our hotel at an old multi-storied stone building, but it took careful looking before we noticed a small engraved sign on the big door with the name of the pensione. I had made this reservation by e-mail, my first use of what was then a new way to communicate overseas, and knew that this time, I had the dates and location right. Still, I had a bad moment when at the end point of our long journey, with our energy lagging and our patience failing, we tried the door of the multi-story old building and found it locked. I felt a wave of anxiousness since, in our present irritable moods, we would not be able to deal calmly with a hotel problem. Al lifted the heavy but well-worn brass doorknocker and found, secreted underneath, a bell to ring. We pushed it a couple of times, not knowing if it worked or not, since we didn't hear any sound. But after several efforts, we heard the crass buzzing sound that released the lock and let us in. Relieved, we climbed two flights of stairs and came to the entrance of the pensione where we entered a pleasant and airy reception area and received the hearty "Buon Giorno" greeting of the hotel manager.

After getting settled, we decided that fresh air would do us more good than a nap. We walked the promenade lined with shops and cafes, following the twists and turns which connect the Rialto on one side of the loop of the big canal, through the old neighborhoods across small canals and piazzas to St. Mark's Cathedral and the often photographed views of the lagoon. Al focused on the yellow signs periodically posted on buildings at intersections indicating directions to San Marcos. Several times we turned the wrong way or failed to turn and had to backtrack when we found ourselves in a blind alley or more often, standing beside a canal with no bridge and too wide to jump.

Still, it could have been worse. Getting lost in Venice can be enjoyable rather than frustrating. You can't get very lost because you are surrounded by water. Eventually, whether you follow people or not, if you walk long enough, you will find your way back to a main promenade, which will take you to a recognizable destination in the compact old city.

We finally emerged from the last part of the pedestrian walkway through corridors between the old buildings and stumbled, surprised and almost by accident, onto St. Mark's Square. Immediately, the sounds and energy of the space, of people, pigeons, the architecture, the hum of breezes of the nearby sea, all enveloped us. One of the most famous sights in Italy, this piazza is enormous, much larger than a football field. The beautiful cathedral with its Byzantine influence from the East is the focus of the square, its architecture and design reflecting Venice's face toward the cultures of the Adriatic. Outdoor cafes lined the sides of the large space and both tourists and local people of all ages strode purposely or strolled leisurely among the pigeons across the length and width of the piazza. The heart and soul of the city, rather than just an open space, is a convergent point entered from all directions by residential and shop-lined walkways.

Taking deep breaths and feeling this vision of San Marcos was easily worth 15 hours of travel, we walked across the piazza to the far end of the rectangular square to get a good perspective of the Byzantine domes and spires and gold and blue colored mosaic facade. We experienced the meaning of the cliché, "it was a breathtaking sight," as we literally opened our mouths in awe at the grand spectacle. A familiar but utterly dramatic visual symbol of Italy, St. Mark's, as St. Peter's in Rome and the red roof of the Duomo in Florence, is frequently depicted on postcards and posters. A moment's observation of the intense color and multiple domes made recognition of the influences of Eastern architecture easy, even for novices like us. We stood at the far end for a while and just looked. I thought, "It's amazing." Al regretted that we had forgotten to bring the camera. "That's okay," I said, "we can buy postcards." We knew that no photographs would be able to recreate what we saw and experienced in our first view of Piazza San Marcos. We strolled on around the square coming back up to the steps of the church working our way through the pigeons and pedestrians, looking from different angles and taking in the full atmosphere of the square.

Having taken in the scene at St. Mark's as fully as we could, we turned right and walked out onto the famous promenade along the lagoon, seen in the magical light of the lifting sea mist. The tension of our arrival fatigue had faded, evaporating, like the sea mist rising from the lagoon.

Al and I walked in the midday spring sunshine along the famous lagoon, enjoying our place in the magic of the grand promenade. The gentle haze in the air, the vapor from the sun-lit lagoon gave us a sense of being in a dream or in a movie. The water sparkled, the gondolas bounced gently in their docks, while larger boats churned in and out of the main docks. We strolled past the quiet and old elegance of the facades of the grand hotels that faced small islands and churches across the sun-sparkled blue lagoon, occasionally climbing steps up and over and down a small bridge over a small canal turning from the lagoon into the city. Water lapped at the sea wall as we walked.

On our first afternoon we just settled in, letting go of home, getting our bearings, collecting information, enjoying the familiarity of Italy and the newness of Venice at the same time. We stopped to read an historical marking on a waterfront building noting that it was the home of Petrarch. I remembered, from the high school textbook I used that Shakespeare and other British poets had been inspired by the love sonnets of Petrarch and adapted his form to English. For some reason I had never thought of him as a real person, just the title of a form of poetry, the Petrarchan sonnet, a name to be learned and taught.

I told Al, "He wrote love sonnets during the Renaissance before Shakespeare. The English poets copied his ideas."

Al nodded without comment, not particularly interested in encouraging a lecture on poetry. Then he stopped to read a poster advertising a violinists' concert of Vivaldi and Mozart. "Look," he said. "Like in Milan." We walked up a few steps from the walkway to study the details of the concert, then continued our way along the promenade, crossing the small bridges over the canals as far we could, until the line of buildings ended and we were stopped by a turn of the canal. As the light shifted to dusk we turned around to stroll back noting the traditional Venetian lamps we had so often seen lighted in photographs of Venice and which create an atmosphere of mystery on a foggy evening.

Returning from our magical stroll, Al noticed the ferry boat docks. Already planning for our next day's excursion, he stopped to study the ferry schedules posted at the docks for the islands of Murano and Burano. By this trip I had come to appreciate Al's taking care of details like this.

One of the nicest vacation days we ever had took place the next morning when we rode the local ferry boat to Burano. Even though Al had checked the ferry schedule the day before, we had learned the hard way that local transportation and schedules can be confusing when one is new in town. Standing at the dock beside a sign that stated our destination, but with no other passengers in sight, we waited and fretted, wondering "Are we in the right place?" and "Did we read the schedule right?" until a few other passengers and eventually the boat itself arrived. Like in the vaporetto the day before, we chose seats outside, this time on a back bench along the stern of the boat. We sat in the sun near the sparkling blue water and felt the wind rush past us as the boat motored slowly away from the dock and then faster as it reached the more open waters of the lagoon. Our fellow passengers were mostly women carrying small sacks of fruit, vegetables, and fish and returning from early morning shopping at the Rialto market. We guessed that those from the smaller islands had ventured into the city center to get ready to prepare the day's meals. Believing that fresh is always best when it comes to food, women in Italy often shop daily.

We went to Burano in stages. At the first stop we had to transfer from our boat to a smaller one to get to the smaller island and picturesque village of Burano. There was no wait and no confusion because there were no choices to make. We simply got off our boat and onto the waiting smaller one.

As we moved from the land to boat to smaller boat to island, we could feel ourselves beginning to unwind, to come down both from the trip and from the year. By the time we got to Burano we were beginning to settle into a relaxed mode, even though it was less than 48 hours since we had left urban life's freeways and shopping malls and computer screens behind.

Quieter even than Venice, smaller, with water flowing around and through it, Burano was a fairy tale, a fragile treasure. In Burano, we wandered up and down the walkways beside the blue water of the narrow canals lined with the tiny, brightly colored homes painted in shades of orange, red, blue and green, the bright Crayola colors that the island is famous for.

Burano is known for lace making and most of the doorways were open, with a curtain of lace giving a semblance of privacy but allowing the air to move freely. Occasionally we would see a woman sitting outside her doorway just a few feet back from the canal tatting the threads for handmade lace pieces. As we walked by, she would look up, smile, say, "Buon Giorno" and go on with her work. From what seemed a respectful distance, I took a photograph of a little boy standing with his grandmother

and dressed in exactly the same color red jacket as the house behind him. For a good hour or so Al and I were content to wander
the quiet side streets and back streets, criss-crossing the small
bridges that wove the town together across the canals.

After exploring the outskirts of the tiny island, we circled
onto the main street which consisted of several blocks of shops
and restaurants. In the context of the small island, we knew we
were in the center of town.

Especially near the water at this time of year, in this part
of Italy, the weather can be a little cool. In mid-March in Italy,
with the weather still unpredictable, sunny days are appreciated
to the fullest. Several restaurants on the shady side of the street
were empty since the noonday diners were opting to sit in the
blessed sunshine at the outdoor tables. Although it was the peak
of the lunch period, the waiter gestured us to a table at the outer
edge of several rows of tables outdoors, a perfect spot in the sun
with a view of pedestrians strolling on the wide promenade. As
we watched the strollers on the "boulevard" of this island town,
we ate fresh mussels cooked with garlic, olive oil, and tomatoes, dipping our bread in the sauce, then followed with a simple
pasta and a carafe of local wine.

We finished our lovely lunch slowly, wanting the afternoon
to last. We listened to the Italian lunch chatter of sociability
around us, watched as people finished up, paid their bills, and
strolled down the promenade, to work or home. The sun finally
shifted behind the building across from us and sitting became
a little too cool to be comfortable. We quickly realized why the
restaurants in the shade across the street had been empty. They
were probably in demand during the hot summer months.

We knew it was time to leave to catch the smaller of the
two boats that would take us to get the larger transfer back to
Venice. Al asked the waiter for the bill, "Il conto por favore,"

and knowing we had been welcome to stay as long as we wanted, we paid and joined the others on the promenade. In Burano that day, we were the only tourists that I could identify.

When we finished lunch, we wandered toward a cluster of lace shops mentioned on our map. On the way back to the dock, I bought a few small pieces of lace for gifts and souvenirs as well as several postcards to remind me later of the bright colors of the houses. Then we headed back to the city, reversing our passage from the small boat to the large boat and back to the main docks near San Marcos. The afternoon started to fade as did the experience of the day, but our memory of it would not. We were officially on vacation.

Later we read in our guidebook that our lunch spot was a highly recommended restaurant. We had been lucky in more ways than one. And although we had enjoyed our tour of the glass factory in Murano in our previous trip and still enjoyed our glass purchases, we had had a more relaxed day all around in smaller Burano. Sometimes the most important tourist attractions take second place to the ones off the beaten track that you find on your own.

***

We took it easy when it came to sightseeing in Venice. There is plenty to do, but the most magical sight is the city itself. We walked and walked and walked. Once we had established that we knew how to get from the Lagoon and St. Mark's back to our hotel at the Rialto, we let ourselves get lost. We meandered without direction along the silent narrow walkways past houses with laundry strung out on pole lines from upper story windows to dry over the waters of the canals. As in a pleasantly designed maze, we followed stone paths along canals just barely too wide to jump across, turning when we had to, backtracking when we came to a dead end of wall or water, until we found one of the small arched foot bridges allowing us to walk up and over to another side. Gradually, we would find our way back to a main walkway.

I don't know if the quiet was the result of no cars anywhere or of the gentle lapping of water, but after a while we began to really notice what quiet is, what an amazing change being in a truly quiet environment is and how seldom, if ever, we experience it. Cities are rarely quiet, and even in our suburban neighborhood, I hear cars go past our corner, day and night, lawn mowers on weekend mornings, or trains, planes, or the quiet roar of the freeway in the distance. At home the hum of my computer and the air conditioner and the refrigerator provide background, even when there is no television or music playing. But gradually, in Venice, we let ourselves go in the quietness of the back alleyways of the neighborhoods and relaxed into the gentle silence. Occasionally we nodded to a pedestrian who passed us. Once we stepped from a walkway into a small piazza, where a couple of older men talked in front of a cafe and boys played soccer in a small area. A fountain and a small church facade completed the quiet neighborhood scene. It was everyday life in Venice, and silent, too, except for the comments from the boys at their game.

We sensed a peacefulness to Venice, a sense of calm among people who seemed a little quiet and reserved, not as emotionally expressive as farther to the south, but not as formal or reserved as in some hill towns. Maybe such a trait evolved from centuries of being surrounded by the water, nurtured as well as protected by it. Maybe islands provide a gentler environment for a city than a hilltop fortress; maybe, in spite of the risk of flooding, living close to water creates a softer touch than living on rock. Or maybe it is because the population is older, more settled, the young tending to move to the towns on the mainland for economic opportunities. And there is a magic to knowing that these people have been living this way for hundreds of years and are obviously comfortable with it. But for whatever reasons, even more than the other cities of Italy, Venice felt safe and serene.

As Al and I walked along one of the wider canals, to a place where there was no bridge, he suddenly said, "Look at that." We saw Venetians, twelve or fourteen adults, standing upright in a small ferry, obviously comfortable in the shallow boat so close to the water. The traghetto, as it's called, takes people straight across the wider canals from places where there is no bridge for a long way. To us, the ride looked precarious, like standing up in a canoe. But nicely dressed men, women and children, carrying shopping bags and briefcases stood straight, facing the opposite shore, as close together as in a crowded elevator with only inches of the little boat to separate them from the sea. With dignity they flaunted all rules against standing up in a small boat. There was not a life jacket in sight.

***

Venetians claim Saint Mark, the New Testament evangelist, as a special protector of their city and also the inspiration for the Cathedral of San Marcos. According to a tour guide we heard, Mark was the first writer of the gospel story, his being the oldest version. He came to the shores of what was then part of the Roman Empire to spread the Gospel's teachings and then drowned off shore in a storm in the Adriatic Sea. The Venetians looked to Mark as their personal presenter of the word of God; their direct line to the Christian message, which allowed them to resist the institutional church that dominated Europe during the Middle Ages and the institutional idea that all salvation led through Rome. All over the eastern part of Italy, it is common to see statues and art depicting a lion with a Bible, symbolizing Mark and representing a resistance against medieval control by the Papacy. Such a symbol made the Venetians more independent from Rome. As I listened to the guide, I liked the idea of resistance to a central authority, decentralized power and greater autonomy of the fringes. "See," I told Al, "religion and politics were mixed together back then, too."

We were aware, as we traveled, of decorated fountains and facades of churches and other public spaces, especially along the Adriatic and in the eastern part of Italy, adorned with a lion with a book across its paws. Al would say, "There's that Saint Mark's lion."

We had visited the inside of the Cathedral of San Marcos with Kirsti and climbed up to the balcony to look out over the square and to see the four large sculptured horses, which we learned later had come from Constantinople. This time we waited in line to take the elevator into the bell tower of the cathedral; the elevator was actually working for once and it took us most of the way up. We had an aerial view of the Piazza San Marcos, the Grand Canal, the Lido and islands in the distance. In the morning sunlight, the movement of boats on the sparkling canals, the expanse of tile rooftops, and the domes and bell towers of churches (even with the cranes and scaffolding that were everywhere we went that year as the Church prepared for the Millenium Jubileo), would have even been worth a hike up the stairs.

After taking advantage of the best morning light for our viewing, we headed for the Doge's Palace, walking along the side of the building next door to the cathedral toward its waterfront entrance. I commented to Al, "It's interesting that the cathedral and the palace are side by side," thinking that architectural placement said something about the relationship between the church and state.

Inside the palace, we were assigned to an English speaking guide who led us through lavish living quarters and governing chambers with some vast paintings celebrating the achievements of Venice. The palace was the seat of power for the Doge, the Venetian title for the number one power figure in Venice during its prime. The opulent palace hinted at the rulers' power and prestige, as well as the wealth and politics that got them there. Although not everyone got to vote, we were surprised to learn that the Doge was elected, but only by a minority of powerful men. Rather than feeling democratic, the palace exuded wealth and power and even a sinister kind of control, suggested by a sculpture of a lion's mouth for secret accusations. An individual would anonymously drop in an accusation of treason or theft. Rather than a democracy style Bill of Rights, the lion's mouth suggested a Gestapo approach to controlling people and to maintaining power in the hands of a few. The box was located outside of a chamber where a Council of Ten would decide on guilt and punishment. The fear of accusation still seemed palpable as the guide explained the process. It must have been hard to keep secrets in a place as small as Venice and, as in other places we had visited, evidence of conspiracy and power plays were signs of the times.

In the largest and grandest room we had ever seen indoors anywhere (a meeting room as big as a football field), we saw the largest painting we had seen anywhere, the Paradiso by Tintoretto, a dramatic composition of densely positioned figures. I wondered if it was possibly the biggest painting in the world. We wondered why we could feel a slight moving in the floor as we walked. The guide explained why the vast area of the floor felt so comfortable. Al understood the structural explanation and, thinking of our own modern dancer daughter, said, "Maggie would like this. It's like the suspended floors that dancers use."

The prison, the most interesting but saddest part of the palace tour, was accessed by prisoners who crossed the Bridge of Sighs from the palace. They would take this walk after their trials had been held and sentencing pronounced. As we walked across the Bridge, we thought of prisoners spending years in dungeon-like cells without seeing daylight. Their last glimpse from the windows overlooking the canal from the bridge must have been more poignant to them than to us visitors. Looking at the underground cells, our first reaction was to appreciate how much better things are in our society where arbitrary power of leaders is limited. But the reality of prison, past or present, was a somber thought. While walking through these dark, small, subterranean areas, I thought that although our legal system and prisons seem more fair and more humane, there is still unfairness and injustice. People without resources still have trouble getting good legal help; we still shut people into small places, even if they aren't underground; cruelty and inhumanity still exist, and when it comes to numbers, we probably have more people in prison in some U.S. cities alone than have lived in the whole city of Venice in the past. I had been volunteering for a couple of years as a support person for adolescents who were incarcerated and felt sad for them as well. We learned that tax money back then provided prisoners in Venice with wine and bread. Prisoners today may have better health care and hygiene and even opportunities for betterment, but they aren't served wine. And in some cases their hope for a better life may seem just as unlikely as those in the dungeons in the Middle Ages. I couldn't help but think that we still had a long way to go in providing justice to all.

After the prison, we were glad to get back outside and see the often romanticized Bridge of Sighs from the perspective of sunlight and the bustle of the lagoon front. We had had our history lessons and dose of social consciousness for the day and were ready for our outdoor lunch and glasses of wine.

***

Al and I had agreed not to hire a gondola, believing we were past the naive tourist stage of paying a lot of money to see sights that we could see on foot. But we heard the rhythmic call of, "Gondola, gondola, gondola," from the gondoliers to us as we walked past their stations and watched the gondolas go under foot bridges and around the narrow canals to another magical part of Venice. As we walked along the canal, we watched the boatmen in broad-brimmed black hats, holding long poles and standing on the tip of their graceful distinctive boats as they skillfully guided them along the water. As the boats glided past the old palazzos, gondoliers serenaded young or old romantics settled in the comfort of the luxurious-looking red and black velvet seats. Less romantic groups of Asian, European, and American students laughed as they sat back in the curved boats gliding gently along the canals.

Enchanted by the scene before us, I said to Al, "Maybe we should ride in a gondola once to see what it's like. The view from the level of the water would be different than from the shore."

When he shook his head, "No," I didn't know if he was being practical about the hundred dollars or a little stubborn about maintaining our status as not your typical tourists. Still, the romantic side of me still thinks a gondola ride might be fun to do someday.

We continued our sightseeing on foot. The size of the city makes it easy to pick a sight and walk to it leisurely, or take the vaporetto without getting lost or exhausted. Whenever we were tired of walking, we got on the vaporetti, which was interesting to ride just for the views. The only difficulties we ever had involved getting off of the vaporetto on the wrong side of the canal from where we needed to be without a bridge anywhere nearby. But finding our destination was never too difficult.

Of all the places we've been in Italy, Venice feels the most otherworldly, especially when you ride along the canal. After a couple of vaporetto rides from the Rialto Bridge to the lagoon front, we got used to familiar sights along the way. We passed art museums and concert halls and recognized facades of churches and mysterious-looking old palazzos with water rippling gently over their boat docks almost to their front doors. Many of the buildings seemed deserted and there was often no walkway in front of them. Some had boats tied right outside their door, suggesting that one might leave a building by getting into a boat. Watching the water lapping at the sides of the old foundations made it clear why they say that Venice is sinking. Al had read about engineering attempts to design wake-free motorboats or shore up the buildings. I could now see why they were necessary.

Al, always good at finding sights off the beaten track, had noticed a short article in a newspaper at home about the restoration of the water-weakened foundation of Santa Maria dei Miracoli, a quiet church tucked into a typical Venetian neighborhood. We set off to find the church, seeing the quest as an excuse for strolling the walkways along quiet canals in yet another neighborhood. As we wove and wound along the narrow walkways, we weren't even sure we could find the church. But, suddenly, as we came out of a narrow passageway, the church just appeared without fanfare or tourists. It stood close to the other buildings of the neighborhood around it. Santa Maria dei Miracoli, or the Church of Miracles, was built and named for a painting of Madonna and Child that was said to answer prayers. The outside of the small church was covered with marble in varying shades of rose and off white, serene in itself, but was made more so as its architecture and colors created a rippling reflection in the small canal that moves past its side. The church was as lovely and calming inside as out, the quietness of Venice making the interior of the church just an extension. There wasn't a lot to do or analyze. The discovery stood on its own. We had by now become familiar with the Italian approach of building a church to honor a sacred painting instead of the other way around. We stood for a while before the small and simple painting of the Madonna and Child that was the focus for devotional candles and special lighting. Al spent some time walking around the interior walls and inspecting the foundation repairs. I lit a candle for a friend back home, something that feels appropriate in old Italian churches. Although there was little to do, we lingered as long as we could, taking in the gentle feeling of the simple but lovely building and its quiet watery setting.

Venice, with its colorful beads, jewelry, glass, carnival masks, brightly colored paintings, is fun for browsing. Shops are full of the same strange kinds of masks, with elongated noses and chins and sun and moon replicas that I'd seen in shops in New Orleans' French Quarter. The masks and photographs recreated the Carnivalia celebrations, the Venetian Mardi Gras. In a continuing education class I had taken that year, the professor had suggested that Mardi Gras colors, purple, green and gold, represented the struggle of the light and brightness of the coming spring of the year with the dark colors of winter. In Venice I bought a series of postcards, photographs with incredibly vivid visuals of Carnival gondolas and figures in costume. The prints showed costumed figures riding in gondolas instead of on floats, the bright contrasting colors of purple, gold and green, and the strangely imaginative masks an easy parallel to New Orleans' Mardi Gras. We had missed Carnival that year but I wasn't sorry. I liked Venice better in its serenity than with crowds. Still, thinking of the excesses of some aspects of Mardi Gras, especially among tourists, I suspected that the Italian-style spring carnival would reflect more celebration and camaraderie than drunkenness or exhibitionism.

On the promenade along the Grand Canal one afternoon, actors dressed in Mozart-era costumes handed out fliers advertising concerts for willing tourists. Declining these offers, we found our own concert. We returned to the small church where we had seen posters for a violin concert of Vivaldi and Mozart and bought our $12 dollar tickets from a window in the vestibule of the church. As we continued our day of strolling in Venice, we enjoyed knowing that we had something special planned for the evening.

After giving ourselves some time to rest in our little hotel room, we dressed in what seemed our least casual combination of slacks and sweaters, the dressiest of our minimal clothes choices, had an early and light dinner and then worked our way across the now familiar passaggio from the Rialto to the lagoon through the lanes and across the bridges in the early darkness. We enjoyed the walk as much as the destination. The church was more than half full for the evening performance. We listened, as eight tuxedo-clad musicians played stringed instruments of various sizes and shapes. This time, as they played, even I was able to recognize parts of Vivaldi's *Four Seasons* and recognize the difference between his music and Mozart. The performance in the cozy atmosphere of the church was both intimate and lively. The appreciative, mostly Italian, audience cheered and applauded and called the musicians back for several encores.

Afterwards, we rode the vaporetto the long way round, deciding not to walk back to the Rialto because it had gotten cool. The churn of the water beneath the flat boat contrasted with the quiet talk of the after concert crowd. The ride back in the evening showed the buildings along the canal lit up at night, but they still looked dark and old and mysterious. "I wonder if anyone is still living there," Al speculated, as we floated past an old palazzo settled into the canal. I thought of Edgar Allan Poe's atmospheric short stories and how he might have described the mood of an old mansion here. And I wondered what stories from past generations those old villas held.

***

Sometimes when I'm in Italy I wonder about how it would be to live in only a small part of a medieval city. Many of us may travel further everyday to go to work or to recreational events than some people of the past did in a lifetime. The change of scenery and tone from city to suburbs, and from activity to activity, is built into our lives as is the mixture of sights and sounds. But in Venice where everything is within reach on foot, we get a sense of what living in a small area would have been like. For Al and me there is a pleasure in seeing so much in a small space. But in the past, the separateness of living in pockets of small, compact areas may have created prejudices and fears of outsiders along with lack of new experiences and a built-in narrowness of focus.

Travel means being open to learning, randomly rather than sequentially. We spent the better part of a cool morning at the museum deepening and broadening our sense of history through art. In spite of the quiet and the protection of the water, in Venice as elsewhere, it's hard to get away from violent chapters of history. Underneath the romantic haze of Venice lie ghosts of the past, echoes of discrimination and violence. The stories of violence seemed distant, strange, other-worldly, hard to imagine in reality and yet the issues of conflict were all too familiar. In the Galleria dell'Accademia, we stood before a large painting depicting the pride of Crusaders off to fight what they thought of as a Holy War. The soldiers carried crosses to symbolize their belief in the Venetian side as the righteous side. We saw evidence that the Venetians were quite fearful of the "heathen Turks" as Chaucer described them in *The Canterbury Tales* in his description of the "perfect" knight who had fought in the Crusades. I had noticed before that some authors from the past, whom we think of as great, reflected the prejudices of the time. Another large painting celebrated the Venetian defeat of the Turks. Large paintings depicted enthusiastically the destruction and defeat of a fleet of invading Moors in a naval battle in the context of their fear of invasion from across the Adriatic. The violent side of Christian history and evidence of both fear of and triumph over the enemy made an impression on both Al and me that carried over to reflection on current events. We saw the fear and narrow thinking of people defined solely by their own beliefs. Confronting the visual evidence of hostilities and fears from the past, even if only in museums, brought its impact home more than reading about it in a history book. We thought of the non-violent movements of the twentieth century as a hopeful sign that at least in the thinking of idealists, we had made progress.

As in many depictions of past wars, a theme of pride in defeating one's enemy relies on a view that the victor is on the side of goodness while the enemy is not. I thought how our own artistic memorials to the Revolutionary War suggest pride in defeating the red-coated British. Other tributes suggest themes of bravery, patriotism and freedom but contrast to later war memorials that more often suggest sadness. I said, "At least we don't seem to take as much pride in conquest or fighting anymore."

Unconvinced, Al shrugged, "Maybe." But this understanding of the religious emphasis of the past, the Venetians' fear of invasion across the sea and their sense of righteousness, the belief that God was on their side against the enemy, made an impression on us just as the resistance to Rome represented by the lion of St. Mark.

The other noteworthy place in Venice, educational and sad at the same time, was the Jewish Ghetto. It's not a vague demarcation or poorly defined neighborhood as in many cities, but a defined area. We walked into the ghetto through an entrance under an archway into an open piazza. The word "ghetto" has an unpleasant ring to it today and it's shocking on one level to see that one existed not as a defacto neighborhood of a certain ethnic group, as today, but as a physically separate part of the city with walls to define it. Living as we do in a society of diversity and civil inclusion, walking under the archway was chilling. But our perception of history is influenced by modernism. We have to reach to imagine what it meant then. Al's thought was that the ghetto might have originally been a place where the Jewish community could hold onto their own traditions in a dominantly Christian society. An old school and synagogue stood with serene dignity within the walls that separated it from the city. Certainly there were long periods in early Christendom of tolerance and compassion and cooperation. But during the worst times restrictions on Jewish areas by Christian authorities limited freedom of movement and commerce. The clear demarcation of the space suggested how separateness could lead to fear and misunderstanding, how blame could be placed, and prejudices and stereotypes develop about those who were "different." Seeing the ghetto, we felt respect for the people who had maintained their culture and beliefs in the midst of a dominant Christian society around them.

When our generation was growing up, we didn't often go to each other's churches or temples except for an occasional wedding or funeral in a different denomination. Lack of knowledge created prejudices, misunderstanding and even fears as well. But how much worse it would have been if the schools and neighborhoods were defined by walls and gates rather than by open streets. The old arguments against the "separate but equal" segregation laws and vague memories of the indirect segregation of neighborhoods of my youth came back to me as I realized how easy it is to project fear and hostility on people with whom we have no day-to-day contact.

Still, as Al and I walked through the Jewish ghetto, looking at the old buildings and noting the Hebrew writings which identified them, we felt the same old peace and quiet of all of Venice's neighborhoods. We saw elderly men out for a stroll, women with shopping bags and boys playing soccer, the same activities we had seen elsewhere in Venice. I like to think, even in days of greater division, that on a human level individual people would still have seen past the divides, that shopkeepers had non-Jewish customers for their good bakeries and kosher meat shops, just as the businessmen used the moneylenders to get loans during the days when the Church forbade their members to lend money at interest. In spite of modern turmoil many of us believe that progress toward enlightenment among believers of all religions and efforts for accepting others of good will is being made. We just have to keep walking around walls and under archways to make the stranger a friend.

CHAPTER FOURTEEN

Monte Sant'Angelo

From Venice we traveled down the Adriatic coast, spending a day in Ravenna where we visited sixth century churches with life-sized mosaics that seemed almost able to reach out and speak to you. One of my students who had visited relatives in Greece had told me about a tradition in her Orthodox family of talking directly to these icons, feeling the inspiration that came from their beauty. By now we had seen a great deal of art, but the breathtaking sight of a line of angels looking down at us from the shining mosaic stones brought them to life in a way that no painting could. "They look so real," I said. "Look at the faces." Al was fascinated by the technique of mosaic. "I guess they had to sketch it first and then different people filled it with the little squares."

Our short stop in Ravenna was worth it for its inspirational value. We can still picture the holy figures coming to life in mosaic. As the colorful facade of San Marcos, the Eastern and Byzantine artistic influence of bright color and living energy and a spiritual humanity impressed us.

From Ravenna we continued down the coast to Foggia and finally to Monte Sant' Angelo. Monte Sant'Angelo or the mountain of the angel, refers to the archangel Michael and is one of those special places that doesn't fit into any of the usual categories and common tourist sights in Italy. It would more likely be part of a pilgrim's itinerary. But that year Al had decided we should go down to the south of Italy along the east coast. "We can see what it's like in that part of Italy," he said. When I had trouble finding tourist destinations in this less traveled area, he browsed through the guidebooks one night and found Monte Sant'Angelo. "Let's go there," he said.

We took the long train ride from Bologna down along the Adriatic Sea, looking first at the water and then at groves of very old olive trees as we went inland. Our destination was Foggia, a small modern coastal city rebuilt after the bombings of World War II. We had chosen Foggia as a good place to stay, a good stopping off place from our train route, the closest stop to get us to Monte Sant'Angelo.

In Foggia we saw the results of the World War II bombings, not in evidence of past destruction but in change. While many cities we had seen prided themselves on their old beauty, their duomo or piazza and medieval streets, Foggia was modern, more like cities back home, with newer buildings, more steel and glass and aluminum, less stone and brick. But modernity had come at the price of suffering serious destruction during Allied bombings in the invasion of Italy in World War II. Unlike the historical evidence of ancient or medieval violence, which we could think of as in the distant past, we were sobered when confronted by the realities of the fighting that took place on European soil only a few decades ago. "It's hard to imagine bombings in Italy," I said, thinking of its romantic beauty. It wasn't even that long ago.

We spent the night in Foggia, and Al studied train and bus connections from Foggia to Manfredonia and then to Monte Sant'Angelo. He settled on a train to Manfredonia, planning to make a bus connection to the mountain. We found the train easily and after a relatively short ride, arrived in the small town of Manfredonia on time. We had over an hour to wait, so once we had found the bus stop to return to, we walked into the piazza of this old fishing town, where old men congregated to talk under the shade of the large trees. We strolled along the sea wall looking down at the fishing boats in the harbor. Other fishermen were finishing the cleaning and packing of their early morning catch and wiping down their boats, having already put in a good morning's work. Feeling confident that we knew both the time and place for the bus, we wandered back through the side streets and even stopped for a quick cappuccino, standing at the bar in a local cafe.

Giving ourselves plenty of time for the 11:00 bus, we headed back from the town center to the bus stop near the station. As we stood on the empty corner, the scheduled time passed. Al said, "It's late." Impatiently, he looked at his watch and at his schedule. No other passengers were in sight, which was not a good sign.

"It'll be here," I countered, trying for patience. "But it is weird that there's nobody else waiting." We waited and waited some more, thinking the bus in this small town was just perhaps very late. But gradually we began to worry that we had again gotten something wrong. Finally as Al continued looking for clues, studying the posted sign that listed the times of departure to the mountain top town, a local man passed along the empty sidewalk. Noticing us, he pointed to the times on the sign and then to a small symbol beside our bus time, as he explained to us in Italian that there was "no bus, no bus" now. Still puzzled, Al found the symbol guide at the bottom of his printed schedule and it turned out this bus was primarily for the summer months and holidays when there was more demand. It didn't run on weekdays, only holidays and Sundays at this time of year. The next scheduled bus wasn't until four hours later. We found ourselves stuck in a small town that we had already toured, our plans to continue to Monte Sant'Angelo halted.

Such is a disadvantage of traveling alone or off the beaten paths of tourism. There was no expert to guide our planning and no manager to help us solve a problem. Al expressed the frustration we both felt, "We're going to waste the whole day."

I couldn't think of a cheerful response since I felt pretty much as he did. Then I remembered seeing several cabs lined up on a street around the corner from the train station. While Al shook his head skeptically, saying, "It'll cost too much. They probably won't take us to a different town," I headed down the block and around the corner to the cabs. We approached the first taxi in the line. A small man, less than five feet tall, in his mid-forties, walked quickly across the street leaving the small group of other drivers standing in the shade. He conveyed a ready to help and quite professional attitude toward his work. After a quick negotiation with the driver who, although he had no front teeth, may have been younger than we were, we got a cab ride up the mountain.

"Taxi?" he asked.

We simply said the name of the town, "Monte Sant'Angelo," which as the major destination for most out-of-towners seemed to be no surprise to him. "Si. Si. Monte Sant'Angelo." We responded. "Quando questo? How much?" He answered by opening both hands to show all ten fingers which he closed and re-opened for a total of four times, telling us the fare would be 40 thousand lire, at that time about $36.00. Without speaking any Italian, the driver made the fare clear to us. We agreed, "Si. Monte Sant'Angelo," and climbed into his cab. For about 20 minutes, the little taxi climbed the side of the white limestone mountain, passing the sheer white stone hillside as we followed the narrow two-lane rode back and forth along the side of the mountain that rose into the foggy mist to over 2500 feet. Since I had paid little attention to the guidebook's description, I hadn't realized that Monte Sant'Angelo would really be a mountain. When we reached the town at the top, we seemed to enter a different world from the town on the sea below.

Al gave our reserved, professional but friendly driver an extra 10,000 lire because we were so happy to be up on the hill. Al said, "I'll bet on a weekday in March he doesn't get that many 40,000 lire fares." Our transportation problem had had an excellent solution. We felt as if we had contributed a little to the pocket of a local cab driver. It was a winning situation all around.

Al had read a brief notation about Monte Sant'Angelo in a guidebook, about the cave where it was said that the Angel Michael had appeared to a farmer. I had paid very little attention to the stories when we planned the itinerary. I was willing to go along on this quest since something Al had read about this cave on the mountain had captured his imagination. Although details varied, the essence of the legend was that the cave had been miraculously discovered. A farmer had been led by a bull to a mysterious opening in the earth leading to the large underground caverns and fresh spring water. The fact that both bulls and farmers might have more likely been on the plains below than on the rocky mountain was not relevant to the story. Our guidebook spoke of ancient myths relating to sacred symbols, in which the dragon may originally have symbolized underground water, making its energy a positive image, a common connection in many early cultures. In Western culture and in the literature books I taught from, the dragon was interpreted as a symbol for evil. But we would see dragons carved over church doors in this part of Italy, seemingly benevolent and suggesting hints of earlier interpretations in legend and art.

We read also about Crusaders stopping at this holy place as a pilgrimage for forgiveness of their sins and prayers for their safe return on their way to the Holy Land across the Adriatic and beyond. The Archangel Michael, the patron saint for crusaders who passed through on their way to the Holy Land, was the reason for the naming of the Mountain of Sant'Angelo, the Holy Angel. I remembered an old prayer about St. Michael the Archangel that said, "Defend us in battle" and "Protect us from evil." What hadn't made sense to a child not going into battle anytime soon made sense in connection to the battle of the crusaders. The prayer was as practical as it was spiritual as the Norman soldiers continued past the end of their lands of Christendom and headed across the Adriatic Sea on their mission to capture the Holy Land. As I looked at the symbols and prayers carved on the walls, I couldn't help but think that, while their crusade was certainly not a mission of "Love thy neighbor" and "Forgive thy enemy," that today's Christians could support, the crusaders, like their opponents, were probably young, nervous and sincere in their own hearts.

For the first time I felt sympathy for the human side of crusading, for young men who journeyed far from home to strange places, whose desire for adventure and fear of the unknown seemed more real when we looked at the carvings they had made in the rock of the cave. We looked at the carvings in the rocks, which were said to be a way of attaining forgiveness of sins, in this last stopping off place, a place of purification, for the crusaders as they went off to battle. There was something calming about seeing these many carvings of symbols, sometimes initials, sometimes just a carved straight line, and realizing the ordinary humanness of many of the people who carved them. Crusaders were on a journey, although their destination would be hard to romanticize. Although they were told that they fought for the honor and glory of God and would be rewarded in the afterlife if they died in battle, they were on a dangerous, unknown journey.

The setting for the cave was a tightly clustered medieval town with a small stone church above ground to acknowledge the more significant presence of the cave below. We followed signs around the side of the church and then carefully down the uneven, irregular and well-worn stairs carved into the stone entrance of the cave. Navigating the stairs without railings made me once again glad we were doing this type of travel while we were still young enough to move easily. We entered a small natural grotto that somehow immediately just felt good. As a pilgrimage site, it wasn't overdone like many of the churches in Italy. Maybe being at the top of a mountain in a small town near the Adriatic, and far away from the old Roman center of church activity helped. There were some small sculptures in niches around the cave and an altar set up for saying mass. But we were able to wander in the grotto for a while before a group came in for the service. We had the space mostly to ourselves with only a couple of other people.

For the most part, there wasn't really much to see. The sculptures were nice and I was struck by the sweetness of St. Michael as he stood with his foot on the creature representing the dragon. St. Michael is shown with a sword as the dragon's slayer, but both the victim and the victor seemed surprisingly nonviolent, unheroic, and simple. Instead of looking angry, triumphant over the evil symbolized by the dragon, or super-powerful, as I had imagined him, there was a sweetness and simplicity about the small figure with curly hair. Even the dragon didn't look very threatening. He seemed to be just quietly playing his part in the drama. Seeing these images of Saint Michael was a very gentle experience. Since then we have become adept at picking out St. Michael and dragon depictions in corners of churches wherever we travel. It is a common image not often focused on in standard tourist notes, but an important symbol from earlier times.

As with many holy places which began in simple anonymity, the grotto had become famous and had been visited by holy people such as Saint Francis and by popes. And the Roman Church had claimed the grotto more formally defining the conditions of forgiveness for the carving in the rock to work. But the essence of the place as a place of faith and forgiveness, of unconditional love and acceptance seemed secure. I imagined the carvers as illiterate and unsophisticated but feeling comforted by the rock they carved.

Sometimes travels become pilgrimages in spite of our intentions. Or maybe all of life is a pilgrimage and meaning simply turns up in a more focused way when we're in a spiritual place. These old pilgrims had walked with reverent intentions. We had traveled by plane, train, bus and cab, as tourists, but to a nontourist type of site. And yet we were somehow moved and satisfied by this experience. Maybe there is a sense of peace and calmness conveyed in holy places that transcends time. Maybe positive energy was communicated to us in spite of ourselves. The reasons why didn't matter. In spite of my childhood ghosts and Al's pragmatic skepticism, the grotto on the Mountain of San Angelo, of the holy angel, made an impression on us. We both liked it.

When the noon church service started, I felt inclined to stay, but Al seemed to have had enough religious experience for one day. We climbed up the stone stairs from the cave to the walkway back to the front of the small church and walked to explore the medieval narrow streets and whitewashed windswept buildings of the town itself.

As the wind picked up, the temperature shifted, and it got gray and windy and cold, very unlike the warm fishing town where we had spent the morning. We walked far enough to the edge of town to look out at the fog, imagining views of the outlying valleys on a brighter day, and looking back at the stacked houses leaning against each other packed tightly together along the ridge of the hill. We felt the difference again between the seacoast towns and the quieter hilltop towns. The people were more reserved.

Hungry and ready to be back inside and away from the hilltop bite of the March wind, we saw the door of a small restaurant, really just a small living room, with six or eight small tables and with a kitchen in back. When we entered, a young girl, about ten years old, came out from behind a thin curtain that hung over the door to the kitchen and took our order for lunch. There was no menu. She simply asked, "Pasta? Vino?" We said, "Si. Grazie." Wine and bread appeared and soon a simple pasta with rich tomato sauce, and we, relaxed and cozily warm indoors, enjoyed our home-style meal. We even had entertainment in the form of a parrot who ironically, since he sat in the small entrance area toward the front door, kept repeating, "Ciao. Ciao. "Good-bye. Good-bye"

After lunch, not wanting to take a chance on missing our return bus, we headed in the direction of the bus stop, giving ourselves plenty of time to find it in the small town, or so we thought. It turned out the bus didn't come into the town center since the streets were so narrow. We learned again, the hard way, that the town was bigger in area than we thought as we hurried down the windy hill to find the open area at its edge where the larger vehicles could wait. We had to race down the hill not to miss our bus, which we knew was the last one out of town for the night.

Our peaceful experience in the grotto underground was framed by confusion on both ends. Looking back I wonder if that's what pilgrimages are about even for the intentional sojourners. Maybe the purpose of a pilgrimage is not really the quest to achieve a goal, but the interlude, the space between activities, the quiet moment or place under the tumult and confusion of life, representing the quiet that exists in us all if we can settle deeply enough. Even as we toured the town and ate our lunch and raced in frustration for the bus, the quiet area, the underground mystery, under the surface of the mountain was still there.

I think now of the way caves have been used in a spiritual sense and with our Mont Sant'Angelo one as my memory. I can still feel the sense of the cave as representing the quiet place in us. We left the town below, we went up to the mountain, only to go down into the simple cave, just as in our lives we make the efforts to seek creative, stimulating or enlightening experiences, but find real peace at a quieter depth.

CHAPTER FIFTEEN

Heading South

By the time Al and I headed to the South, we had become pretty comfortable in Italy and were ready to plunge deeper. This was in 1997 and we had been warned about the risks in traveling south. Friends said, "Don't go to Naples. The Mafia is there." Or "There's nothing there to see," or "It's dirty," or "It's dangerous." Since we didn't know anyone else who had gone, the South seemed a place of dark uncertainty.

Even the guidebooks spoke of pickpockets and advised us to avoid side streets and strolls in the center of the city after dark. They too suggested that southern Italy was different from the north, Rome being the dividing point. The risk of petty crime was greater, particularly in Naples. Both poverty and organized Mafia activity were said to be prevalent in this city and tourists were advised to be more wary.

But our relationship with Italy had grown past the early romantic stage and we were ready to see more, even if it meant uncertainty and possible unpleasantness. Naples and the southern coast rewarded us richly.

One Monday in March, Al and I took a train south from Rome. We planned to change in Naples to a local train, the Circumvesuvio or Circle of Mount Vesuvius, and head to Sorrento, the tourist center on the Amalfi coast.

As we headed south, I was struck by the unexpected drama and beauty of the surroundings. The train passed the bright blue of the Mediterranean on our right and then went through dramatic hills with scruffy but beautiful cactus and other desert-like plants. The beauty of the ride was a pleasant surprise. The hills reminded me of the stark beauty of parts of the Arizona desert or the Texas Hill country.

When we got into the Naples train station, we were braced and ready. Or so we thought. The books had warned us about the many possible cons and razzle-dazzle approaches of pickpockets, so we held our luggage tightly and started through the crowds. We knew we had to buy tickets for the local train and then go through a turnstile to catch it. Getting off a relatively quiet train into a crowded station is always a bit of a culture shock, but was more so in the Naples station. As fair-haired, blue-eyed types, we stood out in a way that we didn't in the north. As we tried to get our bearings and figure out which way to go for our tickets, we were stopped by a short, friendly, middle-aged man, in a suit jacket. He greeted us enthusiastically asking, "Circumvesuvio? Circumvesuvio?" Knowing that as obvious tourists, we would be looking for the train to Sorrento, the man kept flashing his jacket lapel open, quickly showing us some kind of official-looking badge, and saying , "No bandito, no bandito. Officiale, officiale." He seemed friendly and non-threatening. I answered, "Si, si, yes yes, Circumvesuvio," because we did, in fact, need to find the other train. After all, I thought, What could happen? Al had our cash in his money belt, and we were surrounded by people. The man quickly gestured for us to follow him toward the ticket window, where Al held onto our luggage while, with the man's help as interpreter, I bought the tickets to Sorrento. Although Al seemed a little resistant to our guide, his attitude seemed polite and friendly at least on the surface.

"Avanti, avanti." Our greeter hurried us with our tickets, gesturing to a large sign CIRCUMVESUVIO in big letters above the turnstile into the corridor for the local train. People were jogging toward the entrance, indicating that a train was arriving momentarily so the man's hurry up attitude seemed appropriate. We hurried along with him, me wanting to get out of the intimidating hustle of the Naples station, Al just wanting to catch the train. I thought maybe the man's motive in helping us with directions was to earn a tip, a not uncommon occurrence, but Al and I had no chance to discuss what to do. As we hurried with our guide, pulling our luggage toward the turnstile through the busy station, he suddenly reached his own hands to our two pieces of rolling luggage, in order to help us along. At that point Al stopped and said "No," firmly. He tightened his own hold on both bags. Our unofficial greeter disappeared almost as into thin air, sadly breaking the balloon of my belief that he was a one-man welcoming committee.

"He seemed so nice," I said, disappointed.

Al answered, "I knew he wanted something."

Naples rattled me, but no harm was done. Having let down our guard briefly, we had brought it back up in time, or, at least, Al had. And thanks to the guidance and help of our greeter, we did find the entrance to the Circumvesuvio and made the train on time. In its own way our reception to Naples was hospitable rather than threatening, and except for the fact that he disappeared so quickly once our luggage was withheld, I held to the belief that the friendly man just wanted a tip.

Once through the turnstile to get on the local train, we entered a different world. The razzle-dazzle confusion of the Naples station was gone, and we entered the tolerant but subdued world of commuters. The hard plastic seats were occupied with local people on errands or traveling to and from work. In this environment, Al and I were suddenly the biggest disturbance as we pulled our bags onto the car, down the narrow aisle. The commuter train was not designed for even our small amount of luggage near the seats, so we pulled the bags back to an open space near the door of the car. We sat in the middle of the car, in the only empty seats, making only an occasional glance to the end of the car. In a matter of about twenty feet from one side of the turnstile to the other, we seemed to have gone from big city intensity to the calm of small town life.

The Circumvesuvio travels slowly from town to town around the base of the famous mountain. The trip takes an hour, and even though it moves slowly and stops often, much of the length of the ride is related to the size of the volcano. Vesuvius rises gradually from ground level to a height of 4000 feet. Unlike mountains that stand as part of a broad range of hills, this volcano seems to rise singularly from the plain and from the sea. It may be a relatively quiet volcano these days, although it still erupts from time to time, but even in its quiet days its presence dominates the surrounding area. I thought of earlier people's belief that the gods lived in the mountain. That a mammoth volcano like Vesuvius, quiet in its dominance, could erupt powerfully and suddenly seemed metaphoric to me, the paradox of its peace and its power, its destructive capabilities, like many destructive forces in nature, revealing a benevolent side as in creating fertile soil.

"It's hard to believe it can erupt." I said to Al. "It looks so peaceful. I wonder why people live close to it if it's dangerous."

"To make a living," Al practically observed.

I remembered reading that farmers appreciated the soil of the volcanic earth and ignored the warnings of danger from living near the volcanoes.

The Circumvesuvio also passes Pompeii, the ancient Roman city that was buried in A.D. 79 by the eruption of Vesuvius. In the newer city people struggle to make a living partly from the tourists that come to the area. Pompeii is another ancient sight we decided to save for another trip. As a travel-loving friend once said, "It's good not to see everything. That way you have a reason to come back." Thinking of our list of things undone, I remembered once again why we keep going back to Italy. We still have a lot to see.

***

The North of Italy was for Al and me about educational experience, about art and history, but the South was about experiencing the sensual, especially in March when the farther south you get the warmer it is. In the crowded tourist months of the hot summer we might have felt differently, but in March, we, like John Keats in his poem "Ode to a Nightingale," were longing for "a beaker full of the warm south." After our leisurely and long train ride around the base of Vesuvius, we arrived at Sorrento, the end of the train line, and the main tourist town for exploring the Amalfi coast. We planned to use it as a base for exploring the South and for our adventure back into Naples.

In Sorrento, at first things seemed almost too quiet, especially coming from Naples. We checked into our hotel a couple of blocks from the station, left our bags in our room, and, as we had planned, walked to explore the famous and expensive resort hotels high on the cliffs above the sea, thinking we could find a place to have lunch or at least a drink of some kind and enjoy the magnificent views. But as we came out on the high road over the cliffs, where several of the elegant hotels stood, we found one after another of those recommended in our guidebooks still closed for the winter, their driveways barricaded and patios empty. Occasionally we got a glimpse of the height of the cliffs and beautiful views in the distance, but there was no place to enter or get close.

With nothing else to do now that our plan had turned up empty, we walked away from the scenic resorts, back past our hotel and toward the old town center, which had not been mentioned at all in our tourist information. We were feeling a little discouraged. We had spent most of the day getting there and although we had enjoyed what views we had seen and had some adventures in Naples, were feeling like this might be a lost afternoon, too late to take the bus to Amalfi but too early to call it a day. We wandered a bit aimlessly into what seemed to be the town's main piazza and noticed an unromantic restaurant with a view of a few trees and buildings with some outdoor seating. The posted tourist menu indicated this was not a place for locals. We weren't particularly drawn to the restaurant, but we needed something to do, so we sat down outside and ordered a carafe of local wine.

With wine in front of us, Al glanced at the menu. "We might as well eat some lunch, too," Al said disheartenedly, "As long as we're here."

Here in this "touristy" restaurant we discovered our first of many dishes of mussels and the seaside cuisine of the southern coast of Italy. While eating these small tender mussels, fresh from the sea a few feet away, and dipping our bread in the light olive oil, tomato, garlic and white wine broth, then drinking a little of the local wine, we relaxed. It felt good just to be sitting outside after our hours on the train. We began to learn the lesson of the South, that we didn't necessarily have to do or see anything to enjoy ourselves. As we ate, the town of Sorrento began to seem more appealing and our disappointment in the closed resorts lessened. Gradually, our moods of frustration shifted to pleasure as we settled into the relaxed atmosphere of this new area of Italy.

In Sorrento, we discovered the advantages of tourist towns. When there was little to do in cultural sightseeing, there was still something to do as a tourist. After lunch we walked back through the narrow streets of the old town, as we had done elsewhere, but this time along with local color and authenticity, there were shops. The old streets were lined with souvenir shops, pottery shops, woodcarving studios and outdoor stands of local art, volcanic stone jewelry, and packaged food. The shops were fun, not too expensive, ready for cash purchases of impulse-buying travelers. They all accepted credit cards and arranged shipping for larger purchases. We strolled with the other visitors through the town and bought a few souvenirs and gifts. One of my favorites is a small necklace made of the lava rock from the volcano, its small black and bluish colors reflecting just enough light to shine. I also bought pieces of pottery from towns farther south and from then on would notice the styles and colors of ceramics from different locales. I had to keep the size small and bought little bowls rather than dinner plates as they were easier to pack.

We also discovered some of the non-touristy side of Sorrento. It was the last part of Lent, and, as Al and I walked around the town, we saw posters announcing the Good Friday procession that would be celebrated during Holy Week, just before Easter. We weren't surprised when later that afternoon, as it was getting dark, we wandered into a small lighted church and became part of the audience for a rehearsal of the local boys choir. "They're probably practicing for Good Friday and Easter," I whispered to Al, "for the procession on the posters." Although all of the interactions were in Italian, we still were able to figure out what was going on as the priest in charge called out his instructions for the rehearsal; he waved his arms for the boys to line up in rows in the front of the church and then named the songs to be performed. In the back of the church, we stood with the mothers and fathers who entertained toddlers and watched as their elementary school boys projected their voices into the church.

What these young vocalists lacked in polish, they made up for in enthusiasm. They had good voices and sang the religious lyrics with zest and volume. It's always fun to see youngsters, still preadolescent, full of energy and cheer. "They're pretty good," said Al. "Better than some adults we've seen." We stayed until the rehearsal was over and the families headed home for supper. By then it was dark outside. The train ride, good food, some fun shopping and our free youth concert all made for a memorable day.

As we discovered, it's also a matter of adjusting to each new town. Once the strangeness wears off, we get to feel at home. Instead of feeling bored in Sorrento, after we learned our way around each of the streets, we found that familiarity was a plus and that strolling along the streets again, seeing the same shops at different times of the day or just browsing through souvenir shops a second time, became more enjoyable. There was always something to see and comment on. We were learning to apply the spirit of the passeggiata to all of our traveling. Rather than focusing on goals and activity, we started to enjoy ourselves more as we learned to pay more attention to the life that was always going on around us.

***

The next morning, with the bustle of the station in Naples settled into distant memory, we waited in Sorrento's main piazza for the local bus down the Amalfi coast. We knew that some people rented cars or even drivers with cars to take them along the winding coast. But we had read that the local bus accomplished the same effect, and that we could leave the driving to an expert. We knew to sit on the right side heading south and the left side on the return to have window views of the dramatic cliffs, sheer drop offs, distant switchbacks and sparkling sea below.

Once again, we enjoyed the uncrowded aspect of off-season Sorrento, our sense that we were participating in local life by riding the bus, even though most of our fellow riders at that time of day were tourists, some English and some Australians. Al and I enjoyed listening to conversations in our own language for a change and even participated in a few. The other visitors were cheerful and friendly. We learned that the southern coast of Italy and its islands have been popular vacation sites for British travelers for many years. The warmth and bright sunlit colors of the southern seacoast fill the soul of a Londoner, especially at the end of the dreary damp and gray weather of winter. Having lived much of our lives under the often gray skies of the industrial Northeast, we could still see the miracle of blue water and bright sky from the awed and sunlight deprived eyes of a Northerner.

The Amalfi coast road is mostly a narrow two lanes between the sheer drop offs to the sea on the west and the hillsides rising straight upright from the other side. There are no extra lanes for passing or to pull off, except for an occasional lookout space for photo opportunities and buses. There is no place to pull over and no place to turn around. The switchbacks and inclines throughout the American Rockies seem easy by comparison. The only similar drive in our experience was Highway One in California along the Pacific cliffs near Big Sur and Monterey. But even there, most of the narrow and turning road on the edge of the cliffs is closer to sea level than along the Amalfi, which feels more like being at the level of a low-flying airplane.

As our driver swung out along the curves over the high cliffs seemingly heading straight off into the wide blue yonder of sky and sea, several women passengers reacted audibly with the thrill of a roller coaster experience. Al and I felt the same way. We had been warned to expect the constant switches back and forth as we traversed the high edge of the cliffs with only a few feet, if that, of solid earth between us and thin air. We also knew that the bus drivers were experienced and did this ride everyday, and, that even though they drove faster than any of us might have, they were in control and knew the roads, anticipating the curves and the speed required to navigate them. We swished out and back above the sea, occasionally moving down the hillside or around a curved outcrop of jutting land, our bus seemed to hang toward the edge of the sea at every moment.

I remembered having read of at least one serious accident in some past year with a bus somewhere on this coast line, and, while I was never really scared, I mentally took the position that I take regarding airplanes, telling myself that we're all in the hands of God, and our fate is beyond our control, the universe is in charge, and it's not worth worrying about. Still, I hoped that the angels and saints who had been looking over this part of the world for so long would continue to keep an eye on things.

Chivalrously, Al insisted that I sit by the window for the best views, saying he could see as well from the inside seat. I think he enjoyed being able to look out and around on to the scenic road instead of ahead as he would if he were driving. I'm sure he also appreciated that I was not telling this driver, "Don't drive so fast. Don't get so close to the edge," and "Look out!" as I would have no doubt been telling him if he were driving on these winding cliffs.

Even though it was a little hazy, the views were spectacular, especially when we could look down at the sea, out to the clouds, and across to sheer cliffs across an inlet of water far below us, a kind of mirror of the cliffs we were traveling along the top.

At one point along our cliff top drive, we suddenly came to a stop in what became a long winding traffic jam behind a large tourist bus, the kind that travels around Europe making quick stops at scenic places and hard to reach tourist destinations before it moves on to a prearranged hotel site. Another tourist bus had come up the hill around the curve. As the first bus came down and around from the left, the second had come up from the right, using every possible inch of land mass between the steep hillside and sheer cliff. The large buses had become stuck against each other, the downward one edged lightly against the far back of the side of the bus headed uphill. There was of course no way for those of us in the vehicles behind to detour or to go around either of the trapped buses.

We watched from our position above, as other drivers and passengers consulted and advised the bus drivers, first to back down the hill, inches into the hillside and then crawl a bit uphill along the edge of the cliff in order to separate, move round the bend, and then past each other. Since both buses were trailed by a line of traffic, both cars and other big buses, it was quite a production as they attempted to get enough of the line of traffic to back up the hill, inch by inch, so that the bus could back up enough to release itself from its partner, giving them both room to make the tight turn around the rest of the curve. Obviously, the Amalfi coast wasn't built for tour buses, especially those attempting curves at the same time. But after many fits and starts and directions by several men using lots of Italian hand gestures and vocalizing, the situation was remedied. The buses were unattached and swung past each other and we all continued on our way. Al had a great time watching the confusion and its remedy, especially since he didn't have to do anything about it. I felt grateful that we were perched as spectators on our local bus, smaller than the tourist ones and easier to maneuver, and not in our own car stuck in traffic without knowing why.

In spite of the thrill of the bus ride along the winding cliffs, our day traveling the Amalfi coast was low-key. We enjoyed the views and as we worked our way down the coast we unwound even more than before. We focused on nothing but the dramatic scenery of the moment and the immediacy of being on the edge of the turning cliffs, allowing ourselves to let go. Our only stops were at small paths or stairs that led up or down the hills and provided access to small villages.

Gradually, we descended to sea level. Since we were on a local bus, rather than a tour bus with a planned route, we had to choose one destination and then watch for the return bus according to its northbound schedule. The buses didn't travel often enough at that time of year for us to stop at various towns and get back on.

Although we passed several towns which could be possible stops along the way, Al had picked Amalfi as a destination. I pointed out that the guidebooks talked more about and showed photos of Positano, the resort town with hillside steps winding down the dramatic hillside. But Al took the practical approach. "If we're on the Amalfi coast, we should go to Amalfi." When our bus stopped at Positano, many tourists got off, but it looked to us too hard to maneuver the steep hill on foot and, as a seaside resort, seemed not that appealing in early spring weather.

Unlike the resort setting of Positano, Amalfi is situated almost at the center of the coastline and feels older and more rugged. It begins at sea level and rises up the hill. For a day trip the town was more accessible than getting off the bus at the top of the hill as in Positano, walking down roads and stairways to the beach and town at the bottom.

Although little was mentioned about it in our guidebook, Amalfi had just the right amount of sightseeing, local flavor and random discovery for us. We walked down a short flight of stairs through a tunnel under the highway and came out onto a piazza where several middle-aged men stood talking in the morning sunlight, while several boys kicked a soccer ball from one side of the small piazza to the other. With no map of the town or sightseeing plan, we strolled across the piazza and up the hill along the main street past the Amalfi Cathedral. Later we read that the Amalfi Cathedral is a famous tourist destination in season, but for us it was just a surprisingly beautiful sight, its facade decorated with a brightly colored mosaic design, set in a quiet out of the way village.

Above the church, on the high end of the single main road, we could hear water running downhill through channels under the surface where we walked. Occasionally, rushing streams could be seen through grates on either side of the road, flowing down the mountain into the sea. As far up the two lane road as the town seemed to go, we wandered through the open door of a tiny museum. We were the only ones there, surveying the historical tools and farm equipment. Nearby, we looked at an old water wheel that had once used the downhill rush of water as its power source.

We looked south from our high spot above the town and saw what appeared to be a couple of other towns over the next hill. When we had wandered slowly back down to the main level, Al, having seen the domes from the hilltop and checking the guidebook for a name, decided he wanted to walk to the next town. We had seen most of Amalfi and still had plenty of time before catching the return bus to Sorrento. But getting to Atrani, the next town on the way to Ravello required a walk along the edge of the same two lane highway we had traveled that morning; it stretched along sea cliffs and through a dark tunnel, shared with cars. There was no sidewalk. Al set out ahead of me through the tunnel. I resisted, "I don't want to." I was tired after our hike up the hill and maybe I was a little bit leery of going into the tight tunnel when cars might be coming along at any time. As Al disappeared into the dark, I opted to sit near the entrance of the tunnel on the stone wall, enjoying the light and the views of the town behind me and the water below.

For a while I was content to be alone feeling the sea air and looking at the blue water, but, as the time passed, I started to feel anxious when Al was gone longer than I expected. I experienced what poet William Wordsworth once referred to in one of his "Lucy" poems as "a flight of fancy." For a moment I wondered how I would feel if I suddenly found myself alone in this small town in the south of Italy. Open to random emotions, along with random discoveries, I felt a rush of fear at the thought that anything could happen to Al, not just in Italy, but anywhere. As my mind jumped to thoughts about how I would deal with such a situation, I remember taking satisfaction in my brief fantasy that I had some money and a copy of my passport, even if Al did have the original, and was confident enough in my feelings about Italy that I would be able to figure something out on my own, if necessary, even in a foreign country. Fortunately, my imaginings dissipated when Al appeared just behind a couple of men who had come around the bend just in front of him, proving that walking along the road was not considered foolhardy and that pedestrians did walk safely through the foreboding tunnel.

I had a moment of regret that I hadn't overcome my hesitation and taken the short walk through the dark tunnel to see the close up views of Ravello. I consoled myself that there could always be a next time and a return trip.

Ready for a late lunch, we noticed a restaurant on the seaward side of the highway right at the edge of the sparkling blue water but near enough to the return bus stop so we could relax. With its outdoor terrace, the simple eating spot would in the summer probably be packed with tourists. But in March we were among only a few diners and had our choice of sea views. It was not movie picturesque, but in its own way, it was perfect. We again ate mussels, which we imagined were fresh from the sea a few feet away, dipping our bread in the light marinara sauce. And again we just relaxed. It was one of those vacation moments when the simple sensual enjoyment of the food, sun and sea reminded us that this is what life should be like. It was hard to believe that we were several thousand miles from home. We relaxed into the warm pleasure of the Mediterranean experience.

Later, we waited on the landward side of the road for the scheduled bus back up along the coast to Sorrento. The trip back was uneventful. We stopped along the way for passengers who had hiked back up the hill from the resort town of Positano. They looked exhausted from the climb as they laughingly pulled themselves, and their purchases, with relief onto the bus. We had seen the views as we traveled from the south, the striking drama of the hillside town and its many steps that zigzagged down to the sea. I was glad we had not attempted them. For us, Amalfi had been the best destination.

***

By mid-afternoon, we were back in Sorrento. Al announced, "We've got time for one more side trip." Usually I would have resisted, but since everything in this area seemed low-keyed and relatively simple, not like the fatigue-causing afternoons in the larger cities, I agreed. Al looked at a couple of small dots on our map that displayed towns a little bit north of Sorrento, even though the train ended here. Seeing a local bus going in the right direction with one of the chosen names on it, we boarded and headed to the very small town of Santa Agata. We had no expectations about what we would find. Once in the small town we wandered the streets and roads until we noticed a small wooden sign that said, "monasteria." We stepped off the road and followed the path up the hill. We followed the sign and the lane not knowing what to expect. We hiked up the path and the road and entered the open grounds of the old monastery. It was not large, but was situated in a beautiful setting, high on the hilltop. It was set back from the edge of a precipice with views of the sea in most directions. The views from this high point of land were almost as breathtaking as those from the Amalfi Drive. We felt the wisdom of building a monastery in a setting above the earth but in touch with it, the vistas of the sea and sky displayed in a gentle panorama. I said to Al, "Do you think it's okay that we're up here?"

"I didn't see any signs," he answered.

So we walked across the small parking lot to the garden that led us closer to the edge with the best views, Al, as always, wanting to see from the best advantage. As we walked along a path around a garden to the edge, we had the sense of pleasant quietness of only sounds of birds and breezes, reminiscent of the hills above Assisi.

As Al walked around the outward fence to see a view around the bend, I stood on the gravel looking out at the sky and the sea and trying simply to be. At the time I had begun to read a little about meditation practices and part of me was at least pretending to be contemplative, trying to fully appreciate the moment in this lovely natural spiritual setting. It would have been a lovely scenic view in any event, but we felt perhaps a greater sense of serenity knowing we were on a site used for spiritual nurturing.

When an older priest and a younger man walked out to look at our view, we had confirmation that the monastery was still in use. When they nodded, "Buona sera," to us before getting into their car, we felt welcome.

Later, we found a brief notation in one of our guidebooks about the monastery at the top of a hill in Santa Agata. Having found it on our own, we felt a sense of connection to something we never would have bothered to seek out. Someday it would be nice to see what lay behind the gate and within the walls of this simple monastery.

***

The next day we plunged from the serenity of monastic views and the ease of small town touring back into the earthy, intense, high energy experience of Naples. We left our belongings in our safe hotel in Sorrento and dressed in our most anonymous clothes. We found seats on the early morning commuter train, comfortable now with the route past Mount Vesuvius and excited about our day trip back to Naples. Without luggage to worry about, it was less intimidating to do our bit of planned sightseeing.

We had mapped out a route to walk that was recommended as safe, especially in the daytime. From the station we walked across a piazza and down busy streets to the glass canopied buildings of the Galleria, our first stop. Strolling past the indoor shops, we saw very few people, and we wondered about the prosperity of these retailers. Outside, the emptiness of the nearby street in the midmorning felt strange and less safe than the jostling crowds of other Italian cities.

In preparation for our day trip, I had kept warning Al not to bring a lot of cash with him and to be cautious. "Everybody says you have to be careful in Naples," I chided.

He shrugged me off, "Don't worry so much," scoffing at my paranoia about pickpockets and street crime in Naples.

But as we walked down a sidewalk with no other pedestrians, a young man appeared suddenly from a stairwell and asked Al for the time. Al shook his head, "No," pulled up the sleeve of his left hand, and showed a bare wrist. He had put his watch, not a particularly valuable one, on his right hand as a precaution. "Very clever," I said. As our train station greeter, once his bluff was called, the guy who either wanted to know the time or wanted to check out a possible watch theft, melted away.

Overall, our day in Naples was a wonderful experience. The old part of the city was compact and full of life, chaotic but not overwhelming, with small cars jumbled close together on the narrow but busy streets, sometimes getting into gridlock around the tight corners. People, old and young, men and women, moved through the streets and along the narrow walkways in a close jumbled mix of energy past small shops nestled together, selling fresh fish, poultry, cheeses, breads or pastries. Smells from tiny pizzerias filled the air. The traffic jams of small, slightly battered cars gave us an impression of a newly motorized society. Even the taxi cabs were old and small.

Only one other event made me feel uncomfortable in Naples. We were following our planned route, walking down a pedestrian only thoroughfare called "Spaccanapoli" because it divides Naples. Unlike the Galleria area, now that it was lunch time, the Spaccanapoli was full of people. Al and I were walking together when I briefly stopped to look in a shop window while he kept going. For a few seconds I was alone or appeared to be. As I turned from the window to catch up, from close behind me, I heard the murmuring of "bella, bella," and other compliments from a quietly flirtatious young man. The event reminded me of being in Rome in my twenties when locals teasing American and British girls was the norm. The solution to these unwanted attentions then, we were told, was to wear an engagement-looking ring. Now, in my fifties, it did give me a creepy feeling to be whispered to seductively like that on the street. I stepped up my pace quickly and once I caught up with Al, the flirtatious young man disappeared into the crowd. He may have also realized that I was old enough to be his mother, although my own daughter had told me that, even for young women, being with a man was protection from harassment in southern Italy in those years. Looking back, I suppose I should be glad I was still considered young enough to bother.

A favorite sight in Naples was the Museo Archeologico. Here we were awed by our first experiences of seeing ancient sculpture. One of the very best museums in Italy, it contains much of the painting and sculpture removed from the ruins of Pompeii. Later we would be told that visitors to the excavated city of Pompeii are often disappointed that so much of the fresco painting of the houses is missing, but we had accidentally managed to see it all. People who visit Pompeii and find things missing on the walls will find them in Naples. One of the frescoes from Pompeii shows a portrait of a woman reading her book and is one of those living works of art that Keats talked about in his poem "Ode to a Grecian Urn." The muted colors of fresco painting, the subtle shading of rose and gold and tans representing mythological themes pulled us in. We went from painting to painting, Al reading the names of labels while I tried to fill-in with the myths that I knew.

In Florence or Venice such a wonderful museum would have been crowded. But we were in Napoli; there was no crowd. We strolled through the airy galleries looking at ancient Roman sculptures, taking our time, sharing each room with only a few people on this weekday morning and feeling like the place was ours. We had a good time seeing whom we could recognize among the mythological figures in the sculptures and the significance of their objects. Usually the Italian names on the labels gave us clues. We easily recognized Hercules with his lion skin robe and club ready for accomplishing his labors, and holding up the rounded heavens. We looked for a long time at the dynamic sculptures of life-sized figures of the important female goddesses, Isis from Egypt, Aphrodite from Greece, and an unusual depiction of a goddess with many breasts instead of two, symbolizing fertility and abundance of life.

We felt as if we were in a cornucopia of art that had somehow been ignored by the world of sightseeing art lovers. Although we weren't experts, we knew we were seeing some exceptional paintings and sculptures. We felt like scouts exploring an outpost of the art world, discovering something that had been covered over or forgotten by the tourists. We knew that the art lovers who descend on the Uffizi and the Vatican museums during all seasons of the year would love this.

At the museo we even had a moment of excitement when at one point there was a scurry of guards, and doors were quickly closed to isolate part of the upper floor galleries. "Probleme," we were told. "Terrorists," we thought, "Mafioso," but nothing dramatic happened, and nobody said anything about leaving, so, with the few other visitors, we continued our tour.

Naples had neither the sophistication or edginess of Rome. We sensed a quiet but hospitable courtesy. (In the local pizzeria where we had lunch with the local working people, in the museum, even our taxi driver, everyone seemed just a little more warm, friendly and a little less detached both with each other and with us than in Rome.) In fact it seemed to me than Naples had more of what Rome used to have before its modernity. It was how I remembered Rome so many years before.

We saw no other tourists as we walked the streets. We heard almost no English, but when, at the end of our excursion, we entered a candy shop on a quiet street to get directions back to the train station, "Stazione?" the shopkeeper left his customer, came out from behind the counter, brought us outside, and with lots of Italian explanation but more helpfully, lots of hand and arm gestures, gave us explicit directions about the right and left turns to the station. He wasn't frivolous or jolly, didn't smile or laugh, but in his reserved way was very hospitable and helpful. We walked the few blocks back to the station, used our return ticket on the Circumvesuvio and returned to Sorrento. We had both survived and enjoyed our day in Naples.

Al and I both felt in Naples, as we would later in Sicily, that for art lovers and Italy lovers there is much more here than many travelers have discovered. We were glad we discovered it ourselves, without knowing what to expect and we resolved to return. While tourism seems to sometimes be a double-edged sword for less developed areas, we speculated, maybe it would add another source of prosperity to improve the economy of the South.

Being in the warm sun of the Mediterranean seacoast in early spring touched a vital nerve in us. In the season of orange and lemon trees and warmth without heat, the end of winter, but without the white-hot of summer, we had a great experience. Later we discovered Sicily as a destination. We have loved our experiences in the South, especially since we aren't insulated in the tourist experience of expensive hotels and restaurants. But it was not for the faint-hearted or those who want only the best or who don't want to see a little of real life. Seeing a little of real life in these places is what makes it special.

Several years later, we returned to Naples and stayed for several days in a hotel in the Santa Lucia area by the water.

Naples by then had been given some attention by the national government in its attempt to improve the economy of the South. Its historical and art heritage had been highlighted by the tourist industry and tour groups, especially those with a focus on art history, had started to come to Naples. We saw student groups and adults from Asia and the U.S. being led by bilingual tour guides. Naples seemed to sparkle more. (The spring weather and bright blue of the sea, the view of Vesuvius in the distance gave us a more romantic view of this old city.) We learned more about the importance of its history.

We walked more freely in Naples, although we avoided certain areas at night. We felt safer in the Santa Lucia areas near our hotel than in the small streets of the old center. In the daylight, we explored more freely along the Spaccanapoli, finding the famous street where many shops line the pedestrian street, and where artisans make and sell the figures for the manger scenes known as precipio that are part of the Napolitan tradition. One night, to please Al, we even went to the opera in Teatro San Carlos.

This visit was a different experience from the first one. Our sense of adventure was less since we were far from the only tourists in town, but so was our sense of risk. We were able to relax into a greater appreciation of the beauty of the city, taking advantage of better tourist information about the complex history as well as the grand architecture and art of the city. Tourists had become familiar with what Naples had to offer and the more serious elements of crime seemed to have been brought under control. Mostly we were happy to see that the city showed signs of prosperity. Shops were busy both in the glass covered Galleria and in the small shops of the Spaccanapoli area. The late afternoon passeggiata reflected something closer to the high energy that we had noticed in the northern cities. We saw hope that the friendly people of the South who had been at the mercy of neglect and crime among other things were coming back into their own. We looked forward to a return visit.

CHAPTER SIXTEEN

Art

Unlike a skiing, golfing or beach vacation, our Italian travels have no built-in recreational activity. Our entertainment consists of the sights we decide to visit and the random cultural experiences that we happen upon. Planning our days together necessarily forms a bond. If one of us wanted to golf while the other shopped, our travels would be different.

Al and I bring different interests and different knowledge to our explorations. We have taken paths together we never would have taken separately. Beyond the initial sightseeing that all tourists do, each of us broadened our perspectives, seeing and learning things we never would have without pressure or encouragement from the other. These new interests were the threads that wove through our travel.

At first I picked the more famous art and architectural sights, the ones I was familiar with from history and literature textbooks. Al usually went along with my plans, just as glad, on our early trips, not to be responsible for the planning and decision-making. While I saw myself as extending my quasi-academic knowledge, he just enjoyed art as an interesting change of pace from work.

Learning about art in Italy together has been a big part of our Italian experience. We had always enjoyed wandering through museums or galleries at home or as part of a vacation. But we tended to have very different tastes, Al drawn to modern, abstract, unusual, and often dark images while I lean toward the more cheerful colors of the Impressionists or realistic depictions of people in true to life settings. Over the years we had managed to agree enough on what we wanted to live with to buy several paintings, a sign of our ability to negotiate our differences at home.

When we first went to Italy we saw obligatory art such as the Uffizi, Michelangelo's *David*, the Sistine Chapel. But over the years, a greater understanding of how art reflects the culture, history and religious tradition of Italy has enhanced the richness of our Italian experience. We have learned to appreciate art more like Italians. Here, art exists as part of life, with sculptures, mosaics and frescoes in piazzas and parks and churches, not just displayed in museums and galleries. Wherever we walk, we see statues, fountains, and gardens, frescoes painted into the wall of a house or archway, mosaics decorating the side of a building or walkway, sculpted details on bridges or on eaves of government buildings. To see art in Italy all we have to do is look. We'll come across a sculpture of Cupid in a fountain, or a statue of Venus in a park or the lion heads on the face of a building.

We have learned to distinguish between a medieval religious painting and an early Renaissance depiction of a similar subject. We now notice classical themes and political and social content. We have gradually introduced words such as fresco, mosaic, baroque, gothic, classical and Byzantine into our vocabulary, not as definitions learned for college classes, but as art experienced. And we've done this together with Al focusing on certain aspects of the art and me on others. In the sharing of our observations, we have come, not only to know more, but to enjoy the fact that we are learning about art, together.

Experience is an excellent teacher and can also plant the seeds for more knowledge. The spin-off interest from our travels in Italy lasts for years. If one of us finds an article or reference to an Italian artist or work, we save it for the other. And if we go to a museum back home, we bring our shared memories of the multiple experiences from across the Atlantic. Instead of feeling like we have learned all there is to know, we feel we have just barely opened the door to a fascinating subject.

It happened gradually, this coming to know art together and it never could have happened in a classroom. It had to be from shared experiences like waiting on the narrow sidewalk as the long line moved slowly forward to see Michelangelo's *David*. As we waited, Al complained impatiently, "We're wasting the whole morning. We've already seen the other one," referring to the copy of the *David* on the hill. But when we finally got into the Accademia, and worked our way down the hallway of other marble sculptures, toward the *David* standing at the end, we knew the wait had been worth it. In spite of crowds and scaffolding, we were both moved by Michelangelo's masterpiece and spent a good while walking around the sculpture to see again and again the details and perfect balance of the magnificent figure.

Later, seeing the paintings and sculpture in the Uffizi or the mosaics in the churches of Ravenna, we shared the feeling that the out of the way journey had been worthwhile. Although for most of our married life we could hardly have imagined ourselves trekking to out of the way places to look for art in churches that we had never heard of, we felt the same about these excursions.

Seeing great art is an experience beyond words. Great art draws you in, gives you an experience that transcends time and place. You know there is more to these works than the materials used, the marble, or pigments, the design or technique. Although we share our reactions, we know there is more to what we're seeing than what we can describe. Sharing these moments is like sharing a beautiful sunset. You know something important is happening and enjoy experiencing it with someone else.

Al is better at perusing the guidebooks and finding tiny museums or small out of the way art stops that he has read about. He has a good sense of what will be worthwhile and he is usually the one who decides what we'll see next. He also understands the technical aspects better than I do. He can hear a guide tell how the artist blended pigments, painted into wet plaster, or created perspective. He remembers the details and is able to explain them to me later.

My contribution is the story. I know elements of tradition such as the story of the woman Veronica who holds a picture with Jesus's face left on her cloth after she offered it to him to wipe his face, or the tradition that the baptism of Christ with the Holy Spirit is symbolized by a dove, or the words, "Hail, Full of Grace," which the Angel Gabriel spoke to Mary in the Annunciation. I know more about traditional religious art and can explain the symbols.

Having taught high school literature for so many years, I also know classical mythology and can identify Greek gods and goddesses by what they wear or carry and can tell the story of an adventure of Odysseus or labor of Hercules as depicted in a work of art. I get to show that, in fact, I do know something useful, that teaching English involves more than correcting grammar and punctuation on high school themes, and that there is a richness in having a background in literature. Although Al tunes out some of my information and I will never remember as much detail as he does, our individual approaches balance out.

***

In reasonable weather, waiting in line can become part of the adventure. We used to get impatient as a line moved slowly or when tour groups got in line ahead of the rest of us, but now we are more able to just settle in, Italian style, to the experience.

If we look around, there is always something entertaining going on.

When we finally got back to Milan to see the restoration of Leonardo da Vinci's *Last Supper* in the old convent, we knew we would have to wait. It was a sunny day and the line spread across a small piazza in the quiet out-of-the-way neighborhood that is the home of this church. I was carrying some bread and cheese from a small grocery that we had passed en route. Looking around, we saw other people standing or sitting on the walls around the small fountain in the piazza as they waited, munching on their own sandwiches or purchases from a small snack and drink cart nearby.

Pulling out our bread and cheese and sharing a drink, we ate lunch while we waited in line. We chatted with fellow travelers, feeling grateful that so many other European tourists spoke English, and got suggestions for other art stops. We read our guidebook, learning as much as possible about what we would see inside.

Not all art sights are famous. The museums and churches that are highlighted in towns and small cities often have no lines, are inexpensive or free, and easy to access. In Orvieto, the hill town north of Rome, we were introduced to Etruscan art and had one of our most memorable experiences. We noticed a small museum in what could have been a modest two story house on the piazza across from the cathedral and, to get out of a quick rain shower, we entered. The lone security person greeted us and volunteered delightedly to be our tour guide. It was midweek and off season and he was glad for our company and the opportunity to expound on the history of the Etruscans in this part of Italy and the characteristics of their art. He gave us his tour entirely in Italian and, even with our language gap, we got the basic ideas of the identity of the Etrucans and the relationship of their art to the Greeks. Using gestures to indicate an imaginary time line, the guide would point to the century written on the label in Roman numerals and emphasize the B.C. to make sure we understood that the era was "before Christ." Using simple Italian words, noire or verde for black and green, he pointed out the colors on the pottery. From then on, Al and I recognize the deep green bronze of Etruscan sculpture and the clean black figures on the darker orangish rust of Etruscan pottery whenever we see it. Later, in a souvenir shop on the piazza, we bought a miniature copy of an Etruscan pitcher to remind us not only of our art lesson but of the rainy day in Orvieto and our private tour of the small local museum.

When we first visited museums in Italy, Al was inclined in his engineering style to look at every painting or sculpture. Everything was as important as everything else. My more haphazard approach was to move a little faster glancing at things that seemed mildly interesting but spending longer taking in the experience of a work that struck me as beautiful. Now Al has learned to skip over some things and I have learned to look more carefully.

But the best art tours have been when we saw each and every work of art together, staying focused on the same works at the same time. One of the best of these sharing times was on a rainy afternoon in Rome when we spent several hours at the Vatican museum. It was near the end of our trip and we were ready to wind down. We waited under a big umbrella in the long line that wrapped around the outside walls of the Vatican until we finally got into the newly constructed modern entrance of the old structure. Al was impatient with the long wait, although the line moved consistently, and used the time to dash across the street and check his voice mail at one of the few orange phones that took coins, while I held the umbrella and our place in line. By the time we finally reached the crowded entrance, we were both a little irritated with the wait. But when a professional guide offered to take us on a tour of the Vatican collection for a fee, we considered the offer and then Al decided, "No, we'll do it ourselves."

Using our standard Rome guidebook, Al found the section on the Vatican and steered us work by work through the classical and Christian wonders of the halls and stairwells and galleries and courtyard sculpture of this great museum. He would identify the area of the museum, find the sculptures or paintings described in the book and then read the commentary aloud. I loved it. I had my own personal tour guide doing all the explaining while I could stare at the ancient busts of Homer or Socrates or look up at the larger than life-sized statues of Zeus or Apollo or Athena or the female figures in the hall of the muses. Al did not seem to mind doing all the work.

We had enough knowledge of Italian art by then to appreciate much of what he was reading from the guidebook.

***

Our understanding of the great art of Italy increased as our quest for seeing important Italian art became more focused. We had learned that when an art sight is highlighted by several guidebooks and had a status as a tourist destination, it was always worthwhile and often extraordinary. One memorable Sunday, we managed an unplanned daytime stopover in Padua on our way to Bologna for the sole purpose of seeing the famous Giotto frescos in the Scrovegni Chapel. In our earlier trips we would not have been so focused on a particular artist. Giotto would have been only a name vaguely remembered from a college art history class.

The logistics of the stopover were a little more complicated than the short distance indicated on a map. Al studied the yellow posted schedule in the station in Venice, came to the conclusion that we would have about three hours in Padua before going on to Bologna to spend the night. I read to him the assurances from two guidebooks that we could safely check our bags in the train station for a few hours, so we agreed to do it. When we arrived in this totally unfamiliar city, we got lost a couple of times in our walk from the station, as we followed the signs to the Scrovegni Chapel. But we couldn't help but enjoy the warm and sunny spring afternoon, birds singing in the trees as we entered the shady area in front of the entrance to the chapel.

We bought our tickets and walked across the shady courtyard toward the entrance, only to be stopped by an attendant who raised his hand, shook his head and refused to let us go into the chapel. His explanations in Italian confused us, along with the other visitors who waited as the line grew longer and longer. The attendant remained unmovable. Finally we pieced together the reason: To protect the chapel, only so many people were allowed in at one time and at that moment a large student group was inside. Finally, they strolled out and the attendant stepped aside and allowed us to enter.

The wait seemed worth it once we were inside. Now there were relatively few visitors in the small chapel and, with no large groups behind us, there was no urgency to complete our tour. We had the advantage of morning sunlight coming through the windows as we took in the Giotto's frescoes. We could look to our heart's content. Giotto is an artist who speaks more to the heart than the mind. This medieval painter's work initiated early changes to Renaissance art by including human background and perspective, bright colors and joyful celebration of biblical stories; he fused the spiritual aspect of creation and everyday human life.

Walking into the chapel was like entering a magical world, a wonderful impression of color and light. The density of painting on the walls and over the door and altar was like an entire museum crammed into one chapel. We spent almost an hour standing first on one side and then the other, following the three tiers of panels on each side that depicted the chronology of Old and New Testament stories. Al and I took turns identifying the stories we recognized, pointing out unusual background figures or hidden paintings. The richness of detail was greater than many of the other medieval works we had seen. The more we looked, the more stories we saw, traditional narrative subjects such as the Annunciation, the Nativity and the Crucifixion. We studied visual depictions of stories from the life of Mary, her marriage to Joseph, the presentation of the baby Jesus in the temple, the baptism of John the Baptist, and imaginative details from the childhood as well as the adult life and trials of Jesus. Like any good narrative that unfolds in sequence, the chronology of events focused our attention on the drama of the biblical narrative. Even if we hadn't been interested in the content, the colors and light and sense of quiet awe at the artistic achievement would have stayed with us.

Satisfied, but not overwhelmed after our art tour, we took our impressions out into the streets of Padua, walking through the town, where businesses were closed on Sunday afternoons. In a dramatic contrast to the spiritual world of Giotto, coming from an empty walkway around a corner, we came upon a real-life demonstration by workers parading for protection from immigrant labor, complete with marching music and signs. We watched for a while, then, as the time before our train departure was fleeting, headed back to the one busy outdoor cafe we had seen on a piazza. We ate a quick sandwich and drank birra piccolo, small beers, then headed back to the station in time to get our luggage and get on the train to Bologna. Three hours was all we had spent in Padua, but our quick art stop had been well worth the trouble. But we realized it would be hard to explain to most of our friends back home how seeing one small chapel could be worth so much effort.

***

A friend had once commented, as many have, about the riches of old objects, gold and jeweled garments and headwear, as well as ceremonial items, in the Vatican museum that belonged to the Church and had been used for worship. "Why do they still own all of that rich stuff?" Without making any apologies for the historical excesses of the Church, after seeing the treasures of the Vatican Museum in Rome, Al and I could see the benefit of preserving these beautiful objects of ceremony for the benefit of all. What would the alternative be? To melt down the gold chalices? Perhaps. But just as the Crown Jewels in London come from a different time and are preserved for their artistic beauty, at this point in history, it seems better to protect those items in the Vatican for all to see. It's not about the gold and jewels as much as the craftsmanship and vision.

Another friend once expressed her surprise that the Vatican Museum with its Christian identity, would prominently display ancient statues of pagan gods and goddesses, and other depictions from pagan religion to modern viewers. To my mind, the church should get credit for respecting the artistic impulses of ancient artists and for tolerating and often embracing the spiritual impulses behind their work.

Historically, Catholicism accepted and preserved the art of the past, even that which predated Christianity, in contrast to some later Protestant Reformers. The Bible based reformers saw visual depictions of religious figures as idolatries, graven images forbidden by the Bible, removing and often destroying them.

Standing in front of seven foot high sculptures of the goddess Athena, her helmeted head looking out with strength and benevolence, or in front of Demeter, more maternal but again strong with her gifts of grain, or even Zeus with his full beard and small lightning bolt, I am often as moved as when standing in front of a picture of the biblical creator God the Father or of the Madonna and Child. I have surprised myself by feeling inspired by pagan representations of the divine.

In both cases the visual work represents the spirit behind it so, although the images of my religion may mean more and seem more familiar to me, I can be moved by both. All of us personalize our own sense of God or the spiritual, whether through visual art or in Bible stories or only in our imaginations and emotions. My views of God or goodness may not match someone else's, but I can learn something by seeing their visions. I have become more respectful of religious impulses expressed in art from the past and more able to see images from other non Christian religions today in the same light. The same impulse is at work in all truly inspired art. And the same spiritual reality is reflected in the most uplifting works from any age.

All over Italy, depictions in churches include the most familiar Bible stories from both the Old and the New Testaments. The creation of the world usually shows God the Father, designated by His beard, often coming from a cloud to separate the dark and light, to create the world and then human beings. Al has been known to point to the ceiling of a chapel or church and pronounce enthusiastically, "There's God." Like children's art, these renditions are simple and direct, and often quite literal. They show Eve being pulled by God from Adam's side while he is asleep, or Adam and Eve eating from the fruit tree with a lowly serpent in the background. Communicating the content of the story and its spiritual lesson is the most important intention. I look at the paintings and think that much of what came to be the literal interpretation of the Bible harkens back to the efforts of earlier teachers to make its substance known to common people. If we look at the themes behind the paintings, we see and feel what they intended.

Al and I have a good time picking out the representations of the old Bible stories. Somehow their direct simplicity cuts to the heart of the story and the idea behind it. I tell Al, "These are the same stories they teach to kids in Bible school." He agrees, pointing out Noah on the ark with the animals and Jonah being swallowed by the whale.

Both of us recognize the New Testament stories, the Annunciation to Mary by the angel, the Nativity, the visit of the wise men, the flight into Egypt, and the various ministries and miracles of Jesus, the Last Supper and Crucifixion and Resurrection. I often enlighten Al about the details of the less famous depictions.

When an entire series of pictures is lined up on the walls or ceilings of a church, it's easy to see the paintings as Bible lesson. The church commissioned artists as instructors of the common people who would celebrate the drama, color, beauty and inspiration inside the church in contrast to what was probably a more stark life outside. Protestant reform came about when people could read the Bible for themselves but the Christian artists before that were presenting visuals so people could understand the stories.

Just as today, art reflected the issues of the times. Sometimes great churches were built to thank God for helping a certain town survive the plague or defeat invaders. Artistic renditions of slaying a dragon might reflect overcoming death or evil or an enemy. Politics came into play. Patrons would sponsor artists, sometimes for the honor and glory of God, and sometimes for personal reward or recognition in this life and salvation in the next. It was not unusual for a patron to be acknowledged as a witness in a nativity scene or painted among the saved in heaven.

After the Reformation, as part of the countermovement of the Church, baroque art in its very elaborateness, was a protest against the simplicity that the reformers wanted. The triumphal defense of the "true faith" in baroque periods is evidence of the us against them theme of religion that runs throughout history. A baroque church is beautiful but usually seems overdone to us as we look at gold decor and the ornate cupola above us of heavenly angels and cherubs lifting us upward.

***

Al has tried on occasion to explain to someone back home that in contemporary Italy an entire economic operation is built on the maintenance and restoration of its art. The viewpoint that government should not pay to support the arts would seem ludicrous in Italy, where art is a national heritage. After the earthquake near Assisi, officials stated that the most important thing was to be concerned for loss of life or injury to people, but a very close second was the tragic loss of the frescoes in the collapsed ceiling of the church. Before the aftershocks had ended, attempts were being made to find fragments from the irreplaceable art in the rubble to aid in the restoration process that would take place. The concept of sweeping away the broken plaster and simply writing off the loss would be unthinkable in Italy.

But great art is not just a national treasure; on some level it belongs to everyone. Italians think of their art as a national heritage, but also as a trust to protect, not only for Italy and certainly not only for economic reasons the way American pragmatists seem to think of it, but for all humankind. Great art must be protected because if something is destroyed or damaged, it is gone forever.

And the experience of art transcends time and place and culture and religion and gender. Art simply is. That's why we can be moved by religious art of other spiritual traditions.

***

I knew the word "fresco" and associated it with paintings on a wall, but I had forgotten the fact that the paint is put into plaster while it is still wet. Thus the word fresco or fresh. Frescos would last longer than if just being painted on the dry plaster. The process explains why frescos chip with the settlement of the plaster walls and crack with age and why they fade over the centuries. After Al pointed this technical fact out to me, I realized why it is so hard to completely protect the paintings from settlement cracks, or just the wear and tear of time and the elements. Fresco painting reacts like the plaster because to some extent it is the plaster.

Art is everywhere in Italy. Not only are the big churches and cathedrals decorated inside and out with sculpture and paintings, but tiny churches on side streets and in small towns as well. We wandered one afternoon in a small hill town where there was little to see other than the town or to do other than wander. On the edges of the little town built on top of the hill looking out over the countryside, we saw an open door to one of several small churches, kind of the equivalent of a one-room school house in size and concept. When it came to churches in Italy, the more the better seems to have been the rule. These little churches are everywhere even if there is a larger central church, almost as if each neighborhood or subdivision had a church of its own. This church was a little larger than some but was empty with no pews or altar. It seemed to be unused at the time and had very little decoration, mostly just white stucco plaster walls and columns. Nevertheless, on the upper part of a side wall toward the front, working from ladders and scaffolding were craftsmen intent on either uncovering or restoring a remnant of a fresco. The life-size figure of the saint was dim and incomplete, the paint worn with the stresses of age, but the two workmen talked quietly as they patiently went about their business of taking care of this art remnant.

I felt as if I had glimpsed the past, as the men worked with no special equipment and no radio playing, just in the relative silence broken only by their conversation in the cool interior of the church. I thought how the atmosphere inside the church must have been similar long ago. I imagined how in past times, a fresco in one's own neighborhood church must have meant a lot to local villagers.

The fresco wasn't anything unusual as a painting, certainly nothing that would ever be listed in a guidebook. Considering the out of the way location of the church, it seemed that this restoration was being done only for the neighborhood and for its own sake as art. It reminded me of a story a biologist once told of how amazing it had been to see beautiful flowers in the desert surrounded by land that was uninhabited by people. Religious-minded people are inspired by such natural visions of beauty and wonder that seem to give evidence of a Creator whose Spirit overflows even to unknown places. Other creators were at work with much the same spirit in the little church in a small neighborhood in a small town in Italy.

***

Before our Italy trips, we knew that mosaics were small pieces of colored ceramic fitted together to make a picture. I associated mosaics with Eastern and Byzantine culture and pictured them in Orthodox churches. But seeing mosaics in Italy from different times and places gave us a new appreciation of their variety. The ancient Romans decorated floors and walls of public baths, even parts under flowing water, with animal figures and mythological subjects. When we walk on remnants of this art that is 2000 years old, we think of the many footsteps it has survived and, even though the designs of animals of warriors may be faded or less than awe-inspiring, we can't help but appreciate the skill and time involved in laying the tiny pieces of tile into patterns. Now that we recognize and appreciate mosaics, Al will point out even the smallest fragment in a Roman ruin and be impressed by its survival.

With no expectations, we have gone off to see a church noted for its mosaics only to spend a couple of hours taking in the beauty above, below and around us. The best of the mosaics are intense and alive in a way that makes it hard to leave them. Faces in mosaics seem alive and immediate in a way that even the best frescoes and oil paintings don't. You half expect the figures to speak or move, their reality is so great. And yet close up, the miracle of combining the tiny squares of colored ceramic in such a way as to make even a reasonable approximation of a face seems unlikely. Of all the techniques, and with respect to art history experts who probably know better, the mosaic seemed to me the most incredible as the tiny squares of colored ceramics merge into such lifelike forms.

CHAPTER SEVENTEEN

Music

If Al and I discovered Italian art together, I have to admit to more resistance on my part to his interest in attending music events. At home, he is the music person. He adjusts the speakers on our sound system for subtle changes in bass and treble that I ignore and he browses through CDs in stores while I look at books. I usually like his choice of folk musicians or popular groups, but I remember few of the details, sometimes not even their names. I enjoy what we listen to at home, as long as it's not too loud, and the live shows which he occasionally picks out. It's fair to say that most of my appreciation of contemporary music and musicians, I owe to Al's discovery of them.

Al is much more appreciative of classical music than I am. Maybe it relates to his Czech roots that in his mid-life years he discovered classical music, adding Mozart and Bach and Handel to his collection and telling our daughters, "I didn't used to like it either. Maybe I'm getting older." I don't mind the livelier pieces, but I have a short attention span when it comes to just listening. I don't mind classical music as background music at home while I am doing other things, but I like to have something to look at. Given a choice I would rather watch a movie without sound than listen to sound without pictures. I get restless sitting still for very long and classical music performances tend to be long.

I like the lighter approach to music in Italy as well, the American college student choir singing spirituals on the steps of Santa Maria Maggiori in Florence or the gypsy musicians that performed for forty-five minutes in the Piazza Signorini one spring day. The gypsies sang, played and danced, then passed the tambourine at the end for a contribution for their efforts. Al was so impressed with their music he was very disappointed they didn't have tapes or CDs for sale.

Another time, in Rome, we listened in an Irish pub while a young Italian group sang old songs from the 1960s, the lyrics of Bob Dylan and songs of the Band enthusiastically delivered in English with an Italian accent. The group was loud enough that we could sing along without being heard, and we had a great time.

Even the gondola drivers songs inspire me.

But my classical appreciation is negligible and I resisted going to a violin concert or an opera in Italy. "It'll be so boring," I thought, and sometimes said.

But Italian concerts have been a good balance between my need to have something to look at and Al's appreciation of music. The background of the church with its art and architecture and people gives me more than a concert stage to look at. The church concerts provide an informal atmosphere, less serious and intense somehow than in a performance hall at home where coughs and rustling of papers are discouraged. The dress is casual and comfortable and, best of all, the performances are shorter, a little over an hour, with no intermission, no restroom lines, no parking. The only discomfort is the hard seats of the church pews. But the quality of the music is wonderful, with great acoustics. I had to admit, too, that while most theater and film outings would have a built-in frustration because of our language barrier, music transcends language. Thanks to Al, I've learned to appreciate that aspect of music even more.

The first time we stumbled upon a musical experience in Italy together it was by luck. That was the Saturday night we spent in Milan on the last night of one of our early trips; we were staying over on our way home and had no plans. We had already done our sightseeing there at the beginning of our trip and had taken the train back from Florence on Saturday afternoon.

To pass the time, we wandered into the large Tourist Information Center near the Duomo and piazza and started to look at the posted signs in the crowded areas. Al casually studied the listing for a series of concerts in various churches in the city while I looked at maps and travel posters. When he figured out that a violin concert of Vivaldi's *Four Seasons* would be performed that night in an old but small church in an unexplored neighborhood, he was hooked.

The tourist aide sold us tickets for $15 said, "Si, si. Yes," you can wear jeans or slacks. What you have is fine. You should go. It is very nice, the concert!" So we found a sandwich shop, and headed out on our metro ride and walk through a spring rain shower and into the church. Even as resistant as I was to classical music, I had to admit it was a wonderful experience

We entered the magic of the dark church lit with spotlights and candelabra. The use of the old church as a concert hall worked better than might be expected. A large crucifix, with a sculpture of Madonna and Child, and several life-sized saints formed the backdrop as eight male violinists and several other string musicians, dressed in black tuxedos, entered from the sacristy at the side of the old altar.

Rather than tourists, the people at this concert were locals. They were relaxed, nobody was dressed up and people chatted companionably in the pews until time for the concert.

This casual atmosphere was blended with an enthusiastic appreciation of the musicians. The musicians were professional and performed excellently. The church, more compact than the big cathedrals, provided great acoustics. The standing ovations for encores felt more like a concert of popular music back home than a classical performance. The concert was uplifting and fun. And even though I recognized far less than I probably would now of Vivaldi's music, and even though my attention waned and I was ready to leave before the last encore was called, I had a good time. Al had a great time and now we regularly attend live concerts in Italy, He has also gotten me to like the symphony there, something he hadn't managed to do at home.

One evening in Rome we followed the posted signs to a church where an American women's church choir was to perform; admission was free. Unfortunately, unlike the violins in the smaller church in Milan, the women's voices, which were probably adequate leading their congregations at home, were lost in the large open nave of the old Roman church. The audience, small and scattered to begin with in the cavernous space, was clearly disappointed and, by ones and twos, they slipped out, one man shaking his head in disgust as he tossed his program on the pew. We stayed for a while in an attempt to provide moral support for our fellow Americans, but long before the end, even though we felt a bit disloyal, we also quietly slipped from our pew to the back.

Another time Al dragged me unhappily to a more formal piano concert in a smaller room in an old palazzo in Rome. The pianists, a man and a woman, were excellent and the acoustics were good, but my attention wandered and I got restless, more so because in this smaller concert room there was no easy exit.

Whether or not to go to an opera is still a source of irritation between us, operas being inevitably long and more serious affairs. But as often as not, the opera schedule is wrong for our visit, so I am off the hook. The first time we were in Milan we naively tried to buy opera tickets at the last minute for the famous opera house La Scala. Because the performers and opera were well-known, the price for the few remaining seats was $300. We had read that standing room tickets were often available for a mere ten dollars. But standing room in the old theater of La Scala where space was limited meant standing in a small, crowded, even claustrophobic room, listening to the music, but without seeing the stage except for an occasional glimpse between the heads and shoulders of one's fellow attendees. We decided to skip the performance, although Al would still like to go back sometime with tickets already purchased. The idea of seeing an opera in such a well known venue captures his imagination more than mine.

However, one year in Naples we did see an opera when we purchased last minute tickets a few hours before the performance. It was not a famous opera house like La Scala, but at a theater that is supposed to have the best acoustics in Italy. Opera is popular throughout Italy and even on a weeknight in Naples very few seats were empty. People were dressed nicely although not quite as formally as on a Saturday night in Milan. We sat in a box on the ground floor just slightly above the orchestra audience in uncomfortable folding chairs that could be shifted. We shared the box with two men in business suits, who were taking in the performance during business travel. It was a long German opera with three long acts and two intermissions. During the breaks theater goers flowed into the open room at the back for a drink or coffee and a visit with others. Socializing, after all, has always been a part of opera.

During the performance, Al and I listened and watched, trying to glean as much meaning as possible from the Italian surtitles and priding ourselves that we could more or less follow what was going on. Even our little understanding of Italian gave us more clues than any attempt to understand the operatic German. It was a love story in which the lovers struggled against great odds. The straight backed chairs were uncomfortable, but in the box there was room to stretch our legs a bit so somehow I didn't feel as restless as usual. The sounds were pretty, and the lovers were sincere and although I don't really like opera the way Al does, I found myself enjoying it.

The love story ended tragically, of course. The opera was long, so long in fact that one of our box-mates left before the last act. The other man, an Italian who was there on business from Milan and had wanted to hear the famous acoustics of the Santa Lucia Opera House, by the last aria, was rolling his right hand gently in a circular motion, a gesture to the singers to hurry up and finish. I was glad to realize that I was not the only one who, as the final duet went on and on, wanted the tragedy to just end.

Ultimately I have to admit that I'm glad that Al has prodded and cajoled me into these new musical experiences, especially since the Italians contributed so much to opera. I can't say that I'd leap at a chance to hear classical music or go to the opera, and I still prefer easier listening, but some of my most memorable times have been related to these music events. Lately I've reflected at how uniquely suited musical events are to entertainment in unfamiliar places. An easy access to another culture, the musical surroundings are different, but the sound transcends language; the notes and tunes and instruments are as accessible to us from other countries as to the locals.

CHAPTER EIGHTEEN

Eating Italian

I have heard it said that there are no bad restaurants in Italy. And while I couldn't guarantee that to be the case, Al and I have yet to experience one.

Instead of researching for recommended restaurants and making reservations ahead of time as we might at home, we find we eat well in Italy by serendipity. Occasionally we track down a recommendation from a guidebook or from a friend back home, but for the most part we walk, focusing on an area with numerous trattorias and ristorantes. We wander along the narrow streets stopping to read the menus that are posted outside, checking for prices and looking for any variations on the traditional Italian dishes. Sometimes we pass up what looks like a good place, just to see what might be around the corner. Exploration is part of the experience. Eventually we stop and open the door to one of the small street side restaurants. A waiter welcomes us, "Buona sera. Due? Good Evening. Two?" Graciously, he extends his arm broadly, inviting us into a small restaurant where we choose any available table.

Al and I tend to avoid the more expensive restaurants partly because we are usually dressed casually and because we know we can get plenty of good and interesting food without paying a lot. One practical justification for continuing our Italian vacations is that we usually eat better for less, compared to what even a moderate restaurant costs us at home. A couple of courses, a carafe of wine, sometimes with dessert and coffee often comes to less than $40 for both of us. The service is welcoming and gracious, and as my favorite characteristic of Italian restaurants, there is no rush.

Good restaurants, many of them small and family owned, are plentiful even in a busy city like Rome. We can easily find places to eat without standing in a line outside or drinking at an inside bar for 45 minutes just to eat at a new and trendy place. Restaurants don't seem to compete so much for novel cuisine and unusual decors, and restaurant chains, which are such a staple of American dining out, seem absent from the Italian lifestyle. Although there are the occasional Chinese or even Mexican restaurants, for the most part, restaurants in Italy serve Italian food.

We eat simple dishes in Italy. Those who want complex sauces and extreme efforts of originality might be disappointed. But even the simplest food is excellent in that everything is fresh and well prepared. We've never been served a micro-waved re-heated dish. In a small pizzeria, we may wait a little longer for our oven-baked pizzas but they are good and taste like real food, not cardboard. Seafood and vegetables are served in season and according to region. Salads are simple, too. An insalata verde is a green salad and an insalata mista predictably includes carrots, tomatoes and other freshly chopped vegetables in addition to the greens. Marinated mushrooms, peppers, eggplants, zucchini and onions are served as an antipasta, often displayed on a table on platters as you enter. Olive oil and vinegar work miracles on these simple dishes made from ingredients grown and harvested from nearby farms. I once read in a magazine article that the best and the freshest olive oil was kept and used locally and only the next best was used for export. It makes sense that any food close to its source would be better tasting and probably better for you.

Service conveys a certain flair and focused attentiveness to detail even for simple dishes. An insalata mista would hardly pass as a real salad at home where restaurants are always dreaming up original and enormous concoctions for salad and dressings alike. However, in an Italian trattoria, the owner might bring a cart to our table with the greens, olive oil, a light or balsamic vinegar, salt and pepper, and he will dress and toss the salad in front of us.

Wine is ordered and served more casually. Although more expensive restaurants do offer more expensive wines, people tend to spend less time perusing a wine list and rely on the waiter. We order the local wine by the carafe not the glass, Chianti or Montepulciano in the North, white or lighter red wines in the South.

Often, the local wine is newer and tends to be lighter, easier to drink with an Italian meal, not so hearty as the Cabernets that many Americans like especially with beef, but most Italians aren't eating big steaks anyway. Even Al, who usually likes heartier red wine at home, is happy with the vino rosso di casa. There is less fanfare over the ritual of opening and pouring since it is assumed that the wine will be good. Vino is just part of the meal, part of the eating experience, rather than a separate alcoholic beverage or a connoisseur item. Although the introduction of the Euro has changed the currency values, wine prices are still reasonable. We often pay the equivalent of three to six dollars for a small to large carafe, depending on how much we want. It's not unusual in an Italian restaurant to see wine left in a carafe on the table. As part of the meal, wine is not a restaurant specialty for which one pays dearly, as we often do at home, and so we don't feel pressured to swallow the last drop.

Unlike back home, but like in most places in Europe, water is a commodity in an Italian restaurant. Tap water, which is certainly considered safe to drink in Italy, is not served in restaurants so, if you want water, you buy a bottle of aqua minerale. Along with wine, we always order water, senza gas or naturalle, having learning the hard way that water will arrive "with bubbles" unless specified otherwise.

Most restaurants are small and simply decorated. Tables for two can be quickly configured into fours, six, and up, a system that works very well. Empty tables can be moved around easily and reconstructed depending on the size of the party. Regardless of the table arrangements, it is common to sit close to other diners, sometimes elbow to elbow. Italians we've observed seem congenial, communal-minded and tend to be friendly and gregarious. Even in more expensive restaurants, physical closeness to other diners is not considered inappropriate and makes it easy to overhear other conversations and even strike up conversations with fellow diners.

During these early years of our traveling, for the most part, there was no such thing as a nonsmoking section of a restaurant in Italy. People smoked if they wanted to and nobody seemed to mind. Somehow restaurants didn't seem to be as smoke filled as restaurants at home used to be, maybe because there was usually no separate bar or happy hour crowd and because eating is the more serious occupation during a meal, but we learned not to be surprised if someone was smoking near us. Recently a no-smoking ban has gone into effect in all indoor spaces all over Italy. Rather than complicating life by having stages and areas and conditions for smoking, the Italians just moved all smokers outside.

It took us a while to understand the different names for eating places. When I saw BAR written in large letters across the awning or shutters of a small establishment, I assumed it meant a place to drink. Although a bar in Italy may serve wine or aperatifs, it can also be a sandwich bar, a good place to get lunch or a snack. As in a cafe, we can choose from freshly made sandwiches, simple combinations like ham and cheese or mozzarella and tomato. In the case of a ham and cheese or cheese and mushroom, the sandwich is heated in a small oven to melt the cheese and then handed to you in a paper wrapper. We can stand at the counter and eat and drink or take the sandwich with us. It's not uncommon to see people eating these quick meals sitting near a fountain or on church steps or occasionally while strolling down a sidewalk. The panini is the Italian version of fast food, but tastes better and seems healthier than a burger and fries. The lack of to go containers means less disposable trash. Much of our at home garbage and recycling could be reduced by simply using less packaging for take-home food. At home, I try to avoid carryout containers as much as possible.

Al and I usually avoid the ristorantes, which are expensive with a larger menu selection that are obviously for those interested in fine dining and fancy dress. We usually opt for a small, often family-run trattoria or pizzeria, (the name doesn't mean they always sell pizza), or an osteria, with a family style service and sometimes fewer choices that change daily. Any of these eating places will provide plenty of good food and local atmosphere for us.

Often the host of an establishment will simply gesture toward all the tables that are available, and we can pick our own. After we are seated, we get a menu, usually in Italian, although in tourist areas menus may be in several languages, including English. We were surprised at first to be confused by Italian menus but have learned that Italian dishes at home are either very familiar or have English subtitles. Waiters are helpful trying to understand our English and if they can't interpret, will call for someone who can. Waiters sometimes take us back to look at the meat or fish so we know what it is or bring out the main dish for approval before it is prepared, a step that Italian customers sometimes have as well. Although we have learned our way around Italian menus enough to know more or less what we are ordering, we didn't always know exactly what pasta or main dish we would get, but as long as we know that carne is meat and pesce is fish, we usually do okay.

Tourists are often drawn in by a "tourist special" because they feel more secure with a predetermined choice for each of several courses at a fixed price. But it's easy enough to order a pasta or meat and salad without relying on a fixed-price menu. Waiters usually know enough English to make simple translations from their menus. They also tend to know what foreigners like. We have never ordered a tourist special and avoid restaurants that advertise them, figuring they will have tourist prices and fewer local people. We look for the side streets that have restaurants in clusters for more authentic places.

We have almost never had a bad eating experience in Italy, but there was one misunderstanding in Rome. We had a perfect table in an outdoor cafe on the Piazza Navona. We had spent a busy morning touring Saint Peter's and opted to spend the extra money to have lunch in the spring sunshine on the piazza. We knew to expect higher prices but were ready to relax.

Our one sour note came in a misunderstanding about the fish. The waiter had noted that the fish was priced at a certain rate, which Al took to mean the total price. He thought that a small piece of very good white fish would be about eight dollars. It was only when the bill arrived that we learned that the price was by the ounce so the small piece of fish was about thirty-two dollars. Al went on the offensive, not wanting to be taken advantage of. He felt sure that we were being fleeced since we were obviously tourists in a tourist area expecting tourist prices. He objected in English and a little Italian but the waiter refused to budge, insisting that it was the correct price, showing us again the menu price. We ended up paying the bill without leaving any extra tip, although since service is always included in a bill in Europe we were not really able to protest very strongly.

It wasn't until later in other restaurants that we began to notice that fish prices were always by the ounce and often expensive in the cities; we realized we were not being fleeced. However, we have seen many altercations between Italians where each side has his own view about prices, particularly on the trains. Generally both the customer and the official hold their ground emphatically until somehow it all winds down. The customer usually pays up and things move on. Looking back, I feel less embarrassed by my husband's confrontation. Maybe he was just being Italian after all. Whenever we walk through and around the Piazza Navona, we always remember our first experience ordering fish.

Americans often have a stereotypical idea about Italian dinners, that they are always six or more courses. I have heard Americans say that waiters will frown on you if you order fewer courses. But in our experience the pressure to order many courses hasn't proved true. We usually order a pasta or main dish and a salad or vegetable, sometimes an antipasto or dessert to share but never all seven courses. Sometimes we just have one course, a pasta, and wine.

We have watched big celebrations, family birthdays or other celebrations at other tables where the many course dinner appeared, and a group of friends out on a Saturday night is likely to have several courses often sharing antipasti dishes with maybe a pasta and meat or fish course. But at home, we do the same, being more likely to have appetizers and extra courses to slow down the pace of the meal if we are celebrating a special occasion or just want a leisurely evening with friends. Also, an American dinner may have fewer courses but can be a larger meal because our portions are about twice the size. But what is lacking in amount is more than balanced by excellent quality, freshness and attentive preparation.

Growing up in the Northeastern U.S. where cold weather encouraged heartier versions of Italy's cuisine, Al and I associated antipasti with heavy meats like salami and pastrami and assorted cheeses and olives. This type of dish is okay for large groups where everyone gets a sample, but Al and I often opt for a lighter mix of roasted and marinated vegetables such as eggplant, zucchini, mushrooms and tomatoes. Al's favorite early course is buffalo mozzarella, the soft creamy round cheese, with slices of tomato, leaves of fresh basil and a sprinkling of olive oil and black pepper. In this simple but masterful combination, the cheese, the basil, the tomatoes and the olive oil all taste better from being near their source.

Primi piatti or first course includes the pastas and soups. Secundi is the second course, usually what we would consider the main course, the meat or fish or chicken. In a very fancy meal there could be a fish and then a meat course, but rarely. Contorni means the course that follows, usually a salad or a vegetable. In Italy salad is traditionally served after the meal although we Americans are often asked if we prefer it before. We've learned to follow Italian custom, realizing how our big overdressed salads back home often fill us up, making us unable to enjoy our dinner. Another custom we are now comfortable with is having a vegetable served separately after the main courses. A serving of asparagus or green beans or even potatoes seems more significant for having a plate and course to itself. Sometimes I have two contorni, skipping to a vegetable course while Al eats meat or fish and then I'll have a salad with him.

A portion of meat or fish will be about half what we get at home. And yet the size will be plenty. Europeans are often amazed by the sizes of American portions. I'm old enough to remember when restaurants at home did not overwhelm us with the amounts they served. Italians, who assume freshness in their food, don't expect to take leftover portions home. The waste involved in Styrofoam and aluminum take-out containers is not the problem there that it is here.

The concept of smaller portions means that several courses make more sense. A pasta dish before the main course is quite manageable because neither will be large. In the same way, having a vegetable or salad after dinner seems better paced and less heavy.

Courses in Italy are simply a way of breaking a meal apart so that instead of having vegetables with a side of pasta along with our fish, for example, it is all served separately. Having one dish at a time slows down the pace of the meal, which seems better for one's digestion.

Although we may associate rich desserts like cannoli with Italian eating, except for special occasion meals, sometimes with special cakes, Italians are less likely to have a rich dessert than Americans and will have espresso and fruit if anything at all. Asking for a decaffeinated coffee will often bring either a confused look or a small package of Sanka with a cup of hot water. Italians expect coffee to be coffee in its natural state.

At home we were used to having a social drink and taking our time before ordering and would have felt rushed if we were expected to give our order as soon as we sat down. I occasionally used to feel rushed when a waiter would come with our food so soon after we ordered it.

But in Italy the assumption is that we are in the restaurant because we are hungry. After only a minute or two, a waiter will often appear, pencil and pad in hand, to take our order. Occasionally we say, "Momento," and ask for more time, but usually decide quickly what we want, order and then settle in for a relaxed meal. Bread comes, not as a first course, but with other food. Wine is a companion to food, rather than a precursor to it. Having wine with an antipasto or a pasta course rather than drinking while nibbling on bread or breadsticks the way we do at home makes us less likely to fill up too soon on the wrong part of the meal.

Generally, once courses are served, they are eaten at your own pace, then empty plates are removed and the next dish served before too long a delay. Al especially likes the pattern since he is more interested in eating right away. I'm the one who usually wants to delay ordering at home so we can talk, knowing that once we've eaten, we'll leave. In Italy we get to eat and talk and still not feel rushed. At the end of the meal, we stay as long as we want.

Tourists sometimes get restless waiting for the check, feeling that they are being ignored or that the service is lax. But once our final course, dessert or coffee is served, we can expect to be left alone. No matter how long we stay, we don't get a check until we ask for it "Il conto por favore." In Italy no waiter will try to float you out by filling your glass with water, or asking every two seconds if you need anything else, or quickly picking up the bill folder before it has been paid to hurry things along. Not getting a check doesn't mean that we are being ignored, rather we are being invited to stay as long as we want.

In Italy eating is about quality, not quantity, and about enjoying one's meal, not rushing through it. Meals are a community experience. Cooks often come out and speak to the diners.

We feel the positive energy in the preparing and serving of food and in the conversation of other diners, even when we can't understand what they are saying. Even the occasional person eating alone in a little Italian restaurant seems to be part of a community of diners and is treated with dignity and attention by the waiters. While people respect each other's space, it is also easy to greet or nod to people at other tables and we have occasionally had longer conversations, especially with a friendly couple or individual dining near us.

Because service is a respected profession in Italy, and waiters take pride in their work, gratuity or a servizio fee is usually included in the bill. Al usually rounds up the tip, adding a little more in cash to our payment as a kind of thank you and figuring a little extra cash never hurt anybody, but additional tipping is not absolutely necessary.

When we come home, it takes me a good while to adjust to the rush of American restaurants, even some of the more expensive ones. We tend to feel that we are putting a burden on our waiter if we stay too long. How often do people leave a comfortable restaurant setting and then go somewhere for coffee or a drink just to keep the social part of the evening going when they'd do just as well to sit comfortably where they are.

***

Along with figuring out where to eat has been learning what to eat and at what time. Italians basically don't eat breakfast. A cappuccino and a roll will cover them until the noon meal. But an Italian midday meal is substantial, not just a sandwich or cup of yogurt in front of the computer. By 11:30 a.m. or so the trattorias and pizzerias are filling and people who have been at work since 8:00 a.m. and have had only a light breakfast are ready to mangere or eat. When we walk through neighborhoods during the lunch hour, we inevitably hear the clatter of silverware and the lunch time conversations followed by some TV time or just relaxing. Even schools seem to have a long lunch break.

Lunch is the main meal, including the secundi piatti with meat or fish or the heavier pastas like lasagna, eggplant parmigiana or ravioli. People don't rush back to work after a lunch. Since many shops close between noon and 4:00, we suspect offices stay closed longer as well. Although we've never asked, I'd be surprised if anybody was expected back in less than two hours. Wine or beer is part of the midday meal, but not at all an echo of the two martini business lunch in the U.S. that went out of vogue years ago.

While there may be high powered meetings going on somewhere at noon, my sense is that work is seen as a means to enjoy life rather than the other way around, even in modern corporate life. I'd bet that even Italian business executives take longer and more enjoyable lunch hours than Americans. I tell Al, "I bet nobody's eating at their computers."

Judging again by the shop schedules, though, the traditional eight hour work day still exists. Shops open at 8:00 in the morning and close at noon. You can be walking into a store at that time and be politely told that they are "chiuso," closed, as the merchant continues to lock up. The shops open again at 4:00 and stay open until 8:00. If offices do the same, businesses are still getting a full day's work hours. I wonder how Americans would fare with a long break in the day before going back to work. I'm used to thinking that after 2:00 p.m. I'm not very energetic and that a big lunch would make me even less so, not to mention how I would feel after a glass or two of wine. But what if we had lunch and then some time to relax and recoup our energy? Maybe we could and would be more productive in the second part of the day.

Since traditionally, lunch is the big meal there, Al and I during our days in Italy have moved in that direction and usually have more to eat at lunch than at dinner. Dinner is more likely to be a pizza or light pasta and vegetable than a full course.

Al and I used to resist the idea of eating a big meal in the midday but have come to enjoy it if we are someplace where it seems easy to sit down. We won't stop our exploring or sightseeing to find a lunch restaurant, but if we are near one we'll often stop. In March while there are lots of chances to eat outside in the day, that is not the case at dinner since with no sunshine it's pretty cold. Besides, we like participating and then getting a chance to walk with the energy of the meal behind us. Also, restaurants generally don't open for dinner until 7:30 p.m. or even 8:00 p.m., so if we don't eat early we get pretty hungry.

Although in larger cities, meals might be served all afternoon near tourist sights, for Italians, there is no "early bird special." In fact, everybody tends to arrive at the same time, usually 8:00 p.m., much like on a Saturday night back home. Once seated, whether the restaurant is big or small, the presumption is that you are a guest and the table is yours for as long as you want it.

Sometimes we will stop in the late afternoon for gelato or pastries and coffee or sometimes for Campari or beer or whatever. After all, we are on vacation.

***

In Italy we eat regionally. Italy's regionalism can be appreciated by savoring its foods as much as its sights. The same meals being served in the restaurants are probably being served in the kitchens at home.

Without consciously trying to be environmentally sound and probably more from necessity than idealism, Italians have built their cuisine using fresh foods close to the source and following the seasons. They avoid the negative environmental impact of processing and transportation costs. They developed a cuisine of vegetables and fruits, pastas with small amounts of cheese and meat or fish, that is recognized today as being healthy and balanced but was basically a way to feed the people of a poor country. Restaurants tend to offer local specialties using local ingredients. Unlike at home where restaurants import distant cuisines and try to distinguish themselves with original, creative and sometimes elaborate approaches to food, in Italy regional cuisine is presented with pride. There is no apology for serving the same dishes that nearby restaurants have. After all, the trattorias and ristorantes exist mainly for the local people and they like local food, knowing that it is fresh.

Not that Italians don't enjoy a change of pace just as we do. We've noticed Chinese restaurants in most larger cities and, for better or worse, all of the tourist centers have McDonald's visited by Italian tourists among others. But there is not the constant hunger for something new or different that we have in the U.S. On a street with a Chinese restaurant and several Italian ones, the Italian ones are likely to be full and the Chinese one less so. The bottom line is that Italians like Italian food and their preference is for what is fresh, simple and familiar.

I like the pastas everywhere in Italy and the salads tend to be the same from region to region, although the olive oil and vinegar may vary. But seafood has been much better in the South and meat is probably better in the North. Even gelato is better in some places than others.

Milanese northern cuisine uses more butter than olive oil and its risotto, a rice dish that is prepared at the last minute and requires full attention and perfect timing so as not to become too doughy, is their "specialite." In Verona we were told the gnocchi, a pasta made from potato flour that anyone will tell you is hard to make, was excellent. Even my Italian friend's mother gave up on making it in the U.S. because she said the potatoes were never the right consistency. Maybe that's why it's good in Verona, the local potatoes, not the secret recipe. Al and I have ordered risotto and gnocchi in more Southern places and it is fine, but not quite as good as the place where it's especially known. We could find parallel local dishes, for example, Louisiana gumbo, Philadelphia cheese steak or Maine lobsters or trout fresh from a stream, they are all just better somehow at the source.

Tuscany has more meat dishes such as rabbit or veal and is also known for its beans. Even those who do not like beans will want to try Tuscan bean soup with just the right mixture of beans and meat and just the right consistency of seasoned broth. Al, who looks less than thrilled if I serve a bean dish at home, invariably gets a heavy and hearty Tuscan bean soup in Florence. The people have been making it for years and years, so practice seems to make it perfect.

You can order fish or seafood in Tuscany but it appears less often on menus and usually in the more expensive restaurants. The need to use only small amounts of valuable seafood or meat in dishes required becoming creative with pasta or vegetable combinations. The best Italian dishes require more preparation and work than putting something on the grill or rotisserie. Meat comes from smaller animals raised on smaller pieces of land. Italians don't have lots of steak and beef because they don't have the expanses of land to raise cattle.

When we get south to Rome and even more to Naples and beyond, seafood is more prevalent. In the seacoast towns in the Cinque Terre and in Amalfi we loved the small sweet mussels and clams in fresh tomato sauce. This dish in Rome was good but somehow not as out of this world good as the villages near the water.

Just like fish caught fresh that day and corn picked from the field in the morning taste better than store-bought, so Southern Italy's fresh seafood and tomato sauces made from fresh tomatoes and fresh olive oil can't be exported. At home we may get Napolitano tomatoes in cans and they may be better than our local brands, but it's still not the same. Pizza comprised of the same ingredients shouldn't be any different than a good pizza shop at home, but it is. Margarita pizza, thin sliced tomatoes, olive oil, mozzarella cheese and fresh basil leaves and another of Al's consistent favorites, is also best in Naples.

Wherever we go, we drink the local wine, usually red like Chianti in Tuscany and white in the North and South, each good in its own way, complementing our meals.

People used to say that Italian food was fattening. But by now most of us know of the Mediterranean diet featuring the good fats of olive oil, small amounts of meat or fish and lots of complex carbohydrates from fresh vegetables, fruits and whole grains. In Italy the portions are consistently small, but meals are balanced and satisfying. Vegetables are integrated into meals rather than a duty performed because a health expert said, "Eat your broccoli." Garlic and olive oil have a great reputation right now as health foods. Italians have used them forever. Italian food back home may, in fact, be fattening. The difference is that at home when we eat Italian food, the sauces are heavier and the quantities at least double to please American diners. When we're there, we eat well, walk a lot and usually lose a little weight.

When we eat Italian food that Italians eat, it not only tastes good, but is probably good for us. And there is something about the bright colors, the red sauces, green spinaci and garlic, that is satisfying too. Maybe if we feed our souls with relaxation and beauty, we don't need to overstuff our stomachs.

When it comes to food, it is a good idea to follow the saying, "When in Rome, do as the Romans do." McDonald's may satisfy the cravings of the fast food familiar, but we do better with a slice of pizza from a take-out window on the street. Pizza shops are good for quick meals. At a stand, you point to a square of the kind of pizza you want and wait while it is heated up, then handed to you on a piece of waxed paper for eating.

It's possible to eat more cheaply than in restaurants, by having a shopkeeper make a meat or cheese sandwich to go or even prepare a heated sandwich. We have picnicked on a wall near a fountain in a piazza or on a park bench. And if we are staying longer, or looking to save even more money, we will easily cut back on our served meals and be satisfied with these take-out options.

But Al likes to explore new dishes; he appreciates meals as a rare time to let himself relax and be served. While we budget our hotel money, we tend to eat where we can be comfortable and relaxed. While we certainly wouldn't go hungry with fewer served meals, our dining time is a time out from walking and sightseeing and has become another equalizer.

Whether we are inside trying to understand a nearby table's conversation in Italian or enjoying spring air and a view from an outside table, we enjoy the ambiance as much as the food. Whether we're watching other people or just discussing menus and the food, restaurant times are romantic and companionable interludes.

CHAPTER NINETEEN

Becoming Italian

When Al and I cross the ocean, we become Italian, at least in our own minds. We let go of our compulsive, time-oriented ways and our distress at the minor inconveniences in our lives and try to just let things happen.

In Italy life proceeds at its own pace and with its own rhythm. When a hotel manager says that the room will be ready, "In ten minutes," he doesn't mean by the clock. He means, "In a little while," an indeterminate amount of time. Maybe it will be soon but more likely later. Once we accept this, we relax, no longer going back up to the desk every two seconds to find out if the room is ready yet. Now, we leave our bags at the desk and go out for a walk, not caring when the room is ready.

When we arrive, we try as soon as possible to settle into the rhythm of things and become Italian in our reactions. Italian waiters in a touristy outdoor cafe can avoid making eye contact almost indefinitely. We learn that if we just sit and wait, rather than trying, American-style, to get a waiter's attention, we will get served and probably sooner than if we overact. We get used to things the way they are, adapting to variations from city to city and region to region; we get on Italian time.

In Italy things happen soon enough, but there is never a rush. Even in traffic when people are honking their horns, seemingly in a hurry to get around circles and through intersections, much of the intensity seems to be for the sport of it. The beeping and tooting horns are the automobile version of verbal communication rather than driver hostility and road rage that horns often convey back home. Energy is expelled but no harm done.

From our first trips, I have known that our versions of Italy, our sense of the place and of its people, is colored by a romantic notion. This is after all our Italy, not an objective view based on factual research or authentic cultural experience justified by having lived there for years. We are not Italians and not experts on their culture, but only on our subjective experience of it.

But our experiences have formed in us consistent impressions. We know that we can stay as long as we want at a dinner table, that we will not get the check until we ask for it, that we are welcome to relax as long as we want, with or without a coffee or drink in front of us. We know that we will not be given glass after glass of water in an attempt to urge us to leave, as happens in some U.S. restaurants, or feel pressured by the lines waiting for our table.

Italian business owners don't seem to need to have constant growth and improvement. More and bigger is not necessarily better. The attitude seems to be: If one restaurant supports the family, provides work and good meals, why expand? And as Al once said, looking around a small trattoria on the ground floor of an old building, "There's no room to add on anyway."

We enjoy becoming Italian in our feeling of familiarity about little things. We know that if we sit at a table in a cafe and have our coffee served to us, it may cost several dollars, but if we stand at the counter, drinking the same coffee without table service, it will be 50 cents. We know that ordering "coffee" or "caffè" will bring us a cup of espresso, rather than American style coffee. If we want a lighter drink, coffee with milk, we order a cappuccino or latte. We know to leave a small coin beside the cup as a tip, even if we are served standing.

We are used to seeing loose sugar in a bowl on the bar with a couple of communal spoons, no little bags of sanitized sugar and no sugar substitutes. There is also no mess, no torn wrappers, no empty powdered cream containers, no paper to-go cups and no wooden or plastic stirrers. You get a cup, a saucer and a spoon. Occasionally an office or shop worker from down the block will come in and get a small tray of coffees, presumably for coworkers and leave with a round tray and several ceramic espresso cups. Later they will bring back the empties.

Recently in Rome, I was shocked to see my first ever takeout coffee shop, with a sign advertising cups "to-go." I guessed they were targeting the tourists. But thinking of the waste of paper and plastic that we have unfortunately come to see as normal in many coffee shops at home, I can't imagine that Italy would ever go down that road.

Al and I feel a sense of mastery in knowing the little details about ordering meals. We don't expect to get water automatically but order it just like the wine. We know that if we don't ask for water "naturalle" or "senza gas," without bubbles, we will get mineral water. We are used to paying for a bottle of water rather than assuming water will appear, but the cost will be offset by a $4.00 bottle or carafe of pretty good house wine, which is for us a bargain. We don't order soft drinks like Coca Cola or Pepsi but recognize fruit drinks like Orangina as the local alternative. Fewer options keep life simpler and encourage a more mindful enjoyment of one's choice.

We know that for counter service, we should remember to pay first for what we want, get a receipt for our sandwich or croissant and cappuccino, and then hand that to the server. Once we got used to this system, we realized it wasn't about mistrust but has advantages over our reverse approach of eating first and then paying. Deciding and paying first helps the server know exactly what you want before he gives you his attention. You decide what you want, you pay, you get your food and drink, and then you relax. You never have to stand at a cash register, juggling money with your food and drink in hand. And in a station, there is no rush to the check out cashier when the train comes. When it's time to leave, you leave.

Our finest "becoming Italian" moments have been in blending in. As many Italians our age, we dress in dark clothes, a black blazer or sweater and slacks, and dark leather shoes, no tennis or jogging shoes. Although I'm sure we look like tourists in subtle ways, we like pretending.

One year, Al grew a beard and felt and maybe looked more European. Several times that year we were asked for directions by out of town Italian drivers or pedestrians. When they stopped and spoke to us in Italian, we felt as if we blended in for real, instead of just in our imaginations. I especially enjoyed watching Al, who, when some young men in a car asked in Italian about a destination he knew, proceeded to give them directions without speaking Italian. He pointed to a map and gestured with his arm, Italian style, indicating two blocks right, "Due," he said and then gestured straight ahead.

They nodded and drove off. "How about that? They think I'm Italian," he bragged. As tourists we have figured out directions in some cities almost as well as the locals. Al's familiarity with the sights and study of local maps does make him a good traveler's aide. He becomes American again when giving directions to confused looking English speaking tourists, taking satisfaction that he is so familiar with what once were confusing places to us, too.

We try to become part of the culture, and connect with people in little ways. We say "Buon giorno," in the morning, switch to "Buono sera" in the afternoon and occasionally the formal "Buona notte" for good night. Al casually drops first syllables for colloquial use, saying "...sera" to Italians who greet us in the elevator. If someone offers us a candy or cracker on a train, we accept, in spite of our at home injunctions against taking candy from strangers. It's the custom to be friendly and we learn to share as well.

Italian-style, we skip breakfast except for coffee and fruit or maybe a roll. Sometimes we follow local custom and eat a big lunch and a small dinner. Sometimes we sit outside near a fountain eating sandwiches near the ripple of water. We don't feel compelled to wash fruit purchased in the open markets, but do rinse our hands in the public fountains. Following the lead of the Italians around us and the advice of our guidebooks, we drink the water in the public fountain. We have never gotten sick.

We become Italian in spirit and in heart, and less our individual selves, as we happily merge with the culture and enjoy the energy of the present moment. We become one or two among the many in the flow of humanity in the streets and through history. Not just in the crowds walking along the streets but the long passeggiata of the past to the present, the ancients to modern life. It's humbling for us, but in a good way, and it's a relief to let go of roles and responsibilities and just participate in the being aspects of life. Some say history has taught Italians to live in the moment and enjoy the day for itself, and I guess we get more into that. Confronted with accomplishments and triumph, ruins and tribulations of the more than 2000 year history of this part of the world, we in our Italian selves, can't take our real life identities and our missions quite so seriously.

In becoming Italian we realize that, as modern Americans, we are only one point on the circle of worldviews and that although the view from our perspective has value, it isn't the only one. We realize that many of our assumptions about how life should be lived are formed by our culture. We see how we Americans often, rather than seeing ourselves as citizens of the world, in subtle ways expect others to think as we do. But Al and I have many times come upon ideas and practices that seem better to us than our own. We are confronted with the probability that in some ways we are wrong and our perspective is limited. As temporary Italians in spirit, we give up the burden of assuming that Americans are more advanced or that our culture is somehow ideal or superior to the rest of the world. We lighten our mission to change or preach to the world. As individuals we join in the flow of humanity through time, interested not in making our mark or changing others, but in being existentially present.

***

I guess Italians have calendar organizers and day timers, possibly with Florentine bindings and handmade paper, and more recently palm pilots and computer calendars. But our sense of things Italian is that it is the moment that matters and that super scheduling and multi-tasking just isn't the style there. Business seems to get done in a lower-key way with less needless expenditure of energy.

In the spring of 1999, as we Americans approached the Millennium celebrations with a great deal of self-consciousness and U.S. style event planning, Al and I visited Venice. In the U. S. friends were already making reservations for trips to exotic places and planning big parties to welcome this special new year. As we chatted with our hotelier, who chuckled about learning to use his computer from his nine-year-old son so he could use e-mail for reservations, We asked, "What will you do for the Millennium celebration in Venice?"

The Italian looked puzzled until he realized that we were talking about the year 2000, many months off. Then he shrugged and shook his head, "We Italians do things at the last minute."

We had both assumed that a carnival city such as Venice would be advertising big plans for the turn of the century cele- bration. Later, feeling better about our own resistance to friends' suggestions for travel and party plans for the start of 2000, I told Al, "We sure make a big deal out of things at home."

Al agreed, "It's all hype." We recognized more clearly the commercial aspect of U.S. celebrations in contrast to Italy.

As we set out to explore the city, I found myself rethink- ing my fear that we would be the only people in the United States watching the Millennium celebration on television. As our host returned to arranging guest rooms for the coming busy weekend, I was reminded that by thinking or worrying about the future, one often misses the present. I remembered that our plans often did change at the last minute due to circumstances beyond our control or just because we wanted to do something different. Even for us long-range planning Americans, it makes sense to be in the present.

Maybe Italy, situated in proximity to Eastern philosophies, as well as the warmth of the Mediterranean and steeped in his- tory, has a maturity that comes from being part of an older cul- ture. Maybe we Americans, living in a culture of more progress and forward motion, measuring our past in decades and centu- ries rather than millennium, are less patient. Al and I are lucky we can move between both worlds.

Becoming less important as individuals, less goal-oriented, traveling light, staying in small rooms, lightens us up and en- lightens us about what is important in life. By feeling less im- portant in the scheme of things, Al and I become more ourselves. We drop the facades of work and socializing that are essential to our lives at home. In Italy we are anonymous and don't feel pressured to meet the expectations of others and we don't have to put pressure on each other to meet those expectations. Maybe that's why we bond in a special way in Italy. We can really be there with and for each other.

When our kids were little, I was lucky enough to stay home with them. Our generation had fewer options for daycare but also had less pressure to work at least until our children were in school. During that time, when Al came home from work one evening, he asked me, "Well, what did you do today?"

"I just watched," I answered.

It was true. I had sat on the sofa for most of the day and simply paid quiet attention to our one-year-old and three-year-old daughters as they played in the living room. I remember it as one of the best days of my life. On weekends, when our girls were a little older, Al and I would take them to a park or to an outdoor fountain and watch their pleasure in the simple acts of running through grass or splashing in water. Observing their ability to focus on what they were doing, we vicariously enjoyed their lack of concern about the purpose of an activity. They were just experiencing life in its bare immediacy. Being in Italy brings about that same feeling of just being able to watch life and enjoy it without conflict, without thinking we should be "doing something." We relearn the basic concept that doing nothing is really an act of importance, especially when we are tuned in to what's around us and realize how seldom we put ourselves in that mindset. In Italy we settle in, go with the flow of life, join in with the rhythm of the passeggiata. We relax, but with colorful stimulation all around us. We spend time just looking.

***

In Italy, we become more aware of the consumerism and material excess that surrounds us back home. Staying in small rooms with small baths, eating smaller portions, walking and riding public transportation, make us aware of how much we overuse almost everything at home. Using less materially opens us to enjoyment of being present in life. We appreciate the tastiness of the food, the walks along the streets, the sunlight on the piazzas, the views from hilltops. Other than the expense of sleeping and eating and sightseeing, we don't spend a lot of money when we're there, certainly not on shopping. I think of how much shopping and browsing I do at home just to entertain myself. I know I'm not alone since American women are encouraged to buy, to shop for either bargains or luxuries. In our culture life is defined as consumerism. From the vantage point of Italy we see the contrast clearly.

We notice Italian shoppers, who, with their companions, do a lot of looking into the shop windows or in stores, but buy little. We rarely see anyone laden with packages, a contrast to watching mall shoppers at home return to their cars to put parcels in their trunks and go back for more. The small specialty shops for women's hose or men's socks or lingerie or sweaters are not conducive to buying in quantity. Looking at prices in men's shops, Al says, "It's more expensive, so people buy less." I realize how much of our shopping back home is extraneous to what we actually need and how our whole system tends to encourage us to buy more with the "pay less for more" approach. No wonder our closets get cluttered and our houses get bigger.

Discount shopping malls, a popular destination in many parts of the U.S., may exist in Italy, but are hard to imagine. We have never seen one. The bargain shopper in Italy, as in other parts of Europe, is more likely to go to an outdoor Saturday flea market. Even the department stores that we have walked into seem smaller, their merchandizing approach less overwhelming. Displays of expensive designer clothes in the sophisticated fashion centers in Rome and Milan are an exception, but that's not the world of the everyday shopper. And even for designer shoppers, I suspect that less is more, that fewer purchases of long lasting value are the norm.

Grocery stores are either individual shops for meat, poultry, fish, produce, cheese or cheese, pastas, or larger supermarkets. Even these more inclusive grocery stores are small by American standards. You can buy whatever you need but less packaged food, fewer brands and less variation on basics make shopping a simpler process. For me it's so much easier to shop in a smaller store. I was reminded of Italy and encouraged that sensible downsizing could prevail at home, when a grocery chain opened their new downtown store with the stated intention of staying smaller. Even though supermarkets have a variety of ethnicities other than Italian to provide for in our multicultural cities, I noticed only one brand of salsa and one brand of tomato sauce.

So much of America's often maligned materialism, our need to buy bigger cars and houses, to go to malls, the exchange of money that keeps our economy moving, seems to fill a gap. We buy bigger television screens and entertainment centers because we don't have the cultural entertainment of walking in the town piazza. We "shop till we drop" because we aren't quite sure what to do with our time or resources. We work overtime, creating more to buy, and work more to pay for it, because our culture does not have the old roots of enjoyment of life. While employment may benefit and companies profit, it sometimes seems as though we gain the world and lose our souls. Walking the piazzas and sitting on the steps near a fountain helps Al and me see another way of living, one where community is felt by being out with others and a bonding exists even with those who are strangers. It's a way of living we try to emulate when we get home. Sometimes we succeed, spending time in the local coffee shop reading the paper, looking for small family-owned one-of-a-kind restaurants, buying only what we need. But Italian style simplicity is hard to maintain in a culture like ours.

A friend who spent Christmas in Rome commented on the lack of decorations. "Very minimal," she says. "But they don't need it."

"But we do," I say, ironically.

We have to fill the gap because we don't have the basics of custom, beauty and community built predictably into a vast and varied culture.

***

Simplicity in Italy does not preclude creativity. But honoring the beauty and the creativity of the task at hand is the norm, not mass production. When making simple purchases, customers don't seem to get as impatient. We may spend twenty minutes choosing two pairs of decorative socks from a saleswoman in a small shop who seems happy to show us as many colors and patterns as we want. It is just as important to the bakery clerk to help me decide what combination of six cookies I want to try in a bake shop as if I were buying large boxes. The customer feels as if his wishes are being honored, that there is a fair exchange of goods and services. We love the bakeries more than the candy shops and often go in to buy a half dozen or so small cookies of several kinds to snack on in the late afternoon, especially if we're still walking the streets and not ready to sit down anywhere and relax. These simple sweets seem to be just right, tasty but not heavy or overfilling. One large-size bakery cookie at home would be equal to four of these small ones, but I get less sugar and more good taste somehow.

We see individuals coming out of bake shops on Sundays carrying the flat boxed cakes or torta wrapped in colorful layers of thin paper fresh for a family meal rather than frozen or name brand desserts. The goal is not to bring something new to a family meal but to bring the familiar. The colorful ties and paper wrapping, while familiar, also convey a sense of celebration.

Special delicacies like baci, an Italian chocolate kiss with hazel nuts inside, are very good. I love looking in the shop windows near Easter time with the colorful Easter animals and bright layers of paper as people buy presents for the holidays. Buying even a simple candy box will involve packaging with care and creativity using layers of paper in sacks tied with bows like in a nice gift shop at home.

Packaging may be decorative for special occasions but for basic take out it is simple, no Styrofoam or boxes. In fact, most packaging is simple and minimal and practical everywhere. When I read that Americans may recycle more than Europeans, I figured it must be because we consume so much more paper and aluminum and cardboard.

***

Americans tourists get fooled when they order coffee in Italy. Unless they are staying in a large tourist-oriented hotel where American coffee is listed on the menu along with tea for British visitors, Italians don't have the refillable cup of mild coffee that Americans take for granted. In a local cafe or restaurant, ordering coffee or "caffe" results in a strong but delicious shot of espresso. Making good espresso is a matter of national honor and cafes make it well out of necessity. If we want coffee with milk, we can ask for a latte, but our favorite morning drink is "uno cappuccino, por favore," one cappuccino, please, a shot of espresso with frothy milk. Italian cappuccino comes in a small, real ceramic cup with a small saucer, and there are no other sizes. Decaffeinated isn't usually an option but the amount of caffeine will probably be easier to manage than in regular coffee at home. Back home it's still an overwhelming surprise to order a cappuccino in a restaurant and get three times the Italian amount in a large cup.

A morning cafe or cappuccino is part of a small meal to tide us over until the serious lunch meal. We quickly got into the habit of having a cappuccino and roll in the morning and, following Italian custom, we skip milk in our coffee later in the day. We order expresso after dinner. The espresso never seems to have that over-strong bitter taste which I find at home, and even though decaf is usually not an option, the Italian caffe doesn't usually keep me awake.

Generally in the small cafes, the rules are consistent: If you drink your coffee standing at the bar, like the Italians do, it will cost less than if you sit down at one of the small tables. The custom is that if you want to be served and want to sit around for awhile the coffee costs more. We have learned to follow Italian traditions, to drink our morning cappuccino standing at the bar, eating a croissant or sweet-roll along with it. Later in the day if we want to sit outside and enjoy the passersby, we pick a different type of cafe. We know we may have to wait for service, and we know we will pay to sit and be served, even if all we have is coffee or a drink, but now that we understand the rules, it's fine. We know what we are paying for.

CHAPTER TWENTY

Full Circle: All Roads Lead to Rome

Walking along the Tiber and across the bridges, climbing the Spanish Steps, watching sunlight fade behind the dome of St. Peter's, Rome is experienced in glimpses and moments. Seeing it works best in fragments, like the fragments of ancient sculpture that lie around in unlikely places. From views of the ancient Forum as we stroll along the Via Imperiale to the morning energy of sound and chatter as meat and fish shops open and women choose produce in the fresh markets, Rome is simply too many experiences to define or contain.

With its mazes of alleyways breaking suddenly onto unfamiliar piazzas, Rome was at first confusing and overwhelming. Over the years, it has become familiar enough for us to relax in and to enjoy. Our first planned stays in Rome were on arrival; now it has become a ritual to end up there, a tradition to spend our last three days in Rome before we fly home. We unite in our familiarity with the city, once difficult, still challenging, but always full of energy and excitement.

Our return trips to Rome during these years have paralleled our coming to a comfortable place in this stage of our relationship. We circle back to this city finding it a touchstone and place for centering ourselves as we get ready to return home to our lives. Rome has eras that define its identity and help us to manage its enormity. Sightseeing in Rome is like looking through years of photographs and souvenirs: one is in awe of how much there is to take in. Just as our own lives include our collective history, our youth, our single years, our years of work and child rearing, Rome's sights reflect and contain the past.

But Rome isn't only about the past. Seeing only the old sights in Rome would mean missing the fountains and piazzas and parks and most of all the people.

I love Rome. Life goes on with or without us as it has for hundreds and hundreds of years. Rome is the heart of Italy. We have come to love Rome's wild side, its unpredictability and how what seems chaotic and illogical somehow works.

***

When we first went to Rome, I had moments of deja vu. Traveling in my twenties, lucky enough as a teacher to have a summer off to travel with a friend, I cherished the sense of independence and pleasure of being in foreign places at a time when European travel was more of an adventure than it seems now. I loved Rome the best and would have been disappointed if Al didn't like it since it was always the city that called to my soul. I liked the sun and the energy and the welcoming acceptance that even we, as two single unsophisticated young women felt. Even back then I liked watching children playing in a park or sitting by a fountain and just watching the people. But I also remembered the sadness and longing of being in such a romantic setting without anyone to share it with. Although I'm older and less able to look the part of the romantic heroine in Rome, I'm much happier being there with Al.

Like the ancients who said that all roads led to Rome, we seem to feel the most connection to this "eternal city." It's hard to imagine going back to Italy without spending at least a couple of days in Rome. We walk through the narrow streets, get lost, resurface in a familiar area, and enjoy just being part of the intensity of this ancient as well as modern place. We see the traffic circle from the Via Vittorio Emanuele through the Piazza Venezia past the white monument called the wedding cake, because of its layered design, which dominates the circling traffic, and feel that we are in the center not only of Rome but of a conflux of energies. We have a sense of its variety and focus on sections rather than trying to comprehend the whole.

We're never bored in Rome. We never run out of things to do there and wonder if we ever could. We can always find an important museum or church or archeological site or boulevard that we haven't seen or that we want to go back to.

I remember waking up on one Sunday morning to the sound of church bells from several churches all competing in joyful celebration of the Sunday sunshine. The windows were open and the shutters wide, as we dozed in the jet-lagged morning with the sun streaming in and the bells ringing. I realized then that Rome was not ultimately about the historical sights and famous churches; it was about being immersed in experience, moments so full of life that they deserved to be remembered always, memories that, like William Wordsworth said in his poem "Daffodils," could be recalled in "the bliss of solitude," and fill our hearts with pleasure. We all have these experiences when our senses are so alive that we want to preserve them in their entirety, but I seem to have more in Rome.

At first, Al responded better to modern Rome than I did. He reacted positively to the intensity of the horn-honking traffic, the interconnecting and weaving streets piled on streets, the confusion, while I felt a bit overwhelmed by it. It appealed to his sense of a need for action and purpose. I grew to like it as I became more comfortable and it felt more familiar, but Al liked it right away. It may be that Rome is a masculine city today as well as in its empirical past and conveys more of that energy even now.

We have less ego here. Our lives are reduced in scale and there is a sense of relief as we realize we don't need to feel important, that we can enjoy our days with anonymity. It's a relief to be nobody, just another pedestrian on the streets. Al and I can enjoy this feeling more because we have each other for company, basic confirmation and validation of our identities, and comfort.

***

Rome fascinated us from that first Sunday afternoon, when we visited Kirsti, when we had our three-hour tour, the afternoon before we left Italy to return home. We got lost. We walked the entire way up the hill of the Palatine looking in to the Forum, certain that we would find an entrance, a back way into the ruins of the ancient city, but found only fences and walls and had to retrace our steps. Even though we missed getting into the Coliseum, which closed early on Sunday, and waited for two hours for a bus that never came, we still liked it.

Whenever we burst onto a large piazza dominated by three or four imposing stone facades of palazzos or churches, we feel small and insignificant beside the grandeur and endurance of these old buildings. But we like putting our lives into perspective against the magnitude and scope of both present day Rome and its history. As in any walking city, it's exhilarating to lose our individual identities in its flow, to experience Roman culture by keeping our eyes open and blending into the moving energy of the city. We have our own agendas but know that they have no real importance in the scale of things here. Our size is reduced, our lives and our goals, our role in society, our competitive need to feel important and to function significantly as we do at home is diminished.

***

Our second arrival into Rome was by train into Termini Station from the airport. If we had years to search, we could probably not reproduce the circling and turning back and twisting our little taxi took. Diving into tiny streets and circling in opposite directions, we suddenly ended up on the small walkway in front of our multi-story hotel near the Campo di Fiori. Our room was plain and simple, relatively spacious by standards of the old city, with a bare tile floor, a tiny TV, old style dial phone, and a private but small bathroom with shower. We opened the wooden frames inward and the glass casement windows outwards and leaned forward to look down at the small piazza below. On the miniscule plaza small parked cars were jammed together with barely inches between them, occasionally blocking access for other drivers, which lead to energetic verbal confrontations in the street below our window. The size of many backyard patios at home, the piazza was full of pedestrian life and the bustle of activity.

We love staying there. Our hotel is simple and practical, not particularly romantic or glamorous, but the location is perfect and we have become regulars. The location near the market where we buy our morning fruit, and the small shops for cheese, bread and wine and the cafe down the block where we drink our morning cappuccino give us a sense of having a neighborhood home in Rome. Year-by-year, we have come to recognize not only the hotel personnel, but the shopkeepers of the neighborhood. Away from the major tourist sights and congestion, we can easily walk to most of them on both sides of the river.

In the Campo di Fiori or "Field of Flowers," Roman shoppers buy fresh fish, fruits and vegetables for their daily meals in an outdoor market everyday but Sunday. By eight o'clock in the morning, small trucks and carts have brought market goods into the square and, while a few tables sell souvenirs, most of it is food and kitchen stuff for local shoppers. By late afternoon, when we come back to our hotel, the stones of the Campo are littered with fallen lettuce leaves and onion skins, the market stands are gone, and hoses are washing away the day's debris. Around the Campo are trendy clothing shops, bakeries, pesce or fish and carne or meat shops, the whole of Roman experience. I tell Al I could spend a large part of every day in the area of the Campo di Fiori and be entertained. At night and on Sundays, in good weather, the cafes and restaurants along the sides of the open space set up tables on the stones in front of their doorways. Not as imposing as the larger piazzas and, with its cafes less dominated by tourists, the Campo is defined by the facades of the old buildings which surround it, the perfect mix of intimacy and grandeur.

***

Getting around Rome is one place where I have learned to enjoy taking a back seat and giving up control. I'm sure I could find my way back home if we got separated but it wouldn't be easy and there would be lots of backtracking. Guidebook directions are hard to follow since so many of the streets are narrow, and pedestrian-only walkways through old medieval neighborhoods often provide a link between two piazzas. Usually I do better following landmarks, depending on familiarity of sights, but it's harder to recognize things in Rome. So many old buildings and churches and alleyways look alike. The ephemeral nature of Roman life creates an added dilemma. Shops that are open and seem an easy landmark on a busy street during the day are closed at midday. Boutiques, meat and wine shops, with the metal awnings pulled down over the shop windows and locked to cover the display cases during off hours, look like ordinary buildings rather than remembered landmarks. Pedestrian traffic is absent in what was a busy area earlier. I have learned to rely on Al to get us around. The maps are often confusing, and he is better at reading their fine lines.

Al remarked one year, "I can't believe how hard it used to be to find our way out of here," referring to the tiny streets from the Campo di Fiori to the Trevi Fountain and back. Even now it usually takes me two or three tries to remember which side street leads to our regular pizzeria, or to walk out of the Campo past the flower shops if we are headed for the Forum and to turn the other way if we are going across the river to Trastevere.

Ruins are everywhere, giving Rome an other-worldly atmosphere in the midst of modernity. Walking on a busy street with other purposeful pedestrians alongside typical urban traffic, we look up and see part of an ancient temple or down into an area of excavation. Ancient Rome is integrated with the life of the city. A European engineer friend of Al's once told us how hard it is to build subways or other underground structures in Rome because of the constant discovery of more antiquities to excavate or preserve.

One time as we set out from the Campo, we walked down a busy street, crossed in front of the cars, and strolled past the bus stop and stores, when we saw an excavation of a temple site with several Roman columns, a partial pedestal or roof, and scattered pieces of fallen columns. They were set off with a small fence to protect pedestrians from the drop into the excavation. The area was just part of the city scene, like a few trees and benches would be back home. A multitude of cats slept on and under and around the ancient stones and columns, unimpressed with antiquity, but enjoying the protection of the setting of what is called the "cat temple." Cars move constantly around the busy square and, other than visitors such as ourselves, the pedestrians pay no attention to the old structures that are just part of the fabric of the city. Al and I stopped and studied the scene, playing the game of finding all the hidden sleeping places of the multitude of sundry-colored cats on top of, behind and under the ancient ruins.

Now we use the "cat temple" as a valuable landmark so that we know we are on the right street. In more recent trips to Rome, we noticed that an animal protection group now uses the area to raise money and awareness about abandoned cats. They feed the animals and supervise their healthcare needs, creating an official cat habitat out of the ancient site.

One of the best parts of Rome is the ancientness of it and the integration of the old, which is no longer functional, into the modern. Continuing our walk, we noticed ancient Roman columns built into newer stucco buildings, but with the ancient columns still standing and exposed within the new materials. We stopped while Al pointed out old columns built into new buildings as a way of preserving the old building and the integrity of the ruins. They were left exposed in the stucco or concrete, and the ancient columns provided decorative support for the new buildings. "Now that's really recycling," he said.

Al tells people back home about old Rome's use of old structures as foundations of new ones or pieces of old structures within the new. Ancient structures that were often destroyed by invasions or simply abandoned or neglected were replaced by new ones built on top of their foundations. Some ancient sites are only ruins because stones were taken from it to build elsewhere. Reusing old materials, building on top of old foundations and incorporating columns and facades into new design symbolizes how new eras built on the old without destroying it. But it's all jumbled together.

***

Since we were shut out of the Coliseum on our quick three hour visit, we made it a priority on our next visit. Al had studied the map so the next morning we walked from the Campo along the Via Vittorio Emanuele around the wedding cake structure and up the long boulevard near the Forum to the famous landmark featured on so many postcards and travel posters of Rome.

Once inside, we climbed up the stairs of the grass covered ruins and sat on the hard stone seats thinking of Hollywood renditions of gladiator fights, and slightly disappointed that the ruins, which seemed a jumble of large rocks in random formation amid unkempt patches of grass, were not "fixed-up" a little more. Still, consistent with the magic of Rome, we could imagine lions being raised up by elevator from their cages below to meet the gladiators in the arena and other contestants hoping for a "thumbs-up" from the emperors, all for the entertainment of the crowd. Even in a time before the movie *Gladiator* was produced, it was not hard to picture the open-air stadium full of people, probably drinking wine and making plenty of noise, raucously enjoying the weather and the conflicts and the camaraderie, much like the bleacher seats at an outdoor football stadium. Reading that in spite of traditional belief, Christians were not executed or fed to the lions, I was still struck by the focus on violence as entertainment that the arena conveyed. What had been built as a place for games had deteriorated into a raucous entertainment for the crowds. We decided that we could see enough from our vantage point and decided not to take a guided tour. As we started down the stairs and made the turn to head to the outside of the of the Coliseo, I read to Al about how quickly the thousands of spectators could exit as they came down from their bench seats to one of the many exit corridors. "Just like a football stadium." I concluded.

Having seen it once, neither of us have expressed a desire to go back into the Coliseum, although we appreciate its landmark quality as the most recognizable symbol of Rome. Lighted-up at night as part of the cityscape, the Coliseum is not so much about lions and gladiators as a recognizable image, a focus for modern life, a sign that in this city, ruins can be a convenient focal point for community events. It's the starting point of the Rome Marathon, for example.

Leaving the Coliseum we walked down the long busy boulevard past snack stands with fresh fruit, bottled water and soda, racks of tee shirts and tables covered with miniature plastic replicas of Roman and Italian icons, the Coliseum, the Pieta, Romulus and Remus and Michelangelo's *David*. I stopped and picked up several of the smaller ones, "Maybe I'll get one of these for a souvenir," I said. Al frowned at my suggestion. "Junk," he said, as he strolled on.

Returning from the Coliseum, we revisited the Pantheon, the temple built to honor all the gods. Later, it was consecrated and maintained as a Christian church, so not destroyed as pagan temples often were. Fascinated with the merging of pagan and Christian interlocking traditions, I told Al, "See, the church saved some good things."

"Look, the street used to be lower," he said, gesturing down at the excavation of the original foundation well below us. Al was interested in the structural aspect, the columns in the new structures, the excavation around the foundation on the side street of the Pantheon where the ground had settled and the city had itself risen level by level so that the street where we walked was several feet above the original foundation and entrance. What had originally been built above the city level was now lower. The city had risen to its level.

Inside the Pantheon, I was awed by the sacred feeling of its artistry and design, For centuries it was the largest dome in the world with an open circle of light in the center shining in and changing the light and shadow within the huge circumference of the dome. "It's like the Rothko Chapel," I tell Al, thinking of the ecumenical chapel with its natural outdoor light, clouds and sunshine shifting and changing the look and feel of the interior in the same way, although on a smaller scale. Obviously it was not a rectangular, cross- shaped basilica as many early Christian churches, but rather the circular style of earlier temples, which were homes to the gods. I thought about the symbolism of the circle, somehow more contemporary and inclusive, the dome suggesting the natural dome of the sky. If the Coliseum with its focus on conflict and machismo represented the more aggressive and exhibitionist side of Rome's machismo, the Pantheon with its inclusiveness, its rounded dome, circular interior space and overall more gentle and comforting sense, suggested to me a softer feminine balance. I began to see subtle evidence of the more feminine side of Rome.

We appreciate the Pantheon the more often we see it. Even from the outside, its columns and dome face a piazza which slopes down to the building and seems smaller and more people-friendly. Young idlers sit on the central fountain and the few cafes and restaurants feel connected to the whole in the smaller space. The Pantheon doesn't dominate as much as anchor us and its piazza feels like a kinder, gentler side of Rome. Maybe it's the dome that softens the entire space or maybe it's the smallness of the piazza and the fact that it was a universal pagan temple turned into a Christian one, a striking accommodation between old and new traditions that perhaps history could have used more of. Several of Rome's ancient sites hint, perhaps unconsciously, of a recognition of the feminine dynamic to balance the masculine.

The Pantheon has become one of our regular stops along the walk to and from our hotel path. The perfect design and soothing space combine with our sense of privilege to be able to see it more or less regularly. We appreciate the ambiance of the scene in the piazza as well as the grandness of the building itself. This piazza, with a large sculptured fountain nestled near the columned facade of the Pantheon itself, a few feet away, is one of Rome's more intimate spaces. Cafes and expensive hotels and even a McDonald's border the square while pedestrians stroll across it and young people sit on the fountain wall. One time we stopped for a cappuccino at an outdoor table and looked down the slope of the piazza to the Pantheon. Across the single rope defining the area of each cafe and next to us, we even noticed Italians among those who sat at the tables at McDonald's. In postcard shots, the famous columned facade and dome behind seems to stand at a distance. When we stopped at the far corner to take our personal photographic versions of the famous postcard scene, we realized that a photographer must use every inch of distance to get the full facade in the lens.

***

The third time we came to Rome, the Roman Forum was our first stop. Still experiencing a jet lag surge of energy, we dropped off our luggage at the hotel and found our way to the entrance of the Forum on the opposite side of the ancient site from the Coliseum. Even though we had crossed the Atlantic and much of Europe that day, it was early enough for us to buy tickets and still have plenty of time before closing, which, in a practical Italian logic, was an hour before sundown. We rented headsets with recordings, at that time a relatively new addition to museum tours, tuned into the English translation, and wandered happily through the ancient ruins for a couple of hours engrossed in the events that had taken place in this small but famous area. As Al and I paused at the recommended stops in the Forum, we were together, but also separate in our respective worlds of audio commentary. We were purposeful and focused but free of having to make decisions or walk too far. The afternoon was sunny and mild, the sky blue, and the experience of being outside a perfect beginning to that year's Roman holiday.

Ruins require a commentary of some kind; otherwise among old stones and structures, we have trouble knowing what we are looking at. But with information from our headsets, we could imagine events of the past as we stood near what was left of the temples, palaces and gathering places for the Roman Empire. The palace of the emperor was on the hill above and the temples were part of the republic. The close relationship between the emperors and the gods, the connection of the emperor to divinity, is evident in the presence of temples near the palace. The enormous columns were what was left of the Temple to Saturn. I noticed how the temple to the male gods along with the palace and government empirical buildings dominated the scene, unlike in some other cultures where goddesses such as Athena in Athens had the places of honor to protect the city. We saw the Roman Curia, the gathering place for the Roman senators, near the same temples, connecting the gods and the rulers.

But there were women here, too. A temple to Minerva, the Roman name for the goddess of wisdom (known as Athena in Greece), was among the important positions. The traditional story from the Greeks was that Athena sprang from the head of Zeus (or Jupiter), her father, fully armed, an empowered figure from the start. I also pointed out to Al the importance of the female presence in this center of power and commerce as we walked along the Via Sacre and into the home and ruins of the school where the Vestal Virgins, whose job it was to keep the fires of the heart of the city alive, lived. Remembering stories of the Vestal Virgins from junior high school Latin, I wanted to know more about them.

Although many structures of the Romans are impressive even by today's standards, it's striking how much smaller the "streets of Rome" were in the days of the Empire. As we walked along the Road of Triumphant entry for the great Caesar, listening to the tape-recorded reenactment with sounds of animals and people, the ruins seemed out of scale for such momentous events, especially compared with the four-lane wide boulevard for cars nearby. We picture a modern city, but the Rome where Caesar was assassinated was a pretty small place. We project our own time into the past. I said to Al, "It seems so small." He nodded, as we walked back down the narrow road that was used by the returning Caesar and where processions of the conquered slaves from other regions were paraded through the streets. When we got to the place where Mark Antony gave the famous eulogy over Caesar's dead body and stirred the crowds to revenge, I recited for Al a little of the speech from Shakespeare's version of Mark Antony's eulogy of Julius Caesar, "Friends, Romans and Countrymen, lend me your ears" "Yeah, yeah, yeah," he responded, unimpressed, and continued on with the tape. Although as a high school English teacher, I knew about the violent aftermath of Caesar's death and Mark Antony's speech, I was nevertheless awed by being in the real place where the events of the drama had occurred.

It felt good to have a structured activity that afternoon, to walk through the small area of the old Forum, to wind down gradually, rather than come to a sudden halt after the business of work and the rush of leaving home. We were outside, breathing fresh air, moving, but not too taxingly, and focused enough on our headsets and scenes to keep us alert. It was sunny, but not hot, and in our jet-lagged state everything was intensified.

When we finished, we went back to our hotel to take a nap, the sound sleep that comes with jet lag exhaustion, but Al, who with typical discipline had set his alarm, prevailed against my resistance, to get us both up and out the door to wander into the Campo di Fiori for dinner. "That way we'll be on the right schedule," he insisted.

I remember in detail the dinner we had that first night. Even though we were in our most casual clothes, we were welcomed warmly into the ristorante at the end of the Campo. The reds and purples and greens and tans of the displayed vegetable antipasti of marinated mushrooms and asparagus and eggplant and olives and red peppers was our first course and it was delicious. Then we had a homemade fettuccine pasta and some house red wine. For Rome it was fairly cold outside, making us appreciate the warmth of food and light and people. Al had worked intensely on business proposals right up until the day we had left and had gotten some good news from a pay phone call about the results. I remember this as a special first day.

***

With the luxury of more time and visits, we have branched out to lesser known sights. Less visited attractions are a good way to offset the intensity of the inner city of Rome, especially for a good first day transition. In these quiet places we feel as if Rome is more real and more ours.

When we arrived the first day of another trip, we walked across the Tiber River and up into the hills of the Janiculum area, walking quietly through a botanical garden. We looked back at the domes of the city, echoing the design of Saint Peter's; it was not the normal view of the city, but as we walked as Roman citizens rather than tourists, we appreciated looking out at vegetation displays from all the habitats of the world. We ended in a well-labeled herb garden, the first we had ever visited. I had just discovered some of the health aspects of herbs and so had more respect for medicinal properties of these plants. It was fun to see them in their natural state rather than in a plastic bottle and I wondered what part of the plant was useful. Gently touching a stinging nettle plant, I pulled back in surprise. "It really stung me," I told Al. He thought I was kidding until later when I showed him the red marks on my hand.

***

It's hard to find a comparison to a city in the United States. Even in New York, the boulevards and streets are listed systemically on the map, and once you know where you are, you can logically move ahead. New York may be bigger, but Rome is more confusing. We feel lost in a maze, although we know that we will eventually find our way, and we have never felt threatened or unsafe.

We follow medieval alleyways through a mass of buildings that seem to come to blind ends but suddenly jog right or left or open into a piazza. Sometimes we know where we are going and actually have a familiar path to follow, but other times we are regrouping, trying to get unlost and often we are exhausted. Usually our side streets and perambulations are revealing and we see things we wouldn't have otherwise.

Although we go back to the same places in Rome, we never seem to be in familiar territory. There are so many streets and cut through walkways for pedestrians only, alleys that look like dead ends but aren't, that only seldom do we find ourselves on totally familiar ground. Reading a map is hard. Names of streets, if they exist at all, are often carved into the stones at corners of buildings, are engraved and hard to read. Sometimes they are not there at all or have been rubbed to barely readable. A street may be only several yards long, its name may change from one side of a piazza to the other. A piazza can be quite large, like a block or a street intersection, or as small as our living room at home. Sometimes it has a fountain or statue to identify it and sometimes it is just a small intersection of several footways through the old medieval buildings and streets. We have circled several times past a familiar area, missing the one narrow alley that would take us between buildings and through to the big piazza we are looking for. It seems like a map would be worthless but without the maps and Al's ability to read them, we probably would never find our way back to home base.

***

A lot of what happens to us in Rome involves getting lost. But by getting lost and wandering in this way on our own, we see real neighborhoods and views that others don't see. One night we got lost three blocks from our hotel and walked in circles for an hour in thunder, lightning and rain to finally discover that we had made one wrong turn, the first one. Earlier we had walked a short way along the street from our hotel and then up a small alley beside our hotel to the Ristorante Teatro di Pompeo built into part of the foundation of Pompey's Theater from ancient Rome. Inside I was excited when I realized the name represented a reality, that the cave-like room and old wall near our table was part of the original circular theater. I told Al, "This is where Shakespeare said the conspirators to assassinate

Caesar met, on the steps of Pompey's Theater. I didn't know it was a real place."

I enjoyed a chance to share my knowledge of those events of the past with Al. We had a long leisurely dinner and then, mellow with good food and wine, we stepped outside to take the short walk home. The lightning and thunder provided another parallel to the night before Caesar's death when, according to Shakespeare and Plutarch before him, fiery storms foreshadowed the emperor's end. I liked letting my imagination replay scenes of ancient conspirators slipping through these narrows streets during the wild storm. Both Plutarch and Shakespeare used the weather as background for the drama of the conspiracy to assassinate Caesar.

At the end of the short alley, we turned the wrong way, and when we saw nothing familiar, we decided to "just keep on and go around the block" and ended up circling and zagging down streets and alleys passing the same part of the back of the circular theater again and again. We were circling around the walls of the theater from the outside unable to find a side street that would take us back to our hotel on the other side. We randomly chose a small side street of the Campo area going the other way, trying to make a big enough circle to get back, but just got more turned around. Now whenever we wander past that curving wall and see the cafe with the umbrellas, we remember the night we got lost right in our own neighborhood.

I'm still not sure how we were lost for so long in just a few blocks, but that tended to happen to us in Rome. Another time we tried to follow a route that on the map looked like a connection between streets, but kept ending in blind alleys or back in the piazza outside of the old Roman synagogue where we had started. It was a Saturday, the Sabbath evening, and well-dressed people were gathering in the early evening for services. Al and I, obviously not dressed for temple in our blue jeans and jackets, kept circling past. We got suspicious looks from the uniformed young policemen carrying small automatic weapons, who we figured were in the area for security reasons. Al had read that there had been some type of threat of anti-Semitic activities in Rome and commented, "They probably think we're a security risk." We certainly did look out of place circling the synagogue in this non-touristy area. We finally figured out that the streets, which appeared to intersect on the map, were on different levels and one actually went over the other and found a different route. But without getting lost we wouldn't have observed the Sabbath gathering. We would have only seen the Christian side of Rome. Now the area near the synagogue and old ghetto area is on one of our regular walking routes in Rome. It's hard to imagine now how lost we used to get lost in that area.

Pounding the stone pavements in those early years was often the core experience of our time in Rome. Once it took us two hours to find our way back through the medieval streets of an old neighborhood that we knew was near our hotel. We would recognize a landmark, feel like we were back in the neighborhood of our hotel and then lose the thread into the darker side streets again. We passed the same bakeries and butcher shops and outdoor displays of antiques, recognizing them as signs that we had not made progress but had somehow circled back yet again. As we pounded the pavement in late afternoon, circling and re-circling through the old streets, we never seemed to end up where we needed to be but rather back where we had started.

Trying to make Al feel less frustrated, I told him about the book I had read by an Englishman who lived in Rome, and, one day after several hours of being unable to follow his map to an address that he knew was close by, gave up, parked his car, and got into a taxi which took him through an impossible maze of narrow alleyways, old city walls, and tiny piazzas in less than two minutes. He had been very close but just couldn't get there on his own. He determined that driving in Rome should be left to the Romans.

"We're not the only ones who can't find our way around here," I said.

"It's even worse than Boston," Al grumbled, thinking of the lack of logical layout of another old city.

Once, as we worked our way through a medieval neighborhood that we by then at least partly understood, we found ourselves diverted onto a sidewalk path that doubled back over a temporary bridge-like walkway to get over and around yet another excavation of ancient ruins. Not sure where we would end up, we followed the detour through a tightly packed jumble of medieval streets and buildings and stumbled upon a small open area where four boys were playing an energetic game of soccer in a space the size of many suburban patios. We watched for a while, enjoying the unexpected entertainment. These were the moments when getting lost, at least for awhile, was worth the extra time. Later, we came to see soccer as a constant presence, playable almost anywhere, as we saw boys playing in neighborhood piazzas or in front of ruins, in streets and alleys all over Italy. Far too small to be soccer fields, these spaces provided background for intense games nevertheless.

But once the strangeness and unfamiliarity of the old Roman neighborhoods has subsided, one of us will look around saying, "We've been here before."

Finally Al said during one trip, as we walked through a once unfamiliar tangle of streets to get to the river, "I can't believe we used to get lost, walking through here."

***

Our familiarity and comfort level has given us a Rome routine. In the mornings we get up by 8:00 a.m., like the Romans, but with my complaining, "We're on vacation. We should sleep in a little." But Al, who at home is more likely to sleep in on a weekend than I am, is not willing to "waste the day," as he says. Usually we decide the day before what we will do the next morning, choosing a significant sight, excursion, or museum, something to give us a plan and to get the most from the early part of the day when we are energetic.

We first stop in the market in the Campo di Fiori for strawberries, a couple of bananas and an orange, joining the Romans shopping for fresh produce. We wander up and down the rows of stands of fresh fruit, vegetables and herbs. Sometimes a whole stand is devoted to different kinds of mushrooms or nuts and candies. The colorful awnings give weather protection to a vegetable market displaying fresh spinach, lettuces, garlic, basil and an Italian version of broccoli, a leafier variety. We see why restaurant food tastes so good, since dishes are based on the season and the ingredients are so fresh.

We stop for cappuccino at the little shop next to our hotel, which we drink standing at the counter, and then stroll on past the small fish shop's window displays of fresh squid, mussels and fish filets, the meat shop with beef and pork sold separately from the poultry and the fresh pasta shop, all of which are open by 8:00 a.m. and busy soon after. Finally, we wind our way from our neighborhood to the main streets headed for the bus or following the walking route that we'll take to get to the destination of the day.

Al stops occasionally to check his map as we go. We move along purposely and with a goal, but absorbing things along the way. It is enough to have a destination. Just walking in the cool morning, the clear quality of sunlight, the occasional cry of a gull, reminds us that the Mediterranean Sea coast is not far away, even as we cross busy streets and take in the noise and exhaust of Fiats and taxis and motorbikes bustling past us. We walk along sidewalks, not crowded enough for us to feel jostled but always with pedestrians going in both directions, women in black coats and practical shoes carrying string-style bags for their morning shopping, businessmen in suits, contractors cleaning buildings or rehabbing facades. The energy of their presence adds to the scene. We step over streamlets of water sloshed onto stone walkways, which have been cleaned in the early hours. Occasionally, someone suddenly appears from or disappears into one of the ten foot high doors that open directly from the sidewalks into apartments, pulling on the handle in the mouth of a lion that decorates so many of the doorways.

Romans follow their own timetable, too. Stores open early, shops at 8:00 or 9:00 a.m. But you could probably wave money at a shopkeeper closing his shutters at noon and it wouldn't stop him from closing. "Chiuso chiuso," he'll say. Al and I often head for a long lunch, Roman-style, in a small restaurant if it's cool, or at an outdoor spot on one of the piazzas. Sometimes we eat picnic-style near one of the fountains and just pass the time for a while, joining the Romans.

After a focused excursion in the morning, and after lunch, we usually just follow our inclinations in the afternoons. We don't stop or go back to the hotel. Our sightseeing stops tend to be briefer, less intense, a search for a particular painting in an out of the way church or an odd ancient temple. We let ourselves be less focused, sometimes making a park or fountain our destination. Sometimes Al suggests that we take a bus ride, which is another way to keep moving in a relaxed way as long as the buses aren't crowded.

We both enjoy the quietness in Rome as much as the bustle. The intensity of the center, the energy, the noisy traffic, sometimes make me think of Rome as roaring, with the motorcycle engines and cars and quick pace. But oasis of quiet exist in the city. Like the Romans, we enjoy a walk through the Borghese Park above the city or sitting on a bench in other small green spaces. Sometimes we go out of town on an excursion.

We have gotten better at blending into the Roman timetable especially in the late afternoon when Romans like to be out and about to walk and stroll, visit or have coffee or an aperitif. Small groups of men or young couples seem immersed in intense conversations during this end of the day interlude and yet it is not a happy hour atmosphere by any means, but a more purposeful end of the work day period. As tourists, we used to feel out of synch at this time, needing a rest from our walking and sightseeing but not wanting to sit in a hotel room. Now we see late afternoon and early evening as a good time for gelato or coffee or aperitif, especially if we can sit outside.

With the exception of touristy areas and restaurants that cater to tourists, dinner in Rome isn't until 8:00 pm. Usually, we do go back to the hotel for a while before dinner and then, reconnected with local schedules, head out again at eight. We also manage to walk a while after the evening passeggiata either to get gelato or to a fountain or just around our adopted neighborhood.

I remember my dad years ago, instructing us philosophically, "When in Rome, do as the Romans do." We try to the extent that we can, time our lives as the Romans do, so we can enjoy ourselves more.

CHAPTER TWENTY-ONE

Church and State

While the dominance and strong side of masculine power is evident in the powerful architecture and art of Rome's churches, there is evidence of a gentler, more comforting touch, the feminine side, surviving quietly and in small ways. And against the structures of dominance and conservatism, the spirit of creativity shines through.

Christian churches are often built on top of the old Roman buildings, even on top of pagan temples. Santa Maria Sopra Minerva translated means the church of Holy Mary Over Minerva and is built over the site of a temple to Minerva, the Roman goddess of wisdom. I loved the idea of Mary, the mother of God in Christian tradition, being associated with the ancient goddess of wisdom. Seeing the church reminded me of an earlier visit to a Roman bath in England where we saw coins that had been left in the waters by Roman soldiers far from home to honor Minerva, asking for her help. Christians have often had the same attitude toward the Madonna, seeing her as a special source of compassion and help with life's problems. The common spiritual theme seems underlined by Christian churches being built over pagan temples, in places considered sacred by earlier people.

It's not surprising that the Christians would build on the pagans' sacred sites. The sites were already sanctified in some way, and at least some of the new Christians might have made an easier transition to worship at a holy place already familiar to them. And as Al has pointed out, more practically, the foundations were already laid and old materials were available for reuse. I suppose some might object, seeing the pagan connection as unholy, but I saw Santa Maria Sopra Minerva as symbolic, a blending of the old into the new, keeping what was meaningful from the past as new traditions developed. In front of the church is Bernini's small marble obelisk decorated with the elephant whose upraised trunk conveys a sense of joy and seems to celebrate life with its whimsical smile. Its wink of creative good humor seems a suitable companion to the church.

***

I had been to Saint Peter's in my twenties but sharing a tour of it with Al was a priority during our first stay in Rome. One sunny morning we took the Metro to the San Pietro stop and walked the rest of the way, following groups of tourists through the old neighborhood to Vatican City. The Metro stop was a long walk from the cathedral, but as we approached the piazza, we saw that even from tour buses, which parked as close as possible to the church, visitors had a long walk to the entrance.

At Saint Peter's, the central cathedral of Roman Catholicism, only the Pope, as Bishop of Rome, says mass at the main altar. In front of this architectural and artistic wonder designed and decorated by Michelangelo and other great artists, the Piazza San Pietro is one of those spaces that feels so right that it seems transcendent, as it carried us out of ordinary time and place. The life-sized sculptures of saints and apostles along the top of the wall, the marble of the church reflecting light in subtle ways marks this easily as the most beautiful church entrance I have seen. The warm rose-tinted beauty of the facade of the marble church, balanced by the encircling walls of the piazza always make me feel as if I am standing in the arms of beauty and benevolence. We have read that, as an artist, Michelangelo was said to embody a tangible spark of the divine in his creative genius and in this space his artistic gift is obvious. We had seen other famous cathedrals, but even Notre Dame in Paris and Westminster Abbey in London with their wonderful design somehow lack the warmth of the facade of St. Peter's.

As Al and I walked across the piazza toward the front of the church, the beauty of the facade was striking not because of its elaborateness, but because of a kind of elegant simplicity. Since then, every time we are in this space, I feel uplifted and pulled out of myself. Taking a breath, I say, "I can't believe we're really here."

It's easy to see why St. Peter's balanced and lovely design has been imitated.

"It really is wonderful, isn't it?" I said.

He nodded "yes," as we crossed the piazza and walked up the ramp and stairs to the right of the church toward the front entrance.

A visit to St. Peter's is an international experience. We saw nuns, monks and priests of many nationalities dressed in different styles and colors of religious garb and heard multiple languages from tour groups, some of which were on religious pilgrimages. As we walked around the church interior, our first stop was the favorite sculpture of Michelangelo's *Pieta*, to the right of the front entrance. The white marble depiction of Mary with the crucified body of Jesus across her lap conveys the human sadness and tragic loss of the moment as well as the perfect execution of sculpted balance of the master artist. Protective glass, added after an angry and misguided protester threw paint on the sculpture some years ago, made it harder to see the loveliness of the marble in the light and separated us from the more intimate experience of seeing the work that I remembered from my youthful visits to Rome. It reminded us of how we felt after the bombing of the Uffizi in Florence and the earthquake damage in Assisi, that works of art are both precious and vulnerable.

The inside of Saint Peter's is enormous, the nave longer than a football field. We walked up the middle of the church, stopping at the opulent gold decoration of the Chair of Peter by the artist Bernini, and admired the massive gold baroque columns supporting the canopy over the main altar. We looked up at the dome, high overhead, and felt unavoidable awe standing in such a grand and wonderful structure. Beautiful as it was, I somehow found myself overwhelmed by the magnitude and majesty of the space. I realized that although St. Peter's interior is beautiful, it doesn't feel as spiritual to me as some of the smaller more intimate churches and spaces we have visited. I reminded myself that this was a man-made work of architecture, beautiful, but in an overwhelming sort of way.

Al was more impressed with its grandness and elaborate beauty, possibly not feeling the sense of patriarchal dominance that I did. The opulence and symbolism as the center of power of the church triggered some ghosts from my own Catholic upbringing in a more traditional and intimidating time. I'm always surprised that Al's Protestant sensibilities are not more offended by the grandeur of the old Italian churches. But he doesn't worry much about such things, tending to accept what is, with less judgment and analysis than I do.

As the last part of our first self-guided tour, we went down a narrow staircase into the lower crypt that contains the tomb of Peter. His burial place was the original reason for the site of the church, along with tombs and preserved bodies of other saints and popes, including Pope John XXIII. For Americans, used to honoring memories of people through words and photographs, the earlier Christian tradition of honoring the body, and even body parts of the saints, was a cultural leap. As usual, the strangeness bothered me more than Al, who, more distant from the practice (it was not his religion after all), simply found it interesting and weird that a different era would have seen so much spiritual significance and connection through honoring the earthly remains of holy people.

Several years later we went into St. Peter's again on a Monday afternoon and found it closed to tourists except for down the side aisle where we were allowed to walk. The central nave was full of people sitting on folding chairs attending a working man's mass in honor of Saint Joseph's Day. From our vantage point on the side, we had a good, if awkward, view of the altar and the Pope himself. Our viewpoint was crowded behind several rows and to see well required someone tall enough to lean around a marble pillar. I felt like a child with her father as Al picked me up and held me a foot off the floor so that I could lean out and see Il Papa directly with no obstruction. In that moment, even the Pope represented not so much a male authority of the church but the gentleness of a relatively old man speaking to families. Seeing ordinary people filling up the grand space of St. Peter's gave it a sense of warmth and reminded me that even such a grand cathedral as St. Peter's is, after all, for people.

***

Although most often Al and I visit the historically or artistically important churches, hundreds of others, not usually visited by tourists, are still used for worship and prayer. Only the grandest or those with the most famous art are included in most tourist itineraries. As we wander through Rome, we take advantage of open doors and look inside smaller, more ordinary churches that are everywhere, just to see what's there. Some are unadorned and dark when not lighted for use, as if the designers had no money to pay an artist, but the architecture is often interesting.

Although Saint Peter's is the grandest and the most famous, it is far from being the only important church in Rome. On a later trip, Al found one of our favorites described in a guidebook as a twelfth century church built on top of a fourth century basilica, on top of a temple and school of Mithrais, a religion that overlapped the time of early Christians. Late one afternoon, we persevered against his frustration and my fatigue in finding this church of San Clemente on an unassuming street, unmarked, not grand like St. Peter's. It was late afternoon and we had walked a long way out of the way, winding our way through narrow streets in old neighborhoods, thinking we would never find this place and not sure the destination would be worth it if we did. It seemed that early Christian churches were often tucked away in dense neighborhoods in a jumble of short and narrow streets. I imagined the ordinary, unheroic people, who, before the churches were built, might have gathered in a friend's house to share their faith, not wanting to call too much attention to themselves.

On street-level, we entered San Clemente, the uppermost church building, as present-day priests were preparing for a late afternoon mass. We were tired after our long walk. When we finally got inside the church, I opted to sit down for as long as I could, reading guidebook information and resting my legs. Al sat impatiently with me in the stiff-backed pew. When the first bell rang for the mass to start, he stood up and led the way from the upstairs church through the side chapel to a downward flight of stairs and into the earlier basilica.

Architectural history meant little to us before we went to Italy, but now we know that original basilicas were rectangular

Roman buildings used as gathering places for meetings of Roman leaders and citizens. Greek and Roman temples were places for the gods themselves to live, to watch over the cities, and to be honored. Because of their size and tradition as a communal setting, the basilica, rather than the temple, became a model for the Christian churches as gathering places for their communities as the Church grew. At San Clemente, the older basilica was under the later church. It was obviously older than most of the churches we had seen, constructed of simple stone, a long narrow space with columns marking the aisles on either side of the center and a simple stone table altar at the front with a bare cross above. Symbolic mosaics were visible on the floors and decorated tombs from early Christian times were in the back. This space, now underground, since successive rebuildings of the city had raised the street level around it, conveyed an echo of the past, of early worshippers in a simple and serene place. The quiet sanctuary with its simple carvings and cross suggested a sacred atmosphere in its depth.

We walked through the old Christian basilica and then Al led the way down a narrow stairway that turned downward to a still lower level and, the most interesting excavation of all, an ancient Mithraic temple and school.

I followed Al through the marked narrow and dark passageways, across a small bridge where we heard the movement of underground water, past the tiny and low ceiling classrooms of the Mithraic school, a contrast to the larger spaces in the levels above us. Past the rooms we came to a small alcove that displayed the small but lovely white marble sculpture of the god Mithras, killing the white bull, which was, according to our guidebook, the holy sacrifice of the Mithraic religion. Although the unfamiliar subject matter seemed strange to us, the sculpture that depicted the god's relationship to the bull had a special beauty. And although Al is usually more interested in structures and details and I am more interested in stories and colorful images, we were both moved by this white marble sculpture standing quietly in the darkness of the past.

According to the pamphlet we picked up at the church, it was a Catholic priest who had discovered the underground Mithraic School and worked on its excavation.

I pointed out to Al, "See, the Catholics respected the old religions, rather than destroying them." I was struck again with the ability of a new faith to appreciate an old or different one, as in this case. The church hadn't destroyed the older religion, but instead had preserved its historical memory.

The surprise of the lovely sculpture of Mithras with the white marble almost glowing in the dark underground, was the treasure at the end of our journey. It was an adventure we embarked on, on our own, down the stairs and then down again into darker and narrower passages, which were unmarked except by the passage itself. There was an occasional rope to prevent entry into the archeological protected area. Remembering our journey into the underground, I'm reminded of the motif of the journey into the underground passages that occurs in fairy tales and myths, where the hero has to find the treasure.

***

Touring St. Peter's was one excursion but seeing the Pope himself was another. The first time Al and I went to St. Peter's Square for the Pope's traditional noon blessing was a memorable sunny Sunday morning. Al had studied the bus schedules and found the nearest stops on the map, so we were ready to brave our first bus ride in Rome. A little before 11:00, we wandered out to the street and past the cat temple to catch bus number 64 to Saint Peter's. At the stop, and in contrast to the otherwise quiet setting, we were surprised to see a larger group of tourists waiting for the same bus. The first two buses were too crowded to get on so we waited. Finally, we realized that each bus was as crowded as the last. When the third bus came, we joined the others, pushing our way up the steps, which were located in the middle of the bus (the exit is at the front). Al went first through the open doors, and I followed, crushing against the humanity ahead of us, all crushing against others in front of them, as we were pressed from behind by still more riders. Everyone remained in relatively good spirits. Laughing, but a bit anxious at being so crowded, we crammed ourselves onto the bus far enough that the door could close behind us.

It's hard to describe to anyone who hasn't ridden like this how packed these buses can be. The expression, "being packed like a can of sardines" is not nearly a strong enough metaphor, since there is no logical order or line up to the packing of a city bus in Rome. The bodies backed into a Roman bus defy scientific possibilities, as more bodies inhabit a space that appears to be full.

A young smiling woman pulled herself up the bus stairs by holding onto my waist and in the process I felt her hand touch the small shoulder purse that I had put on under my jacket and sweater. Although I thought and still think her gesture was innocent, I pulled back as much as I could. Whether she was honestly trying to get on the bus and keep from falling back off the steps or trying to find my purse, I don't know.

But pickpockets reigned freely on the Saint Peter's bus. Standing with our arms up to hold on to bars or straps, trying to keep our balance as the bus moved forward, left no room to turn the angles of our bodies even by inches, we were totally at the mercy of others. While Al had one hand on the strap overhead, an invisible pickpocket was quick enough and smart enough to take cash from his front pants pocket. In an instant the unseen thief with nimble hands took 100,000 lire (about $60). Fortunately Al's wallet was in a jacket pocket with his free hand on it and his money pouch was well hidden around his neck under his sweater. I was glad the money pouch was hidden, although even that didn't seem foolproof on the crowded number 64 bus, obviously targeted as a good tourist setup at this time on Sunday morning. These quick fingered pickpockets were professionals. And although we saw nobody suspicious, I stayed on the lookout for a Fagan-type character from the movie *Oliver* with his long fingers teaching the boys, "You've got to pick a pocket or two."

This was our only experience of having money stolen in all of our travels, but we would be more wary of riding crowded buses from then on.

In hindsight, it makes sense that the 11:00 a.m. bus to St. Peter's on a beautiful Sunday morning would be a prime target, being crowded and full of unsuspecting tourists off to see the Pope. Italians are less likely to be targeted, less likely to have the cash and cameras that tourists carry, and are therefore ready for such events. A pickpocket is much more likely to find a wrist grabbed if he or she reaches for an Italian wallet or purse and an offended Italian is more likely to let his irate feelings be known.

When we arrived at the bus stop, we were very ready to escape from the crowded bus and gladly joined the flow of people along sidewalks toward Saint Peter's Square. When we entered the broad open space, the festive atmosphere was apparent. Rather than a solemn reverence as one might expect in greeting a religious dignitary, people talked in multiple languages, laughing and chattering in the warm weather. Colorful banners, sometimes large enough to require more than one holder, represented groups from Ireland, Poland, Russia and Spain, with expressions written in their languages and with large scale artwork honoring the symbols of their nation and portraits of a saint or the Madonna or the Pope himself. Although there were plenty of people, we weren't crowded and didn't feel claustrophobic at all, a pleasure after being on the crowded bus. There was a camaraderie among the crowd even as we competed for the best positioning from which to see the Pope.

Al said we should be facing the front of the church, but I knew better. On ordinary Sundays, "Il Papa," as the Pope is called in Rome, doesn't stand on the steps in front of Saint Peter's or on its balcony to give his blessing, but at the window of his apartment residency to the right of the church. Although the only indicator was a large colorful banner that hung from one of the windows, Al, noticing that the many tour and student groups were facing to the right of the church, grudgingly went along with me as we stood in the same direction.

Just before noon, attendants opened the upper story window above the unrolled banner and set up a system of microphones. Precisely at twelve o'clock, the Pope appeared in his white cape, his right hand raised in greeting and blessing as the crowd in the piazza cheered. The Pope blessed the crowd, at first intoning a formal benediction in Italian. Then, more personally, he read the creatively decorated and lettered signs and banners of school and religious groups from other countries, responding to whatever greeting he saw written in the various languages, Il Papa spoke a greeting in each of those languages. As each group was acknowledged, they cheered, "Viva il Papa, Il Papa, Il Papa!" and applauded and whistled, and clapped their hands; the sounds rolled over the crowd and rose to where John Paul waved his raised hand and smiled in acknowledgement. Although Al and I understood none of the Russian or Polish, we felt the chemistry of warmth and shared the good fellowship in this bonding of diverse Christian groups as well as tourists and other sightseers.

Regardless of one's religious loyalties, it seemed impossible not to feel a sense of grace among the people gathered and in the man himself. His sincerity was charismatic, felt, rather than thought about. Like many spiritual moments, it was to be experienced rather than analyzed. Even Al, whose Protestant predecessors saw the Papacy as the symbol of the misguided power and abuses of the medieval and worldly Church, was enthusiastic. It was after all a moment full of human camaraderie. How different from the solemnity or reverence one might have expected. Once again, St. Peter's was about people.

Vendors in the crowd with souvenir trays balanced from ropes around their necks, sold rosaries and crucifixes and postcard pictures of the Pope. I heard an American woman ask one a question and the vender responded, "Si, Si, everything is blessed!" Reminded of the Catholic tradition of appreciating objects blessed by the Pope, I bought rosaries for a friend who had been sick; it seemed like a nice thing to do. I especially liked the rosaries made of rosewood which had a faint scent of roses. It occurred to me that both the rosaries with their focus on prayers to Mary and the scent of the rosewood suggested the gentler feminine side of things. Even in the power center of an historical patriarchy, the balance of masculine with feminine was again subtly present in Rome. They couldn't keep the feminine sensibility out.

Years before I had seen another Pope. By making arrangements ahead of time, I had seen Pius XII in a "semi-private audience" of several hundred people in a smaller chapel somewhere at the Vatican. He was carried in on a throne-like chair as people clamored all over each other to get closer to him. Traveling with a Presbyterian friend on that trip, I couldn't defend the Church against her distaste for such pomp and circumstance; I felt the same. Al's and my visit, to the reflection of a Church that for several decades had attempted to relate better to the modern world, had been a lot more fun.

But my favorite Pope story was from my mother. On her first and only trip to Rome, she and my dad saw Pope John XXIII, the leader who spoke of opening the windows of the church to let in some fresh air and of putting the old wine of faith in new bottles. In the days before his Vatican Council opened the doors of the Church to the modern world, Pope John XXIII broke with the practice of previous Popes by taking the initiative to leave the walls of Vatican City without fanfare, getting in his car to be driven to other churches without warning. Their guide had told them that Romans called him "Pope Johnny Walker." According to my mother, they had just arrived in the church called Saint Paul's Outside the Walls, so named because of its place outside the walls of Rome, to begin their tour, when suddenly lights went on around the old church and some candles were hurriedly lit. Their guide told them to wait and he would see what was going on. Before he came back, Pope John appeared, standing only a few feet away, according to my mother's version, from where they stood in the back of the church near the door. "Your dad could have reached out and touched him, "she used to say. My Protestant mother, always a little leery of the intimidation and folderol of old style Catholicism, was able to put the warmth of a human face and person on the church. It was for her a spiritual experience. Some warmth or charisma from this man who had a reputation of openness and tolerance connected with her and, in a subtle way, changed her feelings about the possibilities within Catholicism.

On one of our trips to Rome, Al and I found our way after riding first one bus, then changing to a second and finally walking a modest distance to visit the church of Saint Paul's Outside the Walls. Inside the church, we followed the usual tour, looking at the significant art and following the history. We stopped for a while to watch skilled crafts persons at work at the painstaking cleaning and restoring of some areas of marble columns. But even though the church dedicated to St. Paul had a grandeur and beauty, with its mosaics and grand architecture and history, for me it was a pilgrimage to the site of my mother's story of seeing the Pope. She had never talked much about the church itself, I recalled. To her, a church was just a building after all, while an Italian Pope was human. Her story became one of warmth and benevolence for me as well.

Sometimes, events or stories about events only have significance after the fact. And sometimes the significance of old stories and events change with new interpretations. From her trip to Rome many years before, my mother had brought me a souvenir gift: a small medallion with a golden haloed Madonna and Child. Not being the type to display religious medals or crosses, I had never worn it. Still I had kept this souvenir gift with other tokens of the past, in a small jewelry box, next to old political campaign buttons and ski lodge pins. Coming home from Italy that year, I happened to notice this medal with the lovely Madonna and Child that reminded me of the religious art Al and I had seen so much of. On the back of the medal was an image of Pope John XXIII, profiled, wearing the traditional red cloak. It's almost mystical how the lovely piece turned up at just the right time among things I owned, but never paid attention to. I began to wear it that spring and still do, especially at Christmas and Easter. Only the size of a quarter, the medal has a certain beauty, judging from the compliments and attention it always seems to get when I wear it. I wear the Madonna with the golden halo outward because it is the prettier side. But since visiting the scene of my mother's story, I have realized that there is significance in knowing the other picture is there as well. I realize that the medallion provides me with mother figure and father figure in a literal version of two sides of the coin.

Another year, Al and I waited in the line that stretched up the inclined walkway along the outside wall of Vatican City outside Saint Peter's Square to get to the entrance of the Vatican Museum. The scene reminded me of the long lines at Disney World. You move along, seeming to almost be at the entrance, but never are, as you turn and enter a new area to wait. Our goal was the famous Sistine Chapel, Michelangelo's masterpiece with scenes from the Bible painted on the walls and, most famously, the ceiling. Later, I would rent a video of *The Agony and Ecstasy* and would watch Charlton Heston play Michelangelo, paint dripping into his face, as he created his masterpiece looking up from scaffolding. I would appreciate even more the awesome accomplishment of the great painter.

The line moved slowly but consistently that sunny morning toward the entrance to the Vatican Museum. Once inside, we joined the herd of people striding hurriedly down hallways, past other chapels with elaborately painted ceilings toward the Capella Sistina. We walked from one hallway or room to another, and Al said, with each new space, "This is it. There are paintings on the ceilings here." Every time we entered a new room with art on the ceiling, we thought we had arrived, but when the crowd continued on, we realized we hadn't. We weren't at our destination until the crowd poured into the large chapel at the end of the route through the Vatican Museum.

At the end of the hallways, after our long hurried walk, we entered the chapel from the side. Because we arrived early, we got to see the Capella Sistina with a relatively small crowd. We ambled around getting our bearings and the general feeling of the space and then leaned back to study the frescoed ceiling, panel by panel. At first it was hard to focus, but gradually as we looked up, section by section, the individual frames stood out. Possibly the most memorable was the image of the Creation showing the bearded God the Father with his hand outstretched as he comes out of the clouds of heaven to create Adam. Divine energy seems to flow from finger to finger suggesting man's being made in the image and likeness of God.

Sometimes high expectations set us up for a let down. Not liking feeling part of a crowd or being rushed to a destination not of his choosing, Al felt ambivalent about our long hike through the hallways to the chapel. After we had walked around the Sistine Chapel for what he considered was enough time to evaluate it, he shrugged and announced, "I thought the paintings on the ceilings of the other rooms were just as good."

I defended the superiority of Michelangelo's vision. "They don't even come close. Remember, people said Michelangelo was a spark of divinity." I focused carefully on the smaller scenes from around the room and across the ceiling, determined to try to take in as much as I could before we left.

I had seen the Sistine Chapel years before and even though friends had complained that it was too small, too crowded, too dark and too hard to see the paintings on the ceilings, I had not been disappointed. Since my first visit years before, the paintings on the walls and ceiling had been cleaned and restored, the bright colors revealed in their original intensity. In the past I had had low expectations and yet had loved the Chapel. This time, having read so many news stories of the years involved in reconstruction, I expected more; my expectations had been too high and Al's as well. Maybe it was because of our long wait and our long walk that the arrival seemed the slightest bit anti-climactic, even to me. Maybe it was just that the detail of the ceiling paintings was easier to see with younger eyes. But I found myself less awestruck than in my youth. But of course we wouldn't have missed this famous sight and would certainly recommend it to others.

***

Several years later we spent the last few days of our annual trip in Rome. We had been traveling for ten days in Sicily and even been out of Italy for a brief side trip to Tunisia. Amazingly, when we got back to Rome, instead of being overwhelmed, it felt like a homecoming, even to me. We were wound down at the end of our trip and approached things in a casual way, again a luxury of our frequent trips. We were lucky enough to get our favorite room, facing the small but active piazza in front of the hotel. It was one of the first times I really wasn't ready to go back to our U.S. home, but wanted to prolong our time in Italy.

One of the days we were there it poured all day long. I bought a large umbrella from one of the street vendors (who always seemed to magically appear with umbrellas when rain started to fall) and we took the now familiar 64 bus from our stop to the Vatican, realizing that on a Monday the empty bus wouldn't be filled with pickpockets. We then stood in line with the crowds to go into the museum. Things had changed since our last visit and mostly for the best. Additional ticket windows, video information, a check room (which came in handy for my umbrella), an escalator, improved rest rooms and several new restaurant areas made for a more comfortable visit. But once we passed these new additions, the old entrance to the museum galleries and route to the Sistine Chapel and back were familiar.

This time we did the chapel last and focused with our guidebook on the wonders of the other rooms of the Museo Vaticano. Over the centuries the church became the recipient of and preserver of all kinds of ancient art, sculptures of Greek and

Roman gods and goddesses and depictions of, by modern standards, strange mythological subjects. One of the best gifts of the Church to civilization is its relatively uncensored preservation of antiquity. Pre-Christian art is embraced for its beauty and its spiritual overtones as well as for its historical value.

For all of the intolerance of some periods of church history, the Catholics had more direct connection with pre-Christian cultures and preserved more art from those times. The Reformation would not have boded well for the ancient sculptures, as they would have probably been seen as graven images and idols by the modern reformers.

Al read the guidebook in front of various works. Some galleries housed enormous sculptures of Greek and Roman gods and goddesses, such as the room of the Muses with the sculptured bust of Homer and Socrates, making me feel closer than I thought possible to the ancient stories that I taught. We both were enthralled by the drama of the famous Laocoon, the complex sculpture showing the torment by giant snakes of the Trojan priest who suffered because of defying the goddess Athena and warning Troy about the Trojan horse.

We were a great duo, Al liked being the tour guide and reading aloud and I loved having a guide. Although I felt a little guilty about his doing all the work, he seemed to like having an attentive and appreciative listener. We had a wonderful day.

As we walked back across the river later the clouds cleared in the western sky and a glow drifted back up the river and highlighted the majestic dome of St. Peter's. Once again, we wished for a camera, but I thought, " I'll remember it without a still photo. Taking pictures would have been a distraction."

***

It would be hard to exhaust the possibilities of art in churches in Rome. We have walked long distances through back streets to find out of the way art. Often the initial quest to find the church is followed by a second quest to find the small corner or side chapel of a cavernous church that houses a particular piece of art.

One of our first was Michelangelo's sculpture of the seated figure of Moses quietly displayed in a side niche of the Church of St. Peter's in Chains. Intending to take the Metro from the Coliseum to shorten our walk to the neighborhood of the church, we ambled one sunny morning from the Campo di Fiori to the entrance of the subway stop at the Coliseum only to find that it was ferme or closed. As we turned to look past security guards to see why, we saw hundreds of runners, warming up, stretching, generally congregating, and generating an incredible energy. We realized that the Rome Marathon was that morning and the Coliseum was the starting point.

Without the Metro as an option, we hiked a much greater distant to the church of St. Peter in Chains, smaller and more out of the way than many of Rome's famous churches. But Michelangelo's sculpture was worth the walk. Looking into the side chapel with only two other viewers in the quiet church, we were able to look at the strong face and into the intense eyes of Moses and study the marble figure as long as we wanted. Unlike the Michelangelo sculptures in Florence or the Sistine Chapel, there was no line and no fee, just us, the sculpture, and, in our imaginations, the artist himself.

Maybe it's because paintings in the churches are fewer than in a museum and so easier to focus on, that we tend to enjoy and remember them. The side chapels are often dark, tucked away from the central nave of the churches and receive little natural sunlight. The first time we sought out such a painting we were disappointed to see it recessed in the deep shadow. As we strained our eyes into the dark niche of the side chapel, another couple arrived and suddenly the chapel was fully lighted for a couple of minutes before it darkened again just as suddenly. A more experienced art viewer, knowing how the lighting worked, had deposited a coin into a small black light box to trigger a timed spotlight directly into the niche and onto the painting. The drama of the religious subject of the painting, the Conversion of Saint Paul, which shows St. Paul being knocked off his horse seemingly by a the brightness of divinity, was increased by the drama of the light suddenly coming on. We commented that the light box was a good solution on how to see the art in the dark churches.

The Church of San Luigi dei Francesi houses one of our favorite Carravaggio's, *The Call of Matthew*. Like a frame from a movie, the painting shows the dramatic moment when Jesus arrives in the house of the money changers and chooses Matthew to join him. The realism of the faces and costumes would rival a modern director as the moneychangers look up from the piles of gold coins on the table. The central figure of Matthew with his hands still on the money as Jesus points to him, singling him out and calling him to change his life, the light, the strong colors, the sense of lifelike figures so close, the dramatic size of the painting all make it special. But neither of us had ever heard of the painting before Rome.

Several people who had toured Rome had recommended the Il Gesu Church because of the grandeur of the interior with the extremely baroque and overdone chapel and elaborate sculptures and altarpiece made entirely of blue lapis. The size and elaborateness seemed more overdone because of its sheer ornamentation. I eventually came to define baroque as the opposite of simplicity. Al and I both liked the quiet church with the Moses sculpture better.

The Christian and especially Catholic aspects of Rome are powerful images, and certainly a visit to Rome requires seeing its most important religious sights, no matter what one's personal views.

CHAPTER TWENTY- TWO

Rome For Us Now

But Rome is more than ancient ruins and old churches. It is a modern energetic city with its own character and, like it or not, with a bit of brusqueness to its personality. The cab drivers are helpful and courteous, but people do not stop on a street corner to help you look at your map as they might in a smaller city or town. If you ask a policeman for directions, you will get help, but with a certain abruptness, as if dealing with tourists is less exciting and more of a chore.

Unlike in Florence, where English can be heard on the streets as often as Italian, tourists in Rome, however numerous, are still a minority, except at obvious tourist sights and hang outs for the young, such as the Spanish Steps. On the other hand, English speakers are plentiful, and it's easy to get necessary information, especially in restaurants, hotels and museums.

Outdoor markets on Saturdays are full of Roman shoppers, young and old, buying food in the Campo di Fiori or sorting through flea market items, antiques and clothing, leather goods, tapes and CDs, collectibles, old coins and phone cards. Taking the time to go to the Saturday markets allows us to mix easily with the Italians in a more ordinary activity. We almost never saw tourists in the tumble of the markets.

As we walk along Roman streets, Al will point out the graffiti on walls, a fact of life in Rome, a seemingly accepted form of public expression. Big spray-painted letters, signs and symbols on buildings and fences don't seem to be considered vandalism to the extent that they might be at home. One year, we read of attempts to limit or clear away graffiti in anticipation of some citywide event, but trains, brick and stucco walls and fences are still decorated. Still, I have never seen graffiti on the wall of an historical building or a church. A basic respect for the beauty of their heritage seems to prevail among Italians. Occasionally, we see some quite creative graffiti, such as the alley fence design of overlapping red hearts that I wanted to photograph on a day when we had no camera handy.

Rome is entertainment in and of itself. We go to museums and churches and check off the sights in our guidebooks but our best experiences are in the city on the streets.

We love to wander through the less touristy areas, the neighborhoods. Rome became more manageable when Al decided we could manage the bus system, a feat I never would have attempted alone. We can ride from one section of the city to another and then walk within that area, still covering old neighborhoods, getting lost among quiet shops and apartments, strolling through parks and enjoying slices of real Roman life.

Across the Tiber River and within easy walking distance of our hotel is Trastevere, Rome's version of the Left Bank. It is one of our favorite places, a compact medieval neighborhood centered around a small piazza. The small piazza is anchored by the church on one side and bounded by cafes, a tabacchi shop, old gold-toned stucco apartment buildings with shutters opened to the air, and an ice cream shop. Other restaurants and bars on side streets among the apartment buildings and shops make Trastevere a destination for local diners and shoppers. Piazza di Santa Maria in Trastevere is our favorite square because it is low-key, very different from the more touristy or busier squares of the city.

Happy to avoid the traffic on the road along the river, we have figured out how to walk from our hotel at the Campo di Fiori across a foot bridge with vendors and beggars to the other side.

My favorite church in Rome is Santa Maria in Trastevere, a more feminine style church, smaller, with beautiful mosaics, the best in Rome. I have started a tradition of lighting candles there while Al sits quietly in the peace of this beautiful neighborhood church, while classical music plays in the background.

Unlike the grander churches, Santa Maria in Trastevere does not dominate its piazza but is integrated into it, providing a nurturing presence as life goes on outside its doors. Children and pets play on the steps around the fountain in the center of the stone square. The golden and red hued stucco of apartment buildings reflects sunlight between the open shutters and the fluttering of occasional laundry declaring the presence of people within. As we sit drinking coffee or eating a light lunch in the spring afternoon, boys kick a soccer ball, families and individuals cross the piazza from one side street to another, strolling or striding, depending on whether they are on business or at leisure.

Occasionally an organized music group performs here in the acoustically effective space. Not infrequently, in a reminder of a less romantic side of city life, a raggedly dressed woman sends a little boy or girl to beg for coins from people entering or leaving the church or at tables in the cafes.

Trastevere has become a regular stop.

***

Going back to the same vacation spots over a period of time has allowed us to develop predictable rituals and routines that we look forward to doing while we're away. As kids at the beach, my sisters and I looked forward to spending one day on the fishing pier and another day riding a ferry boat to a special beach to find seashells. We always went to the same ice cream shop in the evenings, sure that they had the best ice cream in the country. We ate one dinner at a favorite seafood restaurant and another at a favorite home-style place with good fried chicken. Our children expected similar traditions from our annual beach vacations. Looking forward to the familiarity and predictability was part of the fun of going back to these favorite places each year.

In our return trips to Rome, Al and I have found fountains, piazzas and churches that have become their equivalent. Although we always do and see new places, we also enjoy the familiarity of the old. We know the areas of Rome well enough now to touch base in each of them. We look to see what, if anything, has changed. In a tumultuous place like Rome, the ritual of familiar stops is comforting and satisfying.

Seeing boys playing soccer in the same piazzas year after year feels as essential to our Rome as hearing and seeing the waves on the beach. There we noticed what beach properties had been built, improved or washed away by high tides; now in Rome we check how much archeological restoration and recovery has been done and whether an ancient temple or old church that we saw first with scaffolding has been uncovered.

Instead of feeling overwhelmed, we take in with joy, the beauty and wonder of it all. How lucky we have been to get to this point in a city like Rome. Our favorite pizzeria in the Campo di Fiori near our hotel is often full of Romans, eating good pizza in the evenings, tables just far enough from each other that a waiter can reach to serve us. Each year we recall the time the lights went out as pizzas were being served, but the table candles sufficed until the lights came back on and it was fine. While we used to seek the excitement of discovery, now we enjoy the familiarity with what was unknown when we first started to come.

***

We sometimes need to take a break from the intensity of Rome. We have found several easy to manage side trips that can balance out the intensity of the city itself. Their sights provide a destination, but we especially enjoy the opportunity to see the surrounding area of the city.

On one exceptionally balmy day for March, we took two buses and then walked several long blocks to the Roman Baths of Caracella. It was a beautiful spring day and the ruins looked bright in the sunlight as we entered the staggeringly large ruins and walked into what had been steam baths, hot and cold bathing areas, saunas and massage rooms and even a library communal, the high walls still standing after all these centuries. The ancient Romans knew what they were doing, choosing the area with the most sun and the least wind. Only forty-five minutes from the city center, we had entered what was left of a huge spa. The quiet mood was entirely different from the intensity and traffic of Rome.

Another afternoon, Al looked at a map and picked the closest town we could get to by train and we rode to Frascati, about an hour into the hills. With no purpose other than an excursion, we strolled at random, along winding streets past shops, stopping for a taste of frascati, the popular white wine named after the town. We continued along the outer edge of the hillside town, looking at the views out over the valley toward Rome, and finally came into a big plaza below a palatial villa on the hill above. Groups of young people, mostly young men, stood around enjoying the nice weather and the fact that it was Friday.

Hungry after our wine taste and walk, we stopped at an outdoor cheese stand and bought two samples of different looking cheeses and some bread. Then Al spied a cart advertising pork sandwiches, meat freshly cut from the roasted pig, which was displayed in its entirety (head included) on the cart. We ate, leaning against a wall that opened from a piazza behind us to a view of the valley spread out below. It was a memorable out of town picnic.

Another year, with sightseeing in mind, we rode a train with Roman commuters and shoppers past the suburban apartments out to the ruins of the ancient Roman city of Ostia Antica. The business of earning a living and taking care of the chores of daily life was more evident outside the city center. We noticed families on a picnic, women returning home with groceries, young men heading to work or on other errands.

It was our last day of vacation and we wandered, relaxed, Al following the information in the guide book we had bought. This amazing archeological site holds the ruins of a large seaport town that ironically is no longer near the sea since sedimentation from the Tiber River has created more coastline. Even though we spent most of the day in Ostia Antica, we didn't see it all. Not desperate to see every street, we sought out the highlights, an ancient wine bar and bakery, climbed on ruins of old temples, and took pictures of the sculptures of the theatrical masks of tragedy and comedy copied from the Greeks. We wandered along the well-marked ruins of what had been the main street of the old town and then into some of the many side lanes.

Al had seen a travelogue of Ostia Antica that showed the rectangular area of ancient public toilets that we had heard about, so we wanted to include it on our tour and found it on a distant lane in the grid of old walls. But as Al readied to sit down for a posed picture on the ancient structure, he realized we were out of film. He was disappointed, but I couldn't help thinking it might have been just as well.

At Ostia Antica, we were away from Rome but still part of it. It was a town that made the everyday life of ancient people seem more real than the ancient structures in Rome. Walking around the ruins of the old port on a balmy March day was a pleasure in and of itself.

***

Ultimately, the best part of Rome for me are moments, the freeze-frame times of perfection that I can remember clearly and take home with me. The richness of the city experience is not just in its big sights but in its close-up and intimate experiences that seem to occur regularly and are most memorable. We know the Roman experience will never be exhausted, that we can sit in the sun by a fountain in a piazza and watch people and pigeons indefinitely. In spite of the tumultuousness of this high energy environment, these small moments provide times of awareness. We are fully present, not thinking, but every sense caught up in the details of the scene and every sense connected to it.

At the Piazza Navona on the way back to our hotel one Sunday afternoon, I persuaded Al to sit on an empty bench on the large busy piazza for a while to just watch. The Piazza Navona is one of Rome's special places. A large oval-shaped space is defined by three famous fountains, including one of Neptune, one of sea creatures, and Bernini's famous work depicting four of the world's great rivers. Large structures surround the outside of the area, which in ancient times was filled with water to hold boating races during one period of the Roman Empire. Artists, jugglers, musicians and mimes fill the open spaces of the old circus, the carnival-like atmosphere similar to Jackson Square in New Orleans or Fisherman's Wharf in San Francisco. But even without the performers, local pedestrians of all ages mix with tourists and other onlookers to provide the kind of people-focused entertainment so hard to find in modern cities back home. When we cross the Piazza Navona, we always point out the restaurant where, on a breathtakingly perfect March day, we ate lunch while watching the last runners in the Rome Marathon that had been run that morning, trailing in with their own supporters as they completed the race. We had just happened to be there on the right day and at the right time.

That afternoon we saw an old woman dressed against the afternoon coolness in layers of clothing, a long skirt, several sweaters and shoes that looked like bedroom slippers. She was feeding the pigeons, throwing seed or bread crumbs to the ever hungry birds. When the pigeons settled to nibble, children would chase them. Then the woman, waving her index finger, would scold the children for chasing the birds. Then she would feed the birds again. The children were unconcerned about her scolding, only interested whenever a group of birds would settle in. The woman was unconcerned about how she fit into the popular destination spot.

At home, we might be wary of an eccentric older lady scolding children in public, but in a park or near a fountain in a piazza in Rome she was included and was part of the scene. I said to Al, "Where could we do this at home? Where would we just sit on a bench and be so entertained?"

***

The Trevi Fountain in Rome, for all its confusion, is one of the great people-places. But the fountain is not the highlight, rather it's the energy of the people who gather there. Families pose for pictures in front of the large fountain decorated with large-scale sculptures of gods of the river whose waters flow from the high half circle of a wall. The water rushes from the large sculpture, coming originally, I had read, from an aqueduct in the mountains. It is an intimate setting closed in by surrounding buildings, the fronts of their shops out of sight because of the crowds of people who pour into the tiny space from the several side streets to congregate purposefully around the fountain. The soft roar of the water and human voices converge. And although the fountain is one of Rome's most popular tourist stops, the visitors are not all foreign; we hear more Italian than any other language. In fact, for sightseers who stop briefly to throw coins into the fountain made famous in movies like *La Dolce Vita* and *Three Coins in the Fountain*, its high energy crowds may seem overwhelming.

For those with time to settle into the scene, the buzz of life is the real sight. Groups of high school kids sit on a wall facing the fountain, swinging their legs, talking exuberantly and joining in self-guided sing-a-longs with energetic repetitive choruses. Adults eat gelato, resting on white stone benches, which face into the arena of people and toward the rush of water. Some dabble their hands in the pool. Men and women of all ages and nationalities throw coins over their shoulders into the fountain, following the tradition that a coin in the fountain will bring them back to Rome. Standing or sitting near the edge of the water, they advise each other whether to face the water or away from it, whether to use the right or left hand, what shoulder to throw the coins over, and whether to throw one coin or two or three for the best results. Others, more timid, stand in the street above, hoping their long distance toss will make the water.

Like the passeggiata, the Fontana Trevi embodies Italian time. It is not about the beauty of a sight but the experience. The dramatic figures and flowing waters of the fountain is the objective, but the essence is simply to be in the unifying space, and to enjoy the high energy of togetherness. As we sat on a low wall one afternoon between a young Italian couple and some American college students, I said to Al, "How could you tell anyone what this is like unless they've been here themselves?" So much is going on, yet sitting by the fountain becomes a kind of meditation in motion, as you let go of thoughts and identity and melt into the surrounding energy. In these moments, our senses are heightened, but, as we observe, we develop another sense, one of an encompassing stillness that holds the vibrant scene together.

The first few times we stopped at the Trevi Fountain, Al had trouble seeing the point of staying. His attitude used to be, "Okay, now we've seen it and photographed it. What do we do now?" He has by now gotten into the spirit and will even throw in a coin. "It's worked so far," I tell him as he shakes his head. "We keep coming back." He no longer resists when I find us a small piece of empty marble wall near the fountain where we might squeeze between a family with a little boy on one side and two teenagers on the other. We settle in to just observe and participate for as long as we are comfortable. Al might watch for opportunities to help photograph couples or families in front of the fountain, even though he resists asking someone else to take pictures of the two of us in a posed picture. How nice for couples to get home and have a photo of the two of them together instead of separate snapshots in front of the fountain.

Life at the Fontana di Trevi encompasses drama as well as innocence. Immigrant salesmen from third world countries, clearly non-Italians, carrying trays of rubber toys or cheap jewelry, weave in and out of the crowds, enticing parents and children to buy their inexpensive wares. When the word goes out that the "polizia" have arrived on the other side of the fountain, suddenly the salesmen bundle their wares and take off running. In some ways they seem more out of place than the occasional beggars, more of a tradition in Italy, but over the years these young salesmen have become part of the fabric of Roman diversity.

For those who stay longer than the seconds it takes to snap a picture, there is a rhythm to the Trevi experience. We wouldn't want to spend an entire afternoon around the Trevi Fountain or even several hours, but after our mini-retreat, we have a natural sense that it's time to move on. Or maybe we just feel someone else might enjoy our seat.

After one of our pilgrimages to see the Carravaggio paintings in Santa Maria del Popolo Church, we walked into the grand circle of the Piazza del Popolo as people entered from an archway on one side, which is the old entrance through the protective stone wall into Rome. There's a tall Egyptian obelisk and a fountain with steps in the center, and two avenues that lead in a V-shape to the Spanish Steps and the Via del Corso, the pedestrian crowded area known for designer shops. Two domed churches appear to be identical, but in order to fit the churches into a narrower space, the artists created a deliberate illusion of sameness by making one dome narrower than the other.

We had been here before and taken note of the architecture and checked it off of our list of tourist sights. We had climbed up to the Pincio Park as well to look down on the piazza, and had finished our official sightseeing here. But one particular spring morning, we discovered what the Piazza of the People was really about.

On this sunny spring afternoon, as we walked across the center of the large piazza, enough space for the two of us opened up on the circular steps near the fountain and obelisk. In the center we came upon a young couple in tee shirts and jeans who stood to leave. This time, I convinced Al to sit down on the steps with the other people, the majority of whom were younger than we were.

Looking out over the space from its center, we watched the constant motion of people crossing this grand space from both directions. Our first intention had been to sit down to relax for a few minutes without having to take a table at a cafe. But, once we were comfortable in our prime spot, we settled in to watch whoever or whatever came by: pigeons, bicyclists, old men with canes, dogs, tourists with cameras. Although there was motion all around us in the constantly changing scene, we were still, relaxed, enjoying not walking or standing or focusing or learning.

Time passed and it was after noon. We were hungry but enjoyed the mood and spirit of the piazza, and we didn't want to leave the area. Al suggested that we look for a sandwich shop. Reluctantly, I gave up my seat and we walked across the circle of the piazza to one of the side streets, found a cafe, and bought sandwiches and beers. We took our picnic back onto the piazza and, joining other noontime diners, found new seats, this time on the periphery of the circle of the piazza on one of the benches in the shade. From a different perspective at the edge away from the center, we had the view of the whole of the circle as we slowly ate our sandwiches.

With food and drink, we stayed a long time, entertained once again by the constant pageantry of the activity of lovers and children and birds and dogs and working people, feeling a sense of solitude but not loneliness, of peacefulness in community, of being part of the whole and yet not responsible for doing anything. Ever since then, one of our favorite Roman traditions has been picnicking with other noonday Italians, sitting on one of the benches on the edge of this piazza in the shade.

***

Whenever we go to Italy, we love to be in surroundings that are so different from ours at home. We experience every texture of sight and sound and sense, which are sometimes over-whelming. To be someplace where things are old rather than new, where life is lived in such different ways, where language and traffic and even birds sound different and yet to be comfortable is a wonder to me. When we come home and sit in our den and look out on our familiar backyard, I sometimes think, "Were we really there? And only weeks ago?" Maybe that's why I developed the need and desire to go back again and again to see if the wonder will still be there.

Somehow cafes and fountains form my special moments in my mind's eye. Like the poet William Wordsworth, who used the phrase "emotion recollected in tranquility," to describe the reliving of cherished and special moments filtered through time, it's easier to hold on to and relive these places and times.

One year I noticed that we seemed to have found a comfortable rhythm for our stay, which we continue to follow when ever we go back to Rome. Rome was cleaned up here and there for the Millennium year called the "Giubeleo" or Jubilee by the Church. It was nice to see some of the buildings less dark with their rose or golden hues revealed. The last day we revisited the Piazza del Popolo, had another cafe lunch and watched the people. Later, we sat on the Spanish Steps with the young students leaning back in the sun and some older people on an excursion. Two Italian women bought a rubber mold after the African salesmen demonstrated all the humorous shapes and faces. They sat on a wall a few feet from us and amidst the turbulence of people talking and walking, thoroughly enjoyed their Sunday afternoon outing. Instead of sitting in a café spending money on foot and drink, we just hung out entertained by the human interactions around us.

One magical evening we walked through the last drizzle of an afternoon rainstorm across the bridge near the synagogue.

Looking down the river, we drew in our breath as the pink and gold light of an early sunset shone around the marble dome of St. Peter's. The light was again so beautiful as we looked down river at the dome of St. Peter's that we almost went back to the hotel to get our camera. It was that special light in the late afternoon at the end of a rain.

A couple of years later Al took a photograph of the same scene early one evening after a drizzle, the sun barely showing through the clouds. I later had the photo enlarged and framed for Al. We love that photograph.

One Sunday we sat in a cafe on the Campo di Fiori and looked at the spring sun shining on the square. Because it was a Sunday, the fruit and vegetable market was not set up, and the area was filled with strollers and groups in conversation. Families with their babies and children walked by after church or settled at nearby tables for an outside lunch. Couples sat at the small tables drinking cappuccinos and eating croissants and small sandwiches. The tourists blended in so that sometimes couples I thought were visitors spoke Italian. The chatter of Italian conversation, the old piazza circled by six and seven story buildings of medieval stone, the sheer abundance of life observed and shared overwhelmed me. In my intensity, I said to Al, "If heaven is how you imagine it, this could be my heaven." I think Al knew what I meant. There is something spiritual about such moments. It's how someone might feel looking at a beautiful mountain range or desert or sunset, the ecstatic feeling that we could stay in that moment forever and be happy, the fullness of the Italian scene filled me.

Later that day Al and I sat at a small cafe across from the church of Santa Maria in Trastevere, a smaller venue this time and less busy. It was late afternoon and a little cool, our last afternoon before going home. We had ordered a Campari and soda and sat huddled at a little round table eating the peanuts and pretzels from our small bowl of snacks, trying to keep the dozen or so pigeons from joining us at our table. Once the food was gone they left too and we stayed, reading the *International Herald Tribune*, the English language paper with its section about Italy's news. Our little cafe table faced the fountain in the piazza and the facade of the church, the life-size mosaics of the Madonna and saints that the church is known for directly across from us. There were few people around this weekday afternoon. Some boys kicked a soccer ball around, and occasionally someone walked across the piazza from one side street to another or entered or came out of the church we had visited earlier. In contrast to the Sunday morning activity on the Campo di Fiori, there really wasn't much going on here. This became one of our good memories as well, a quiet contentment of companionability such as we might have at home reading the papers, but instead we were on this old piazza across from the gentle church, witnessing the pieces of life that passed by. My mind can take me there again.

***

So now Rome is a type of homecoming. The city which overwhelmed us has become a place where we feel a connection. I say to Al, "We need to come sometime and stay longer in Rome. We need to see what it's like in the fall or winter."

Always the realist, he answers, "It'll be too cold," and "I don't have that much vacation." But mentally I put "staying longer" and "visiting in different seasons," on my "hope to do someday" list. There is more to discover here, now that we are comfortable and know our way around. Like fishermen who, as they cast in their line and never tire of casting, knowing there are always more possibilities in the water, we know Rome will always provide us with something new. "When we retire," I tell him, "we can stay longer."

CHAPTER TWENTY-THREE

Postcards, Souvenirs and Photographs

Al and I don't shop much in Italy but we always buy post-cards. Even the smallest town has a postcard display at a news-stand or in a tobacchi shop. Postcards are simple, inexpensive and easy to carry mementos.

When we first traveled to Italy, I would spend time choos-ing a variety of postcard scenes to represent the highlights of our trip. A few days later, I would realize that Al had mailed all of my carefully chosen cards, leaving only the least interesting in my little sack. Now I buy duplicates of the best postcards and put my copies in my luggage. When we get home, I'll come across my cards and enjoy the feelings and vivid memories of these places, especially when life has returned us to everyday routines. When I find old cards, I sometimes think it would have been nice to date and write postcards to ourselves over the years. One year, sitting in a cafe and getting Al to make his picks of the best, worst, fun-niest and most interesting moments of our trip to list beside mine, we did write and send ourselves a card from Rome. And when the card arrived a couple of weeks later, it was fun to reminisce.

Al enjoys taking on the challenge of buying stamps. Our trips to local post offices, where agents often speak only Italian, are part of our sightseeing, a regular activity, especially fun in the smaller towns.

I try to buy a few cards in each new city and from each museum or historical sight. Our photographs will be personal but won't match the quality of the colors and light of a major building like St. Peter's or the Pantheon. Postcards that focus on one sight are better than collages. Especially for aging eyes, larger figures make more of a statement than small ones. In a display of local loyalty, cities seem to display cards and souvenirs related to themselves. We won't easily find a picture of Florence's *David* in Rome or of the Coliseum in Venice. Now I try to buy souvenir cards early in our visit to each place.

Along with our pictures of famous buildings and cityscapes with the tile roofs, the domes of famous cathedrals, we always get postcards at museums. I have postcards of classical sculptures in marble that I display at school. One is of Hercules holding up the earth for Atlas, another of the hero wearing his lion skin robe with the head still on as he fights against a monster. Zeus, with his curled hair and beard, throws his small lightning bolt, Venus stands with her son Cupid, sometimes shooting his arrows and sometimes standing beside his mother, love personified, also decorate my classroom. Although I'm often tempted to buy the poster-size of something famous, I usually resist, knowing how hard it will be to carry it around and keep it from damage. Postcards are easier all around. I enjoy having this one souvenir and can always justify buying them.

At school I post pictures of the Coliseo explaining it was where the gladiators fought. I also purchase postcards of some things we didn't see, such as the bright blues and greens and gold of costumes of Carnivalia in Venice and masks representing the sun and moon. The masqueraders ride in gondolas and the close-up pictures show more than most people would see in a crowded parade. The strangeness of them appeals to my teenage students and I point out the struggle between the light of early spring and the darkness of winter that is symbolized in the colors of the costumes. Since the same theme occurs in some early British literature selections, I am able to teach through my postcards. But mainly I just like to look at them.

In our kitchen, along with photos of our kids, I display something from our latest trip. Right now a spring view of the Dome of St. Peter's from a bridge down the river is beside a recent picture of our daughters. I can be there again by looking at the simple postcard.

The cards not on display or sent are in a box on my dresser to review at my leisure. Sometimes the cards were not good choices, the colors too muted, the scene too small or vague. The defined subjects, the particular buildings or close-ups of works of art like sculptures convey more than the landscape or city scenes. Still, how can I resist buying an aerial photo of a hill town we've visited or the expansive countryside view?

***

People sometimes ask us what we buy when we're in Italy. Travelers look for an idea of a place's bargains or specialties. Some people get a lot of pleasure out of shopping wherever they go, browsing in stores even if they don't plan on buying. Al and I don't travel with an intention of shopping. Maybe it's being at an age of wanting to accumulate less rather than more, or maybe it's not wanting to deal with shipping or carrying too much in our minimal luggage. Except for our unexpected weakness with the glass salesmen early on in Venice, we haven't made any significant purchases to bring home. Occasionally, I have looked longingly at a large piece of decorative pottery, but inevitably the cost for shipping wasn't worth the item, so we moved on. We pass through customs easily since we are well under our limit.

Sometimes, I bring home souvenir pieces to friends and our kids but have learned to focus on practical items, a small bowl that can be used and put away, rather than a pottery figure. I hate burdening someone else with a souvenir that I thought was cute or pretty but that is only meaningful to us.

In earlier years, we did some bargain shopping, particularly in Florence and Rome where silk scarves and ties, and leather goods were good values especially at the outdoor markets. We bought Kirsti a briefcase in Florence the year that she set out on job interviews along with a couple of leather purses and my favorite decorative Florentine note paper and picture frames. In fact, lined leather gloves and wool scarves from Florence, for fairly good prices, provided Christmas presents some years for our girls and friends in cooler climates. Wearing our own, we can feel a connection back to Italy.

Although Italian style and fashion design is known around the world, we don't worry about labels or quality. Our purchases are things we don't see at home. Al still wears a couple of small print silk neckties with cleverly designed elephants and horses in the pattern. When he wears it we remember that it was fun to buy; he has nice silk ties that he bought for six or seven dollars in street markets.

We do bring back souvenirs and these have added to our year-round enjoyment of our once a year vacation. If we're lucky, we stumble on some distinctive local craft or folk art and just happen to see something we both like. If we go purposely seeking a souvenir piece recommended by someone else or suggested in a guidebook, we usually don't find anything special. But if we are just wandering along a street or past a street vendor or craft shop, and we happen on an unusual object, and if we both like it, we'll get it. Our pieces tend to be small so we can carry them easily and to represent something from one particular place in

Italy, but mostly we just get them because we like them at the moment. We remember the whole scene of buying each one.

In my kitchen window in a glass vase are three small wooden tulips of rose, peach, and pink on green stems. They were inexpensive, not particularly unique except that I bought them in an outdoor market in Milan on a spring Saturday. I liked them then and I like them now. They sit on the window ledge inside the glass, echoing colors of the tall hibiscus that grows past the window outside. A still-life artist might think they were intended to be together.

We have a couple of small paintings, watercolors from street artists, a contemporary rendition of one of the towers in Florence, and some traditional watercolor views of the Pantheon and its piazza, and Roman cafe scenes. On impulse in Trastevere in Rome one day, I bought a three-by-six inch painting of matrimonial figures, a man and woman in Renaissance-style dress. Five years later we happened on the same small shop as we were wandering the small side streets, and I bought another miniature, this time of church bell towers. I remembered the artist from years before, in her thirties with full dark hair and a friendly warm manner who also was the salesperson; we interrupted her work to package our purchases.

At home, in our kitchen, a small wall ceramic depicts the coastline of the Cinque Terre and even has the name Monterosso written across the bottom, usually a mark of a tacky souvenir. But Al and I both liked the deep blue water of the sea and the recognizable towns on the hills. Al reluctantly agreed to put a nail into the side of our white wooden cabinet to give the ceramic a safe home, even though this meant damaging the wood.

On an end table in the living room sits a ceramic creamer in the shape of a little round woman, in colorful peasant dress, with a handle and a spout. A souvenir that could easily be classified as "junk," she happens to have just the right face and just the right color tones on her clothing to qualify as a nice little piece of folk art. Nearby stand small copies of ancient Roman and Greek pottery, a Greek pitcher with the body and face of a man worked into the figure and an Etruscan water pitcher with a warrior painted in the representative black on orange design. Our "art" reminds us of the many originals we saw in museums.

The longer the time passes since we have visited these places the nicer it feels to have souvenirs from them. Unlike other souvenirs we have bought over the years, these little pieces connect us emotionally, taking us back to places where we found them. A circular wooden carving four inches in diameter depicts in bright colors the details of the circus area in Lucca. In a shop there, we found this charming piece jumbled among less appealing clutter. A small ceramic cup painted in blue with yellow lemons reminds me of the citrus trees in the south of Italy along with two decorative plates on my kitchen table of a man picking oranges from a tree heavy with fruit. These bright little objects focus my attention even amidst the normal clutter of my kitchen table. They cheer me up in the here and now as well as reminding me of the colors and light of Mediterranean Italy.

One of my other favorites is a small, clay holy water font, painted in aquamarine tint and white, a circle of terra cotta angel faces in the center. These common and inexpensive pieces were discovered in a shop in Rome. At home they are impractical, but the unique detail and artistry brightens our living room. I don't know where I would find anything like this other than in Italy.

Sometimes the experience of buying an object and the care given to the ritual of paying and wrapping even the smallest purchases from small shops and craft stands is what we appreciate most. In Leche, Al chose a weather-worn small bust of a sea captain from a newspaper stand, a reminder of Italy's south east coast. We had seen more expensive and more elaborate pieces of this local style of painted papier-mâché in store windows, but here on the street on a cold and windy late afternoon, he chose the nicest from the selection of ten or so set on a stand near magazines and newspapers. This artistically rendered bust of a weathered sea captain shares a place on the top of our television set with the Greek figure vase.

As I look around our house at other material things we have accumulated over the years, I feel ready to pack up or give away many of them, but not our Italy souvenirs.

I have miniature houses copied from the colorful small houses in Burano, the island near Venice and colorfully painted clay vases from Sorrento and other small towns south of Naples and Amalfi, each a unique style and color.

One of my favorite purchases was from a shop in Sorrento which had beaded necklaces hanging on outside racks. These beads, according to the handwritten sign, were made from lava rock, of Mount Vesuvius, as is much of the land all around the volcanic regions. I picked out a short strand with interesting dark blues and blacks in the small shiny stones and am often asked what kind of gemstone the necklace, for which I paid the equivalent of seven dollars, is made of. I still regret that I didn't take the friendly shop woman's advice and choose two more for my daughters.

Certain items lose something in a different environment. One year Al carried home a bottle of Limoncello, the aperitif served gratis in many restaurants around Sorrento, but it didn't seem to taste the same here. We didn't have the right glasses and the lemons hadn't come from trees down the road. And instead of a waiter surprising us with an icy cold after-dinner glass, I had to pour it into a small wine glass here and serve it myself. A bottle of Mandolaro almond liquor, so delicious as a dessert there, seemed a little sweet for home. But the one unlikely food purchase that we enjoyed for a long time was the quart bottle of olive oil from Apulia that Al decided to carry home one year because he had read that the region had the some of the best olive oil anywhere. We used it gently and sparingly on mozzarella and basil and tomato rather than for cooking, and it stayed good to the last drop.

***

Al and I take too many pictures with too little planning. Rather than selecting a few of the "best" to enlarge for our album, we keep them all. Some we have enlarged for framing or selected for Christmas cards. Most are not significant to any one but us, especially not the mundane street scenes that remind us of places we have walked. Others are still in envelopes and boxes. When we get home, life takes us quickly back to the present, and on our side of the Atlantic, even our latest pictures get put aside after a couple of quick looks, as the business of daily life takes over. Still there is nothing like running through a set of pictures from a trip several years earlier to have us remembering and pointing out to each other what we enjoyed about a simple building or bridge or figure.

EPILOGUE

Our Italian vacations are over within two weeks. But like a visit to a health spa or retreat, our Italian sojourns enrich our lives in a shared enthusiasm for things Italian.

After we get home we have the leisure to reflect on our experiences. The intensity of foreign travel recedes along with memories of problems we encountered, and we can enjoy replaying impressions and experiences. We have become secondary Italians, Italiaphiles. With each trip our interest in things Italian are broadened and we enjoy sharing them. If we're feeling out of sync with each other about something or irritated over a domestic issue, Italy can often bring us back in tune. Seeing a television commercial with an Italian fountain and piazza will draw both our attentions. Like skiers follow ski events and golfers who watch golf matches, we feel a connection to Italian election proceedings in the *New York Times*, having tried to interpret campaign slogans on billboards in Italian cities and talked to Italian taxi drivers about their takes on the candidates. An Italian theme or setting is enough to make us see a movie. We rent *Death in Venice* or *A Room with a View* and point out scenes where we have walked. Anything with Italian subtitles is worth a look.

We seek out Italian restaurants, the small, one-of-a-kind family-run places in unassuming old houses or buildings. We compare menus and ambiance to restaurants in Italian towns. I probably never would have eaten a mussel at home if I hadn't had them in a seaside Mediterranean restaurant in a tomato and garlic sauce with a glass of wine. Now, when I order mussels, I associate them with our vacations. When Al read the history of a local family who had started several Italian eateries and discovered they were from Sicily and returned to visit family every year, we were there within the month, not only to try the food but to look at the photographs on their walls.

I cook more Italian food, trying to imitate the simple dishes we have eaten when we were there. Untalented gardener that I am, I grow fresh basil and use the freshly picked green leaves with buffalo mozzarella and tomatoes for caprese salad. Having seen how Italian cooks prepare fresh fish, I now use a standard recipe of fresh oregano with lemon and olive oil.

Al and I get questions about why we don't use our travel time to explore other places. But during this phase of our lives, Italy has been a theme that enriches our shared experiences by being integrated into our lives after we get home. The pleasures of Italian culture connect with our lives more than we could have imagined. We read travel articles to get new ideas about places to go and towns we might have missed, but are as likely to read about where we've been. We read to relive our experiences now that we can picture things in our minds and read about places we haven't been and make plans to go there and get ideas for the next trip.

After a tentative first few years, now Al always looks forward to the next trip. If I ask him if he had a good time, he always says, "Yes," or "Sure," When someone once asked him, "Weren't we ready to get home after traveling for two weeks?' he answered, "Once you get all the way over there, you want to stay."

The years when we thought we might not be able to go or when we had had some particular problem at home, we were especially grateful to be there. Each year we, both individually and as a couple, and the circumstances of our lives are different. In this ten to fourteen day separation from all that is familiar, away from family and friends, routine and work, from separate rooms to retreat to, we make discoveries about ourselves and each other. And there are often surprises.

Travel forces us out of our boxes, our structured defined ways of thinking, not only in cultural understanding but in our relationship. On a trip, the unpredictable happens and we have to deal with it, for better or worse.

When we return home, we try to make our vacation mood last. But quickly life pulls us back into the reality. We miss the freedom of standing outside our social identity and living on Italian time outside the structure of routines. We miss traveling together in our one-to-one passeggiata, our journey that continues less for the sake of a goal than for the movement itself. We try to remember that in Italy it's not as important where we go or what we see but that we are experiencing it together. We try to apply the patience of our Italian mindsets to our lives and each other. In Italy the journey and the destination really do become one, and the moments of the journey of married life do as well as we try to apply insight to our lives.

Gradually the past days of our travels become part of the present and our experiences across the ocean become part of our lives at home. Though the reality of our vacation ends, our shared experience of it continues. As then becomes now and there becomes here, our footsteps merge and two become one. Our treasure of two weeks of together-time infuses our times at home with its spirit. We find ways to continue our passeggiata.